ORDERLY FASHION

A SOCIOLOGY OF MARKETS

Patrik Aspers

PRINCETON UNIVERSITY PRESS

PRINCETON AND OXFORD

Copyright © 2010 by Princeton University Press

Published by Princeton University Press, 41 William Street,
Princeton, New Jersey 08540

In the United Kingdom: Princeton University Press, 6 Oxford Street,
Woodstock, Oxfordshire OX20 1TW

press.princeton.edu

Library of Congress Cataloging-in-Publication Data

Aspers, Patrik, 1970–
Orderly fashion : a sociology of markets / Patrik Aspers.
p.   cm.
Includes bibliographical references and index.
ISBN 978-0-691-14157-2 (hbk. : alk. paper)
1. Clothing trade—Social aspects. 2. Fashion merchandising—Social aspects.
3. Industrial sociology. I. Title.
HD9940.A2A87   2010
306.3'4—dc22   2009041616

British Library Cataloging-in-Publication Data is available

This book has been composed in Sabon

Printed on acid-free paper. ∞

Printed in the United States of America

10   9   8   7   6   5   4   3   2   1

For Caroline

Contents _____

Preface

THIS BOOK APPROACHES the global fashion industry with a focus on markets. Its perspective is that of economic sociology and it addresses the question of order. The study is substantially based on observations and interviews, though I do not refer to the names of firms or persons. This is done not only to maintain the anonymity of those who have contributed to the research project, but also, and above all, to stress the general and theoretical points and to facilitate application of the approach in other studies. Large bodies of literature, such as those on business economics, business organization, and industrial economics, all of which have made important contributions to our understanding of the real economy, are acknowledged, but not discussed at any length.

Martin Heidegger, in "Schöpferische Landschaft: Warum bleiben wir in der Provinz?", remarks that philosophizing is like being in a blizzard. He also celebrates *Einsamkeit* [solitude] as a work strategy. Though I fully agree that scientific work, to be successful, must to some extent be characterized by *Einsamkeit*, one should not always be alone. Two relational thinkers, Pierre Bourdieu and Harrison White, have inspired the approach I have developed, but the main input comes from the phenomenological tradition.

This book would probably have been written even without the help of most of those I shall thank, but the outcome under such circumstances would have been rather poor. Several people in the field have helped me gather the empirical material that supports the thesis I present here. Their kindness has been of great value to me, and obviously a precondition of the study.

This book is the product of a major project on the global fashion industry that started in 2002. Many people commented on drafts of chapters during 2006 and 2007, at the London College of Fashion, the London School of Economics, the Stockholm School of Business, Växjö University, Stockholm University, and the University of Konstanz. I would especially like to thank Göran Ahrne, Jean Pascal Delouze, Ingrid Giertz Mårtensson, Mark Granovetter, Oskar Engdahl, Herbert Kalthoff, Karin Knorr Cetina, Per Anders Linden, Árni Sverrisson, and Richard Swedberg.

In the early phases, Emil Uddhammar was my colleague in this project. I have had many interesting discussions with Emil, both in Sweden and during field trips to India. The associates at Skeppsbron in Stockholm, who have been present throughout the project, Kay Glans, Erik Wallrup and Peter Elmlund, made this a very special work place.

I am very grateful for the kindness shown by Nigel Dodd and Don Slater who let me spend one year (2003–2004) at the Department of Sociology of the London School of Economics. I was also very pleased to be a guest of the London College of Fashion, at the research centre for Fashion, the Body, and Material Culture—spring and fall 2006—where Joanne Entwistle commented on drafts of my book.

My colleagues at the Department of Sociology at Stockholm University have been helpful, and some of my work on this book was done there. I am also grateful for a scholarship from the Swedish Research Institute in Istanbul, which made it possible to spend a month in Turkey.

Since April 1, 2005, I have also been based at the Max Planck Institute for the Study of Societies in Cologne, which is an extremely stimulating and at the same time very supportive and friendly academic milieu. My colleagues—and especially the research group on markets, with Jens Beckert, Brooke Harrington, Thorsten Kogge, Mark Lutter, Guido Möllering, Geny Piotti, Irene Troy, and Raymund Werle—have been very supportive. The mutual reading and discussion of papers that I have had with Jens Beckert has been of great importance in sharpening the arguments I present here. I am also grateful for the comments, help, and assistance of Alexander Dobeson, Nicklas Baschek, Natalia Besedovsky, Sebastian Kohl, Cynthia Lehmann, Mike McGee, Isis Neuerbourg, James Patterson, and Thomas Pott. I would like to thank Richard Baggaley of Princeton University Press, and the anonymous reviewers who provided very constructive reviews.

The research reported here is part of a project "Identity and Globalization" that was launched with financial support from the Margareta and Axel Johnsson Foundation. The support of the Foundation has been crucial for this project. I am also grateful for the support from the Max Planck Institute for the Study of Societies in Cologne, the Department of Sociology at Stockholm University, SCORE, and the Swedish Research Council.

June 2009, Cologne

ORDERLY FASHION

Introduction _

THE PURPOSE OF THIS BOOK is to study social order in the global fashion industry. The issue of order entails the question: Why is social life not in chaos? But instead of addressing the question of order head on, which would be naïve due to its complexity, I have chosen to zoom in on branded garment retailers—that is, chains that sell clothes to consumers—to investigate order in relation to their activities in markets. It is the order of the branded garment retailers (BGRs) and the markets in which they operate that is the central empirical object of this study.

Why is order essential in markets? What, in other words, would it mean if a "market situation" was characterized by chaos? The short answer is that without order there would simply be no markets, and so, as I shall show, any realistic definition of markets implies order. Why order is essential in markets may be illustrated by discussing a hypothetical fashion consumer "market." Imagine entering the local mall, but finding no stores. Instead, all kinds of items are being sold here and there, by individuals whom you neither know nor recognize. They also operate as buyers of the items. On top of all this, you do not recognize any of the brand names of the clothes, and you do not know for how much they are being sold. In such circumstances, an actor is unable either to predict or to calculate; there is no "market" from the buyer's perspective. Turning around to look at the market from the perspective of the sellers, who do not know who their customers or competitors are, not to mention prices, and furthermore have no access to quality standards that might provide information on what garments mean, the "consumer market" is in chaos, or rather, there is no market: no "buyers" or "sellers" exist, and no principles for evaluating the goods. Moreover, if suppliers of garments cannot identify retailers, or if the retailers must organize production themselves, there is no supply market for garments. Imagine, too, that there is no credit market, and it is soon hard to imagine an economy at all. Finally, if there are only a few fashion magazines, all of which put out only a single issue before they go out of business and whose advertisements consist of pictures of people wearing clothes, one would be bereft of accredited advice on fashion, which in these circumstances would depend on one's trust in the value of a single magazine issue. More fundamentally, for something to be in fashion—a notion that is tied to change—there must be at least some order; something, such as a set of fashion magazines that have distinct identities that do not change as quickly as fashion itself.

This study of order in the fashion industry will show how order and change are interrelated.

The fashion industry is indeed ordered. However, only when there is a product or a set of roles filled by actors who mutually create and reinforce the goods and/or each other's identities in interaction over time is there a possibility of predictions in the market, which is a practical and concrete consequence of order in a market. This is to say that actors have stable—and largely shared—perceptions of the market, enabling them to coordinate their behavior (cf. Fligstein 2001: 76). Knowing nothing, and so being unable to predict, bespeaks chaos. If we want to understand markets, then the question is not whether markets are in "order" or in "chaos," but how order is created and maintained. In this study, it will become clear in relation to the empirical material how order is created, and how it can be created in different ways in different markets. It will also become clear how order in one market relates to order in other markets.

I begin by considering the question of order in the final consumer market for fashion garments. I look at the relationships between branded garment retailers and their consumers. Branded garment retailers (cf. "marketers" Bair and Gereffi 2002: 35) have their own design and marketing departments, but normally no production units; to get clothes to sell they rely on suppliers. I focus on large and medium-sized branded retailers in the global fashion industry, such as C&A, Gap, H&M, Macy's, Old Navy, Topshop, Next, French Connection UK, Marks and Spencer, and Zara, as well as smaller retailers. These firms may have hundred, or even thousands of stores in one or more countries. The study does not present an analysis of firms and specific markets, however, but rather presents ideal-types. I have studied only Swedish and British retailers, and manufacturers in India and Turkey who produce the garments that retailers sell. The study concentrates on what are perhaps BGRs' two most central markets: the market in which they sell garments to consumers and the market in which they buy the garments from manufacturers. Appendix I describes the materials and methods employed. I focus on European conditions, though there are also many similarities to the U.S. industry. (Studies of the U.S. market include Gereffi 1994, 1999; and Taplin 1994.) One important difference between the European and U.S. markets is that the latter demands production of larger series. A second difference is the lower importance of fashion as a factor in the U.S. market. One practical implication is that U.S. purchasers typically attract larger manufacturers than European purchasers do. Furthermore, U.S. purchasers more often work with, for example, vendors in Mexico than do European purchasers.

The uncertainty (Beckert 1996) that characterizes the fashion industry (Godart 2009) is one reason for its selection for this study of social order.

Moreover, the global fashion industry is one of the largest in the world (see Appendix II for trade statistics). The industry covers a wide range of activities, from large-scale production of cotton, through handicraft production and advanced marketing, fashion photography, and design, to corporate control, sourcing, and of course consumption.

Furthermore, fashion is a cutting-edge business, and what happens in it has implications for other industries. Skov (2006), for example, has studied garment and fashion fairs and finds that a large number of visitors are not from the fashion industry. Her explanation is that people from other industries are there to pick up trends. Finally, it is an industry to which all of us as consumers of garments have connections.

To make it easier to understand the different actors, markets, and institutions that make up this industry, I have included some of the most important in figure I.1. It is possible to view this figure as a description of a material flow, in which input goods are gradually refined to end up as garments in stores; however, I will show that it is more fruitful to view this industry with the meaning of fashion as one's point of departure—that is, to read the figure from the bottom. This will clarify how the reverberations from the consumer market reach the production market "upstream" along the production chain, and show the great importance of the production of cultural meaning in this industry.

Many other actors are involved than those depicted. The state is often seen as playing a unique role in relation to markets (cf. Fligstein 2001). States lay down legislation in the countries in which BGRs operate as buyers and sellers. There are, in addition, organizations such as the WTO that also affect the terms of trade. This large industry reaches around the globe, though production is concentrated in some countries and consumption in others. Ever since Marx, this industry has been pivotal in debates on inequality and working conditions. Opportunities to affect this industry are unequally distributed among its different stakeholders, from workers in Bangladesh through designers in Paris to consumers in the United States. Its development has caused some people to lose their jobs, but others, both businesspeople and workers in developing countries, have seen their living standards rise. These changes experienced by the fashion industry must be related to social transitions of a political, ethical, and economic nature, such as quotas.[1]

A considerable body of research has been generated on this industry, which at this point may be summarized in three points. First, garment production has over time become more separated from the consumption of garments. Second, the production of garments is still hard labor for those who actually produce them. The third and final point is that global markets can promote the development of participants. I expand on these points in Appendix III, but they are reflected throughout the book.

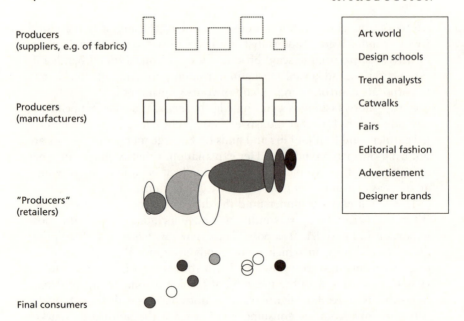

Producers
(suppliers, e.g. of fabrics)

Art world

Design schools

Trend analysts

Producers
(manufacturers)

Catwalks

Fairs

Editorial fashion

Advertisement

"Producers"
(retailers)

Designer brands

Final consumers

Figure I.1. Markets and actors in a production flow, schematic figure. The dotted actors in the production flow (top left)—that is, suppliers of various input materials, such as fabrics—are included only to show how the chain continues beyond the two markets of the production chain included in this study, those between final consumers and retailers, and between retailers and manufacturers. Retailers are seldom producers of the garments they sell in their stores, but they are nonetheless "producers" of fashion. The names in the box on the right hand side of the figure represent actors and arenas responsible for further symbolic production of fashion garments. Seen from the top of the figure, we can observe the material flow, seen from the bottom, we can observe the flow of meaning.

The Aims of the Book

This book aims to contribute to three fields of research. The first is sociological theory. The discussion of order shows that order must be seen in relation to smaller units of analysis—to this end I look at markets as partial orders. The second is fashion, which I examine from a sociological perspective that includes the economy. From this perspective, fashion is a result of interaction between producers and consumers (cf. Fine and Leopold 1993). I develop my own position on fashion in more detail throughout the book (Appendix V contains a concise assessment of research done in this field). Fashion is a highly informative and relevant area of research, not only in society, but also for sociological theorizing.

Unfortunately, this field has been neglected by social scientists. The final field is economic sociology, and in particular the discussion of markets. I address five shortcomings of contemporary economic sociology, which I discuss in Appendix IV: (i) the limited attention to value; (ii) the realist assumptions despite claims of social constructivism; (iii) the attempt to merely "add something on" to economic theory instead of asking sociological questions; (iv) the limited attention paid to the global economy; and (v) the neglect of consumption. In the following, I turn to the central issue of order.

Order

I would argue that the question of social order is central to sociology. This is not a controversial statement (see, for example, Alexander et al. 1987: 13); the discussion of order among social scientists can be traced back to Hobbes, if not earlier, though it was Parsons who made it an explicit, basic, and central issue in sociology (see, for example, Parsons [1937] 1968; Spence Smith 1992; Wrong 1994; Beckert 1996: 824–27, 2009; cf. Eisenstadt 1968, 15: 23–36; Berger and Luckmann [1966] 1991: 57).[2] The issue of order is important not only to sociologists, but also to economists (Nelson and Winter 2002: 23), and to social scientists in general (Hayek 1973: 4). Sociologists—in focus in this book—agree that order is a central question, but they are less in agreement on what it is and how it should be studied (Alexander 1987: 11–12).

Max Weber's notion of *Ordnung* covers what is called social order (Weber [1921–22] 1978: 31–36; cf. Swedberg 2005: 185–86). This refers to forms of behavior oriented to norms, rules, or traditions, based on various interests (cf. Swedberg 2004b). Weber distinguishes between two forms of *Konvention*, which is similar to what we would today call a norm, namely *Sitte* (*mores* or *tradition*, such as informal institutions) and *Recht* (*law*, such as formal institutions). *Recht* means not only *law*, but also *right* or *correct*. Weber argues that in terms of the principle of *Recht*, order can be like a standard (for example, "ethischer Maßstab"). He informs us that order was originally created by tradition (Weber [1921–22] 1978: 31–36), but separates the creation of order from its perpetuation. Thus, once an order is created, the reasons for orienting oneself to it—thereby perpetuating it—can differ.

Parsons, a translator of some of Weber's works, also speaks of social order. He ([1937] 1968: 91) discusses two forms of order: normative and factual. Normative order, according to Parsons, "is always relative to a given system of norms or normative elements, whether ends, rules, or norms. Order in this sense means that a process takes place in conformity with the paths laid down in the normative system" ([1937] 1968: 91). This form of order is contrasted with disorder and chaos (cf. Frank 1944). Factual order connotes the antithesis of randomness, and Parsons says that this order is based on scientific laws and logical theory. Parsons, following Pareto, says it is possible to establish a factual order out of a normative order—that is, one may establish scientific laws concerning the empirical normative order (Parsons [1937] 1968: 92).

Parsons assumes a firm "ontological base" (realism), and frames the problem as an epistemic issue. Parsons is explicit about this when he declares his position, which is:

> realistic, in the technical epistemological sense. It is a philosophical implication of the position taken here that there is an external world of so-called empirical reality which is not the creation of the individual human mind and that is not reducible to terms of an ideal order, in the philosophical sense. (Parsons [1937] 1968: 753)

Parsons argues that scientific theories are not part of the world ([1937] 1968: 753–54), a position he calls "analytical realism" (Parsons [1937] 1968: 757). This position "legitimizes" an objectivistic approach to science in which there is no feedback between the field of study and the scientific knowledge of this field, a notion that few would endorse today (Aspers 2007). There is also a tendency in Parsons's early work to ascribe values to actors rather than to investigate them empirically. This is reflected in Parsons's approach to order that essentially implies that, in the end, only cultural values can explain social order (cf. Parsons and White [1961] 1970: 186).[3] Additional weaknesses include the functionalist dream and the grand theory approach (cf. Hedström and Swedberg 1996, 1998; Hedström 2005).

There is also a structural approach to order. Mark Granovetter discusses order in the economy, arguing that "social relations between firms are more important, and authority within firms less so, in bringing order to economic life than is supposed in the market and hierarchies line of thought" (1985: 501). Granovetter's structural approach is in conflict with the value approach of Parsons; one may say that while Parsons stresses content, Granovetter stresses form. I shall argue throughout this book that one cannot focus on only one cause of order.

Economists, too, have addressed order. The mainstream economic—and liberal—idea sees order as something that emerges spontaneously. This means, however, that how (market) order emerges is not problematized; it is merely a natural consequence of *homines oeconomici* coming together. The economists, moreover, do not use the term "order," but rather "equilibrium." There are two radically different views of how social order is created and maintained in markets. The liberal view of markets (cf. Smart 2003: 89–96) is that they are arenas in which "monads"—or *homines oeconomici*—sign contracts with each other and in which order emerges spontaneously. The other view is that order emerges and is maintained largely because of the state and its policies (cf. Fligstein 2001). According to Fligstein, "A stable market is defined as a situation in which the identities and status hierarchy of producer firms (the incumbents and challengers) is well known, and a conception of control that guides actors who lead firms is shared" (2001: 76). Though Fligstein's definition, which stresses the structural components of order, is useful in many markets, I will show that it does not apply to all markets.[4]

The sociological question of order is more basic than the economic question of equilibrium, which refers only to stable prices in a market with given and identical products without entrepreneurs (cf. Kirzner 1973). But as has been shown, many markets do not operate according to the logic assumed by most economists (for example, White 1981, 2002). Moreover, the sociological issue of order is broader than the economic version that is built on the notion of market equilibrium in switch-role markets, such as the stock exchange (Aspers 2007). Claus Offe has expressed the view, shared by many sociologists, that "the market and its mechanism...can hardly be invoked as a self-evidently superior contribution to social order" (2000: 88). Markets are more than the price mechanism, and order in markets depends on order in other parts of social life. Before further discussing order inside and outside markets, I will briefly discuss what order is.

The Social Construction of Order

I define *order* as the predictability of human activities and the stability of social components in relation to each other (Hayek 1973: 36).[5] Order is a matter of degree (Wrong 1994: 9), not something that either is or is not (Waldenfels 1998). Order, moreover, is often seen as the antithesis of chaos (cf. Giddens 1976: 98; Waldenfels 1998: 18), or "noise" (Luhmann [1984] 1995: 214), a point also stressed in relation to fashion (Gregory 1948: 69). There is also much to say about the genealogy of the term.[6] However, when sociologists study order, in most cases the problem is already "solved" (Luhmann 1981: 196), since we are already in the world (Heidegger [1927] 2001) that we take for granted.[7]

Hobbes, Parsons, and other sociologists, I argue, have addressed social order, but they have not addressed the ontological level at all. Parsons, to take one example, says it is "convenient" to "classify the object world as composed of three classes of 'social,' 'physical,' and 'cultural' objects" ([1951] 1970: 4). This is also to restrict the problem and to give the researcher an empirical-independent and superior position based on the assumption of realism.

One way of putting this is that social scientists have been faithful Christians, believing essentially in the Book of Genesis. In these terms, the social world has been seen as something that is there to be discovered. In my opinion, this is not a valid assumption. The approach I shall present enables us to analyze and understand order even if we assume that the world is best characterized as a global social construction (Hacking 1999). To analyze order at the level of social constructivism is another way of saying that the social constructions that give rise to social order are entrenched. I thus see *social* constructions as meanings that result from social interaction and become entrenched.[8] By *entrenchment* of meanings I propose that socially constructed meanings are established due to active or passive processes that make them difficult to change (cf. Berger and Luckmann [1966] 1991). All meanings are entrenched, but to different degrees. Meanings should not be restricted to cognitive processes or to discourse; practice is also a way of entrenching meanings. A social construction is entrenched in other constructions, which is to say that any entrenchment is only relative to other entrenched constructions. The most entrenched social constructions, in other words, are taken for granted or, relatively speaking, are more difficult to change than others. This means they can serve as building blocks for other social constructions. Social constructions are conceptualized as intersubjective meanings and are seen as constitutive of social interaction.[9] Actors orient themselves to this socially constructed world, of which they are a part, and the existence of order means that its inhabitants' expectations are often correct (cf. Luhmann [1984] 1995). This social constructivist approach means that constructions of both ideal and material "objects," including our theories about them (cf. Goodman 1984: 21) and ourselves (cf. Heidegger [1927] 2001), make up the world. Order in the branded garment industry, for example, is based on other and more entrenched meanings of the lifeworld that are not specific to this industry. What I have presented so far is the basic idea of order at the level of assumed (entrenched) meanings; I will now turn to the more practical question of order.

I shall concentrate on a number of interrelated units that I call partial social orders, an idea that draws on Bourdieu, Luhmann, and White. To analyze the construction of *partial order* in markets—that is, order that is limited in range but not necessarily local—is to study order at the concrete level without assuming order. Moreover, my approach of studying markets as partial orders resembles an idea voiced by Parsons. He viewed the "economy as *contained* in 'society'" (Moss and Savchenko 2006: xxi). Though Parsons's idea points in the right direction—the integration of the economy and the non-economy—I think his notion of reifying society as an entity ("above" its parts, so to speak) does not promote understanding of interrelations or social effects.

Each partial order draws on the order of the lifeworld and other partial orders, but it does have some autonomy, too. A final specific consumer market for fashion is an example of a partial order in which actors are structured in two roles: sellers and buyers. They come together and define each other's identities around the value of this market—meaning, what it is about, which in this case is "affordable fashion." In other words, not all actors take part in this market, only those—sellers and buyers—who orient themselves to "affordable fashion." The BGRs' identities are also determined in social formations that are non-economic. This is the case, for example, when non-governmental organizations evaluate garment retailers according to how ethical production is in the supplying factories. No money is involved in this case, but the BGRs are evaluated according to a value, namely ethics, which they have not determined. Garment consumers do not directly take part in the evaluation, but this information is relayed in the media and affects consumers' opinions of BGRs. It will be shown that branded garment retailers can control their identities in the eyes of consumers only to a certain degree. I will show how order in the final consumer market for fashion garments can be explained only if one considers how BGRs' identities are determined in interdependent markets, but also outside of markets. This is to say that markets are economic partial orders that are ordered by other markets, but also by non-economic partial orders.

Outline of the Book

The rest of the book is divided into seven chapters and five appendices. The study begins with an analysis of the final consumer market for fashion garments. The first chapter focuses on how branded garment retailers constitute one market among other fashion garment markets. In chapter 2, I focus on how BGRs "gain" their identities in the final consumer market for "affordable fashion garments." How order in this market is made and sustained is not clear, and in chapter 3 I analyze several markets and non-markets that affect and stabilize the identity of branded garment retailers in their consumer market, such as advertising, the look of their stores, and how they are evaluated in terms of how ethically production is organized in "their" garment factories. Chapter 4 shifts the focus from the consumer market to the global producer market, in which BGRs face manufacturers. Chapter 5 studies the same production market, but analyzes it from the manufacturers' perspective. In chapter 6, I focus on how BGRs are positioned in the stock exchange, where BGRs face investors. In this market, identities of firms are translated and aggregated into economic terms. Chapter 7 summarizes the findings of the book, and contains discussions of partial orders.

Chapter 1 _

Garment Sellers in Consumer Markets

THE PURPOSE OF THIS CHAPTER is to begin the analysis of order in the final consumer market, focusing on the different kinds of fashion garment sellers. But what is a market? I define *market* as a social structure for the exchange of rights in which offers are evaluated and priced, and compete with one another. This means at least three actors are needed for a market to exist: at least one actor on one side of the market, who is aware of at least two actors on the other side whose offers can be evaluated in relation to each other (cf. Aspers 2009; Simmel [1908] 1983: 83–84). The market is a form of economic coordination in which actors have a choice; they can decide to sell or buy, at the price they are offered. Market actors—that is, sellers and buyers—are characterized by different interests, or, in the words of Geertz, "under whatever skies, men prefer to buy cheap and sell dear" ([1978] 1992: 226). Though originally markets were tied to a particular place (Swedberg 1994), this need no longer be the case (cf. Knorr Cetina and Bruegger 2002). A market, in contrast to individual transactions, must have some stability over time. Formal or informal rights are exchanged in markets, and prices are means for the economic evaluation of at least two competing offers.

This book studies how identities, products, and values contribute to make a part of the social world—namely the fashion industry and, more specifically, its markets—stable and so, from the perspective of the actors, predictable. Predictability in a market means knowing what is produced, who the actors—that is, the people and organizations—are and how they become what they are. This knowledge is also what people need to "predict" what will come into fashion. Only given the order of a market is it possible for actors to understand and "predict" fashion, or at least have some sense that they are not mistaken concerning trends. Fashion, which is characterized by change, as already mentioned, can be understood only against the background of order. To explain order in the final consumer market one has to bring the actors, buyers and sellers, as well as the offers—in this case, fashion garments—traded into the analysis. Order in one market usually depends on its context, which is largely made up of other markets. This suggests that markets should not be analyzed in isolation.

I begin this chapter by introducing the central notion of identity. This notion is then used to analyze the different types of sellers of fashion garments in the final consumer market. I focus on fashion garments and disregard other items these sellers may offer—for example, shoes and perfumes. I proceed with a discussion of the differentiation of consumer markets for fashion garments, which is a way of observing how sellers relate to one another. This chapter analyzes four different types of fashion garment sellers: branded garment retailers, privately owned shops, independent designers, and haute couture. Based on this I will discuss competition and collaboration at the level of markets. This analysis provides a background for the focus on branded garment retailers in the rest of the book, but it also clearly shows how markets and their different actors are related to each other.

Identity

We cannot start with the assumption of order, or simply take the identities of the branded garment retailers for granted, because this is partly what is to be explained. How does it come to be, for example, that there are such firms as branded garment retailers (BGRs)? The concrete theoretical entry point is the question of identity (see Cerulo 1997 and Brubaker and Cooper 2000 for overviews of identity research). According to Husserl ([1922] 1992: 117–18), at the most general level identity refers to a similarity between two "things" over a period of time. A thing, in sociological terms, can be a body, for example, which anchors a name and a narrative, in which case we can talk of the identity of a human being. I define *identity* as a perceived similarity bound by a narrative pegged onto a "thing-event" (cf. Goffman ([1963] 1968: 74–75).[1] The perceived similarity refers to the socially constituted cognitive framework of identities, which is to say that the similarity does not have to be pegged onto an object; an event—for instance, a fashion fair—or a place can serve as a peg (Miller et al. 1998: 19–24). The narrative brings the "thing-event," in association with activities over time, into a meaning structure (cf. Ricoeur 1992: 140–68). It is important that a narrative, so to speak, supports the peg, given it is not evident what is seen as constituting the similarity (cf. Somers 1994: 618). Identity refers to what one is, and should be contrasted with what one does (a role).

Differentiation from other identities are further requirements of an identity, and points at the relational aspect of identity (cf. Emirbayer 1997).[2] The "thing-event" can be a commodity, a brand, or a set of aspects seen together, so that it stands out in relation to the environment over time. I start by analyzing BGRs' *collective identity*—that is, the identity that all BGRs share, and which sets them apart from other collective identities. This level is constitutive for the other levels, to be discussed next.

Market Differentiation

Seen from a distance, anyone who is selling something is competing for consumers' money. In other words, in a "perfect" neoliberal world virtually every individual apart from the seller of a commodity is a potential buyer of this commodity or service (von Mises [1963] 1966; Nozick 1974). In such a world, with no firms, transaction costs, or sunk costs, there would essentially be no retailers, just egological economic actors signing contracts and maintaining a multitude of relations at arm's length, switching between being buyers and sellers.

Though many economic actors—such as those who sell garments to final consumers—at least at first sight appear to be in a structurally similar position (cf. Burt 1992), this cannot be the starting point of a sociological study; the situation must be investigated further. A closer look will enable us to see their different identities. Moreover, the empirical fact that there are many different markets and many different actors within them must be accounted for.

Markets have been made over time, dividing and differentiating the production process. As a consequence, actors have become associated with roles (cf. Braudel [1975] 1992; Durkheim [1893] 1984). The idea of fixed roles (White 1981; Aspers 2007) for buyers (who are often producers) and sellers (who are often consumers) adds an important dimension to the analysis of order in the final consumer or "edge market" (White 2002: 320). Branded garment retailers are sellers of fashion garments and they constitute a collective identity. But how does this collective identity—which means that one can speak of a market identity (White 2002: 2)[3]—come about?

We can understand the formation of collective identities, focusing on the fashion industry, in relation to specialization and differentiation. Today, mail-order firms, private stores, independent designers, branded retailers (for example, Topshop), haute couture design (for instance, the house of Christian Dior), *prêt-à-porter* or ready-to-wear (Louis Vuitton, for example), and other alternatives are available for consumers. The different ways of buying and producing garments, and the different ways in which fashion is produced—which are the main factors together with correlated prices—have generated different markets over time. These markets are based on different values, and producers in them constitute different collective identities (White 2002). These are different markets because sellers and buyers, in their practice and perceptions, treat them as different markets. This requires explanation, however, and in this chapter I shall discuss how the cohesion and evaluation of a market must be related to social structure.

Branded retailers sell a large proportion of the garments traded in the Western world. Nonetheless, consumers seldom spend all their money on clothes in just one market. Because of constrained budgets, access to stores, or their different fashion preferences, many wardrobes are put together by combining basic and more fashionable garments, from different firms and in different price ranges, though most people spend the largest share of their garment budget on clothes from BGRs. This means consumers often buy commodities in more than one market. It is unlikely, in contrast to business-to-business (B2B) transactions, that the sellers know the consumers as individuals. Instead, ideal-type consumers represent the buying side, which means one person can represent several different ideal-type consumers. The exception is the haute couture market, in which named designers dress the wealthy and celebrities (cf. Agrawal and Kamakura 1995; McCracken 1989; see Marshall 1997 on celebrities) of different kinds. In these cases, as with *prêt-à-porter*, sellers and the public may recognize the buyers. Thus, when Paris Hilton or Kylie Minogue appear on a red carpet, some portions of the media take careful note of what they are wearing.

The differences between types of sellers of garments may be grounds for collective identities and their corresponding markets (cf. Zuckermann 1999). These differences cannot be reduced to production quality (for example, the types of fabrics used), but must be sought in the eyes of the consumers and in the relevant institutional factors (cf. Kawamura 2004: 73–81). In the following, I discuss four different types of sellers, representing four different markets: the branded garment retailer, haute couture, the independent designer, and the private store, concentrating on BGRs. From a theoretical perspective, any dimension can be a reason for differentiation (cf. Bourdieu 1987), but only some are seen as meaningful by the actors—garment sellers and above all their consumers—who orient themselves to these dimensions and thereby construct them.

I shall not carry out a more detailed empirical analysis of all the different types of sellers. I have used general knowledge, from my own observations and documents in the business and public press, as well as the academic literature to create table 1.1. In this table, I focus on the dissimilarities, which should not conceal the fact that they obviously share many things, besides selling garments. In my view, the dissimilarities presented in the table are enough to set them apart, in their own as well as consumers' eyes, so that one can talk of different collective identities (cf. Philips and Zuckerman 2001: 383–84). The different ideal-type sellers

TABLE 1.1.

Differences between four selected ideal-typical garment sellers in contact with final consumers

Dimension	Branded retailer	Privately owned shop	Independent designer	Haute couture
Value	Affordable fashion	Safe fashion	Alternative fashion	Conspicuous fashion
Promotion	National media, TV, billboards	Consumer networks and local media	Personal networks and shows	Journalists and shows
Production chain	Global buying chains	Buys from importers	Buys input materials, in-house production	Buys input materials, in-house production
Stores	Standardized	Personal	Studio/home/personal	Studio/exclusive
Price	Low/moderate	Moderate	Moderate	Very high
Organizational structure	Several divisions, including buying, design, and marketing	One owner and perhaps a few employees	Small and part-time self-employed	Small-scale in-house production according to the customers' needs
Consumers	Virtually everyone, but focusing on certain groups	Different niches or broader groups	Friends and those who want something special	Celebrities and the wealthy
Fashion profile	High/ mainstream	Varies	High / avant garde	High
Visual examples	Figure 1.1	Figure 1.2	Figure 1.3	No figure*

* There is no figure to illustrate the visual appearance of haute couture since this form is not oriented directly towards customers "in the street."

of garments are unlikely to be found in reality, but they capture the differentiation and segmentation among garment sellers that has occurred over time.

The different values constitute the main difference between them. But one cannot understand the values as the sole factor that orders these markets; the social structure is also central. The table captures not only things that are observable to consumers, such as stores and the way they market themselves, but also aspects that are of most interest in relation to BGRs, such as organizational structure. Furthermore, competition largely takes place between firms operating within the same market (category), as discussed by White (1981, 2002).

The central difference between these markets is what the market is "about"—in other words, what is valued in it. How can we understand the different values of these four garment markets? Values, I assert, are central social constructions for understanding order. I define *value* as the determination and rating of a "thing." This definition captures the complexity of value; it is a way of separating things from one another, but it is also a scale to be used for evaluating those things covered by the value. This means that different things, such as a service, a cultural expression, an action, an institution, a commodity—or any other thing—can be rated according to the value of that thing.[4] When people adhere to a value it becomes an entrenched meaning (cf. Heidegger 1997: 38–40), which means it is taken for granted. It thereby contributes to the "partial order" that the market is. Values are social constructions made in the public arena (cf. Arendt [1958] 1988: 164) that guide people; adherence to one over another indicates they prefer one thing (state) to another (cf. Luhmann [1984] 1995: 317). Husserl ([1900] 1975: §14) has analyzed the process of the constitution of values, and he draws an intimate connection between evaluation and value, an idea he shares with Parsons (1991: 38).

A concrete consequence in fashion markets is that though all sellers stand in competitive relations to each other, the different values make them different in the eyes of consumers (cf. Boltanski and Thèvenot 2006; Biggart and Beamish 2003: 455–57). These collective identities are created if they differentiate the products sold by the price policies, not just in terms of the products' visual appearance and the way they are sold (figures 1.1–1.3).

Though one can separate markets according to values, in practice it is very hard because the very idea of fashion—in contrast to the market for, say, crude oil—is to change the products often. In fact, the social structure of buyers and sellers based on status is the ordering principle in fashion markets, as the meaning of this structure is relatively more entrenched than the fashion garments sold in the market. I define *status* as the rank position of identities that result from evaluation, and which are relatively stable over time. Status, of which a position has more or less, becomes an ordering principle when there is a lack of generally accepted scales of values; in other words, when it is unclear what the offer of the market—the product—"is." In a status market, order is maintained because the identities of actors on both sides of the market are ranked according to status, which is a more entrenched—or, in other words, more taken for granted—social construction than the thing (value) traded in the market, namely fashion garments. Thus, while fashion changes every month, the structure of firms that are positioned in relation to each other (White 2002) remains relatively stable in this market, as in most other markets (Burt 1988). In the following, I elaborate on the status order, which is a social construction that must be seen in relation to standard markets. "Standard" refers to markets in which the scale of value—what is sold in the market—is more entrenched than the social structure of incumbents in the market.

Figure 1.1. A branded garment retailer—one of London's high street fashion fixtures. (Photo taken in London, 2006.)

Figure 1.2. A privately owned shop—part of London's high street fashion. (Photo taken in London, 2006.)

Figure 1.3. An independent designer exhibits her clothes at an outdoor stall. (Photo taken in London, 2006.)

Different collective identities ordered by status tend to be geographically concentrated (Aspers 2009). With the notion of status, we can also explain some of the observations that are at least indirectly observable in the photographs (figures 1.1–1.3), namely the spatial distribution of markets. Markets have been specialized, and this is the case in all old European cities, as reflected in the markets' names. Consequently, in London, as in Stockholm, stores from the different segments are found in different places: compare the luxury shops in Bond Street with the large BGR stores in Oxford Street. Thus, the photographs are not intended to capture the products, but rather the combined effect of the product and the context of presentation that consumers observe.[5]

BGRs' stores are concentrated in shopping areas or districts, and frequently the fiercest competitors, such as H&M and Zara, are to be found on either side of the same street. Some more high fashion brands have their own stores or are "incorporated" within luxury department stores, such as like Selfridges, Harrods, and Liberty. It is of course not the physical dispersion that is the most important issue here; it is through the concentration of firms with certain identities, and the corresponding status that gives them meaning, that the place becomes meaningful. In view of the fact that many of these garment chains, such as Zara and H&M, are better "known" than most local areas, they are increasingly giving meaning to places, rather than the other way around. It is because of this that malls try to attract the "right" firms and labels. Only when a place has meaning can new entrants draw on that meaning. In other words, a brand that is "picked up" to be sold at Selfridges (cf. Entwistle 2006) acquires meaning from this very fact (that is, it becomes more of a high-fashion brand). It is then possible that, after some time, the place becomes a more strongly entrenched social construction than the individual firms that originally made it up.

All of these types of garment sellers face competition from the market in which they operate. To put it another way, differentiation (which in this market is not collectively orchestrated but the result of a developed monopolistic competition), division of labor, and strategies, diminishes competition, or at least diminishes the number of direct competitors. Competition also exists between the different markets, and the spatial distribution reinforces this. The individual firm within a market, however, cannot do much to affect which market consumers prefer. It must concentrate its activities on competition between the firms within its market.

Types of Sellers

In the following, I expand on the different ideal-types of garment sellers. I do not discuss firms that sell non-branded garments or brands that no one has ever heard of—two kinds of products or sellers that lack market identities. I shall not discuss mail-order firms either. Instead, I will look at three different garment markets that are related to the consumer market in which the BGRs operate, which is the topic of the next chapter. I begin with the private store—that is, stores owned by an individual and that are not part of a larger chain.

Private Shop

What is the central value, and what is its meaning, in the market in which privately owned shops compete with each other? Such shops are defined by the mixture of brands they sell, which are usually more expensive than those sold by BGRs. The supply chain, with many intermediaries, is extended and slower than BGR chains. The slowness of the supply chain, and the centrality of brands, means that one can talk about "safe fashion" as the central value. The turnover of a private shop is usually not large enough to allow its representatives to visit many fashion shows, or to go abroad for "inspiration." The number of items bought of each type of garment is small. Private shops can buy their stock of garments from centralized retailing outlets or permanent fairs in which importers trade with many smaller garment sellers, as I observed during my own fieldwork.

London has several districts in which shop owners can buy from wholesalers. Near Finsbury Park underground station are more than 50 shops/wholesalers. The following are typical examples of signs the sellers post in their window: "Manufacturer and wholesaler of ladies fashion wear," "Not open to the public," and "Factory Prices Direct to the Public." This area is ethnically mixed, and shop owners and staff tend to be immigrants, some of whom have connections to production units in their home countries. Such shops are of relatively low status. There is even an outdoor market, and some advertise primarily on the basis of price: for example, "Trousers from £5." In Stockholm, a business park excludes the public from the B2B market. This market is important in enabling private shops to create the specific fashion mix that sets them apart from each other.

Shop owners may also buy from traveling salesmen or, in some cases, from within their ethnic business network. A private shop must represent several brands, something normally associated with requirements as well as rights, for example, to be the sole representative of a brand in a certain area. This often means shops must comply with demands made by designer brands concerning such things as how the clothes are displayed, pricing, and what other brands it may represent. Representatives of branded designers and others anonymously visit shops that represent their brands, look around, and either directly comment on what they find, or more likely let their contact know about potential problems. In this way, they control their identities, but also the identities of the shops.

Private shops have different price policies; some sell brands with a high fashion profile, whereas others sell brands that are more conservative. To concentrate on a certain type of garment often means concentrating on certain consumers, and so smaller shops may try to survive by creating niches. Selling fashion to sailors, golfers, or 50+ businesswomen are examples of niches. In a smaller city, a shop may be the only outlet of a brand, which entails a monopoly situation or monopolistic competition. A niche of this kind, however, can be restricted to a local area (for example, a shopping center or a smaller city). The shop and the clothes on display are the primary means of advertising. They may advertise locally, but the suppliers of the brands are responsible for advertisements in fashion magazines and the like.

Independent Designers

What I call an independent designer is a self-employed, often young person who may be struggling economically to establish a market niche. Such designers are, together with *prêt-à-porter* and haute couture designers, "creative workers" (cf. McRobbie 2003; Aspers 2006b). Though prices may not be particularly high, the supply is limited and enables buyers of these clothes to develop a personal style. The value in this market is best described as "alternative fashion," which includes cutting-edge fashion.

Independent designers essentially produce the garments themselves or with the help of networks of other self-employed persons or small businesses, and they buy the bulk of their fabrics and other materials from local distributors or let their garments be produced by foreign suppliers, frequently mediated by agents. Though it is the dream of almost all students who graduate from design schools (cf. McRobbie 1998) to set up their own label, few succeed in doing this. As a result, they may start competing with ready-to-wear design. But it is often a futile struggle involving a seemingly never-ending "start-up process," the outcome of which is often that they end up in the design department of a larger retailer. The alternative, which is difficult, is to raise capital to move into large-scale production. The situation of independent designers and their working conditions resemble those of other self-employed persons in the "creative" sector, such as fashion photographers (cf. Aspers 2006a).

Those seeking to become or to establish themselves as designers need visually to manifest their connection to the collective identity of fashion designers, for example by sometimes outrageous designs. During my fieldwork, I visited a competition for young would-be fashion designers, whose clothes were also on display in small booths. Catwalk shows had been arranged with experienced fashion models. In fact, the most extreme fashions were worn by the designers themselves, rather than the models or the visitors. This was one way for the designers to obtain at least some recognition. This visual connection to the fashion system is particularly important because such designers do not, strictly speaking, yet count as such. They are on the right track, but ultimately it is out of their hands whether they turn out to be established fashion designers. This requires acceptance—in other words, someone else must evaluate what they do. But they can at least try to look like fashion designers, for which the assent of others is not required. One can see this as a way of creating bonds with the collective identity of fashion designers by mimicking the visual dimension of the culture. The way would-be designers dress reflects the fact that their being is often closely connected to their work role (Bovone 2006: 378).

Designers determine neither their identity nor, one might add, their being. They can only hope they will make it in the market; only in their dreams can they unite what they want to be ("fashion designers") with what they are ("people who attend design schools"). The competitions they take part in are one way of getting closer to their goal (though it can sometimes take them farther away from it), depending on the status bestowed upon these would-be designers in the process. Participation in such competitions is therefore fraught with anxiety. As a yet-to-be-established fashion designer then, one is "inherently nothing"; neither one's name, face, or label is known.

Markets are another way of obtaining recognition. A problem is that independent designers often have few consumers, most of whom are young and with little purchasing power. This kind of consumer wants something a bit different, but because independent designers are virtually unknown, they cannot charge much for their products, while facing high production costs due to a small series. Profits are therefore elusive. The markets in which independent designers take part are organized differently from the BGRs' market, for example. Independent designers' products are often not made for the mainstream consumer, but for those demanding a higher fashion profile. This often means they are involved in unconventional marketing. Hauge (2007, III, IV: 10–19) describes how small firms and independent designers try to stay "cool" by associating themselves with "cool" people and "cool" places. In London, Brick Lane and between Portobello Road and Ladbroke Grove underground station are examples of such places where one finds independent designers who offer their limited production to consumers on market stalls. They may also show their clothes in temporary fairs. An independent designer usually lacks economic resources, and to advertise would indicate that one is no longer "independent." One might even say that independent designers are involved in an inverted economy (cf. Bourdieu [1992] 1996: 148–49) in which one cannot be an "artist" and at the same time have a large "audience." It is also through face-to-face interaction, gossip, and informal contacts that recognition is acquired. Another source of recognition is awards, which endow designers with status. Social capital—or in simpler terms social class—is in this case extremely valuable in coming into contact with those who decide which young designers ("rookies") will take part in fashion shows.

Business-to-business markets constitute another channel for reaching out to final consumers, but few independent designers are represented in stores. Selling clothes in stores requires that someone on "the other side" of this market, the economic audience (cf. Zuckermann 1999: 1429)—in this case, buyers from stores—appreciate what they do. Buyers operate as an economic audience that evaluates designers' market potential, which is to say that the relationship to the audience "constitute[s] one of the bases for evaluating the producers and their products" (Bourdieu 1993: 46; cf. Goffman [1959] 1971). In this way, recognition is distributed (a process that can be identified in many cases, not only in this market).

Haute Couture and High Fashion

Haute couture is another word for high fashion, and it comes with an aura of exclusivity. In terms of pricing, it constitutes the top end, and is a constant source of fascination to students of fashion. The myth of the creative genius is nurtured in this market, though the explanation of its status both today and in the past cannot be reduced to either creativity or production quality. Far more important is the institutional system of La Chambre Syndicale de la Couture Parisienne, of which the different fashion houses are members (Kawamura 2004). This meta-organization (Ahrne and Brunsson 2005, 2008) has long controlled this segment, much like a guild. *Prêt-à-porter* (sometimes called "ready to wear") refers to less expensive designer labels, made for a larger group of consumers (Kawamura 2004: 73–88). There are of course differences between haute couture and *prêt-à-porter*; the latter uses subcontractors (cf. Storper 1997: 150), and the clothes are not custom-made.

Haute couture pieces are unique and created for individual customers, such as royalty and the wealthy (and of course fitted to the bodies and preferences of the customers, cf. Storper 1997: 149–51). Production takes place in-house (in so-called *ateliers*—and the materials used can be very costly (incorporating, say, diamonds). Customers are willing to pay large sums to make sure they have unique garments to be worn at public events. Even well-known French fashion houses, such as Chanel and Christian Dior, have limited production in haute couture. They may not do more than, say, 20 bridal dresses a year, and the total number of garments sold by a fashion house may not exceed 1,500 pieces. This is a diminishing fashion market; 200 Parisian fashion houses existed in 1946, but in 2003 only 11 still made haute couture (Kawamura 2004: 79).

Though the logic of haute couture resembles that of the independent designer, much more money is involved and the collections are given much more media exposure (Kawamura 2004: 63–71). Haute couture can be termed, borrowing from Veblen, "conspicuous fashion." These garments are not directly advertised; instead they are the focus of attention of fashion shows. What is exhibited at such shows is made known to the public through the editorials of the fashion press, the Internet, and so on. Reports show pictures not only from the catwalks, but sometimes from "backstage," where the models change clothes, and from parties. Information control is still exercised, for instance by means of hired photographers whose pictures can be controlled. Today, however, *prêt-à-porter* is the dominant market segment in "high fashion," and it is this that is reported from catwalks rather than haute couture.

As Kawamura (2004) has pointed out, fashion segments that are less expensive than haute couture—*demi-couture* and *prêt-à-porter*—have grown to some extent at the expense of haute couture. I will also comment on these segments, since today they are of great importance for fashion. The *prêt-à-porter* segment, which is defined in terms of membership in La Chambre Syndicale du Prêt-à-Porter, includes such names as Pierre Cardin, Cerruti, and Torrente (Kawamura 2004: 80).

It is worth examining in more detail these high-fashion segments and how fashion is diffused and generated. Information is central, and it is spread in, say, celebrity gossip publications that feature pictures of celebrities attending high profile events of various kinds, like film premieres. Red carpet shows like the Academy Awards visualize the connection between designers, brands, and their customers. The celebrity industry includes the numerous magazines whose main selling point is the pictures taken by paparazzi photographers. These magazines can include the names of the stores the celebrities shop at, what labels they buy, and what kind of food they eat, as well as the people they associate with. One cannot understand fashion without considering the intimate relationship between fashion, celebrities, and the diffusion of what celebrities do and wear. The importance of this social game underlines one of the main points of this book, namely that fashion is a phenomenon that lacks an underlying quality dimension.

To illustrate how fashion design is embedded in the world of celebrities, and how neither the quality of the clothes nor their fashion importance are the primary grounds for what is discussed and what "matters" in the world of fashion—a subject to which I shall return—let us look at how one fashion journalist at British *Vogue* commented on a designer who happened to be the daughter of actor Jack Nicholson. The comment does not begin with a discussion of her clothes, but with several references to Jack Nicholson, as well as to Hollywood (where she lives). Most fashion shows reported on are accompanied by pictures presenting the garments. In this case, however, the picture was of Jack Nicholson. We are told that "[Jennifer] Nicholson began mingling at a very young age with legends such as Diana Vreeland, Angelica Huston and Lauren Hutton" and "her past and present culminate in rich, polished designs with the right blend of Hollywood and history."

A few lines later, we are informed that "[w]hat sets [Jennifer] Nicholson apart from other designers is that she does not just re-create the looks she was inspired by as a child—she plays with the original silhouette and recalls old Hollywood for today's modern woman." Her style, to give us some idea of the quality of the clothes, "is just what Hollywood starlets, such as famous clients Paris Hilton, Rose McGowan and Ashlee Simpson, would wear if they were at the beach all day and at Hollywood parties all night."[6]

Most of another report is devoted to everything but the clothes, focusing instead on the guests.[7] "In the front [where the most prestigious guests are placed] there was Kelly Rowland and fellow Destiny's Child buddy Michelle Williams and—only a few seats along chewing gum and shielding themselves under the pop of the pap bulbs—were the diminutive yet mesmerizing Olsen twins at their first outing of Fashion Week. A high standard front row for the duo who dress for excess."

Though in these circumstances the importance of design "quality" might be questioned, high fashion—for example, haute couture—is still important. It operates chiefly as a source of inspiration to other designers and fashion firms. The costs of the design and production of garments for shows are very high, and it is difficult for fashion houses to make a profit on garments alone; in fact, losses are more typical. However, such houses can exchange their symbolic capital as high-fashion designers, and cash in on the production of other items, like perfumes, jewelry, cosmetics and accessories that can be bought by broader groups of consumers. Expansion into the *prêt-à-porter* segment also allows them to increase sales volumes. This is a form of brand extension (Forney, Joo Park, and Brandon 2005), in which a brand in one market is transferred to another market. The products are usually related to a certain lifestyle, such as "young people who like to do sports," to make the transfer easier. The prestige of fashion garments is used in other fields to sell mass market products, incurring royalties. Moreover, high status car producers and watchmakers advertise in the same magazines as high status designer brands, which is a way of cooperating that benefits both, as status may "leak" between actors (Podolny 2005), which is a metaphor for the fact that status is relational.

Actors who have an elevated status position are aware of how they can contribute to such status leakage. Many examples could be cited to illustrate how the ideal-type garment sellers discussed here are connected. Madonna (who of course is no designer), Stella McCartney (who has a fashion label), and Karl Lagerfeld (who has his own company and is a designer for Chanel), among others, have all designed for H&M. Most of the garments were sold quickly, and some even ended up in Internet auctions. In this way, the designers not only receive a financial reward, but free advertising in the general press. The BGR, as a consequence of this association, gains status. But how is the difference maintained between the same designer's ready-to-wear products and those they design for retailers with less status? In other words, how does a noted ready-to-wear designer avoid having their status tainted by association with their designs sold in main street stores at much lower prices? A reporter asked one of the designers, Stella McCartney, what the difference was between a blouse that costs €30 [sold by H&M] and one that costs €300 by Stella McCartney. She replied, "If there was no difference I would have no future. There is of course a difference in quality, but this line [referring to her clothes produced by H&M] is of good quality. One should remember that I have my garments made in Italy, and I make a few hundred. H&M makes thousands and thousands of them." The last point is important, but the culture of this market more or less forbids her to discuss her status, which is the main factor explaining why she can sell garments under her own name for €300 a piece, rather than the inherent quality of the clothes. An unknown designer who also has her garments made in Italy cannot sell them for €300; she would merely be a "nobody" selling extremely overpriced garments that probably very few would buy. In this case, "quality" is to some extent a "myth" that both consumers and producers contribute to, and which the latter draw on to justify selling garments at a high price. We shall further discuss this point of connecting sellers and buyers with price later in these pages. If we compare the type of sellers just discussed with the BGRs, it is clear that the latter operate in a market that is largest in terms of volume, but they are not the most important when it comes to fashion. Next, we discuss how the different garment sellers analyzed are related to each other in the forms of competition and cooperation.

Competition and Cooperation

Though markets are characterized by competition, this does not exclude cooperation. Garment sellers in markets make up a collective identity, and in one sense they relate to each other as competitors (cf. White 1981, 2002). In phenomenological terms, however, these types can be seen as representing different competing markets instead of one single market. If all firms competed with each other, there would be thousands of "brands," which of course would be too much for any consumer or producer to keep track of.

Understandably, consumers know more about the firms in one or a few markets than in others. This has partly to do with consumers' focus of interest, conditioned by who they are, their identity. Other aspects, such as where they live, their budget, and their fashion interests also matter. Finally, consumers have limited cognitive capacity to "know" a large number of brands. It is therefore difficult for both consumers and producers to obtain an overview of a market. One consequence of this is that in a market such as Turkey, which has hundreds of "brands," there may be only a few that people remember and can relate to. In the period of the making—or the transition—of markets, one may observe this oversupply of brands, which means that in fact no market is in place.

There are consequently two kinds of competition: between firms that are seen as being "close to each other," but also between types of sellers. Thus, one may talk of two different competitive structures: one between actors within each market (Simmel [1922] 1955: 147, 155–56; cf. Bourdieu 2005), and one between markets. This view contrasts with the economic textbook and neoliberal idea of the market in which all market actors compete directly with each other. Many markets are a result of the state and are maintained with the help of the same (Fligstein 2001). Though this is not directly the case for the markets in which the BGRs operate, they are nonetheless often at least partly organized, often by the BGRs themselves. Marshall (1920b: 256) calls markets organized when "those who deal on it are in effect a corporation," and mentions stock exchanges as examples. Thus, organized coordination takes place in markets, often with the help of business organizations. Membership of trade associations and the like is often associated with policies or ethical rules, or informal collaboration. This organizational differentiation may contribute to the demarcation of markets. Guilds are a historical example of organization and controlled competition.

Markets, regardless of the degree to which they are formally organized, differ from each other. Some markets center on garments that are more fashionable—for example, independent designers—and others on less fashionable items, such as mail-order firms and discount outlets. There is in this industry, as in many others, an orientation (Swedberg 1999) towards actors with status (cf. Podolny 2005; Benjamin and Podolny 1999) in terms of the level of fashion. This means actors with less status observe and follow what actors with more status do, because those with more status have more power to define the underlying value of fashion in that market. These high-status firms can use their "freedom" to do what they have to do to keep their position, namely being innovative. Firms with more status, however, take little note of what firms with less status are doing in terms of fashion (cf. Aspers 2006a: 91). This means there is something of a "trickle down" effect on the production side of the market, which of course is not a recent phenomenon (Marshall 1920b: 118). The number of "knockoff" garments sold by BGRs that are more or less copies of fashion brands with more status is evidence of this. For example, supplements to some British magazines, as well as certain gossip magazines, regularly feature pictures of original designer garments next to the cheap copy available in the local mall. Thus, a Gucci blouse or a garment worn by Pink or some other celebrity might be shown next to a picture of an almost identical blouse made by Marks and Spencer, or another retailer that sells it for less than £20. This is very concrete and visual evidence of how fashion is copied and how it trickles down from the high-end firms to firms with a lower profile and which sell clothes in a very different price range. Thus, the combination of fashion and reasonable prices with high turnover—short lead times—is likely to have been important in increasing the amount of clothes involved in today's quickly changing fashion cycles.

In schematic markets, the collective identities of sellers, as well as individual firms' market niches, can be found. The individual firms occupy market niches. Borderline firms also exist, but normally are not clearly defined as members of one collective identity.

Each of the ideal-type consumer groups in the market acquires its identity in the same way as sellers, namely in relation to each other and as a result of what they wear (and of course what they do, though there is no room for an analysis of this here). When sellers and people "representing" the different ideal-type consumers transact, ties are created across the market interface that affect actors' identities.

Variation as well as entrance and exit from the market are most likely to take place at the top and low ends of each status rank of producers. One finds the least entrenched social structure at the different ends of the markets, and it is also where competition from adjacent markets is most noticeable. The firms located in the middle of the market are more likely to stay put. Thus, the top end actors may orient themselves to other markets, as may those at the lower end, who may consider shifting to another market because they have little to lose, and hardly any power to change the rules of the market (Phillips and Zuckerman 2001: 386; cf. the discussion by Fligstein on incumbents and rivals, 2001). Consequently, some markets, and their incumbents, have a different status and a higher fashion profile than others, meaning that what is fashion in these markets affects what is fashion in other markets. This also indicates that markets are embedded in each other (White 2002).

Struggle

Market actors operate in an uncertain and aggressive business environment, and hence have an interest in controlling it. This they can do by a number of means. Actors compete in markets by means that they control individually. Actors can, individually or collectively, use their power, for example, to affect and change the way in which markets are ordered. This means that the market creation process cannot be seen merely as a process in which actors watch each other, as White (1981) suggests. By shaping the market so its structure suits their purposes, market actors can exercise some kind of control. This can also take place in political processes (Fligstein 2001). Market actors may have different interests and there is often a struggle between market actors, such as buyers and sellers (or between kinds of sellers or buyers). The struggle is about defining the rules of the market game that governs competition (a topic addressed by, for instance, Marx, Weber, and Bourdieu). "Struggle," as I use the term, refers to organized interests participating in the market seeking to change its conditions—for example, its culture, rules, or values. In addition, there is competition, which is a "contest " involving use of the various means available and tolerated in the market. In an existing market, struggle and potential change take place in the context of what is taken for granted in this market. Hence, change due to struggle can—at least analytically—be separated from change that is the result of actors trying to out-perform their competitors. One can therefore identify competition or collaboration at two different levels. This means that legislation and economic policy—say, manifested in the struggle between markets that those sharing a collective identity have in common—can be handled by actors who collectively collaborate at the industry level, while at the same time competing in the consumer market.

Collaboration

BGRs collaborate and promote their collective interests in a number of ways (cf. Hall and Soskice 2001: 9–10). Before the quota system was abolished, many Swedish garment retailers, who competed fiercely in the consumer market, organized to try to remove import duties on garments. Firms in the garment industry also collaborated to create standardized garment sizes. There are other ways in which they can collaborate, as one BGR representative told me: "Maybe not sourcing, which is very competitive; one does not want to give away one's best suppliers. But there is much collaboration elsewhere. We collaborate in the development of a code of conduct, as well as on environmental issues. Thus, one tries to collaborate instead of fighting each other; it is actually pretty funny." Swedish garment retailers have, for example, been invited to fairs and been asked on study trips to various developing countries by state agencies—to study potential manufacturers, which is a way of building a common base for collective action and collective identity.

The state can be a vehicle for groups with different interests (see Korpi 2001; Woll 2005; White 2002: 88; Fligstein 2001), such as when creating standards and trade rules. I call struggle political when it takes place in the political arena, and involves the state and possibly stakeholders outside the market. Various forms of taxation are perhaps the clearest example of political influence in markets. However, laws and regulations sometimes target specific markets. Not only markets affect politics, of course, and one can also identify effects in the opposite direction. Thus, if a market is (politically) autonomous, it means its actors (on one or both sides of the market) are not easily affected by politics. An autonomous market, however, can affect how it is regulated by the state.

Struggle and Collaboration in Fashion Markets

Let me exemplify how organized interests can take political action. To promote their collective interests, or merely to exchange information, firms may join hands and create meta-organizations (Ahrne and Brunsson 2005, 2008). However, not all actors in an industry have the same goal, which suggests that struggle also takes place between actors on the same side. In most European countries, a line divides those who do not have any production units of their own and so import garments, and those who still have some production in Europe. These two kinds of players, who both appear on the side of sellers versus final consumers, are likely to see customs duties and free trade from different perspectives.

EURATEX, which is an association of European garment and textile producers, see their role as follows: "As the voice of the European textile and clothing industry, EURATEX's main objective is to create an environment within the European Union which is conducive to the manufacture of textile and clothing products."[8] EURATEX thus supports garment and textile producers within the EU.

The Foreign Trade Association (FTA) has different interests from EURATEX. The FTA represents the interests of all European importers, not only in the garment sector. The following statement by the organization explains its aims: "As a non-profit organization we campaign in the political and public arena for free global trade and a multilateral trade system and we oppose protectionism and bureaucratic restraints."[9] The organization also says something about its members: "Traditionally, the import interests of the large retail companies and of the respective associations are above all represented in the FTA."[10] These interests often collide with those of EURATEX.

This form of conflict between actors in the same industry goes on in many countries today, such as the United States (cf. Bonacich and Applebaum 2000). The identification of conflicts between capitalists is not a recent finding, of course; Pareto emphasized it strongly in his discussions of rentiers and speculators (Pareto [1915–16] 1935; Aspers 2001). The issue here is that actors who may be competitors in the same final consumer market have different interests in the production market, which they pursue collectively through various trade organizations.

The struggle between these two opposing groups could be seen in the so-called "Bra Wars." After quotas became less restrictive (on January 1,

2005, when they were supposed to be abolished), the import of clothing to Europe from China increased dramatically. In the fall of 2005, some import categories of clothes, among them bras, were blocked because the quotas had already been filled. As a result, the goods stayed in the ports where they had been unloaded. A deal was struck after a proposal from the European Commission that the quotas for 2006 could be used in advance, thus limiting the import possibilities from China in 2006 in these categories. Though the war essentially involved the EU and China, I would like to stress the role of the Europe-based Free Trade Association. One of the FTA's legal counsels said, "Our members are losing out from this," referring to the increased costs and the potential loss of these imported garments.[11]

Seen from the perspective of EURATEX, the Brussels-based group of textile producers that lobbied for the restrictions, the import restrictions were good, and they are reported to have said that the compromise that the European Commission proposed would benefit retailers at the expense of manufacturers. The president of EURATEX, Filiep Libeert, stated: "We find the Commission's proposals to be unacceptable and are confident that member states will find more palatable alternative solutions," referring to the abolition of the quota system and the use of the 2006 quotas in advance.[12]

This debate clearly shows the different interests of competing firms in the final consumer market "upstream" in the production chain. In this case, the conflicts are handled by "political means" to fight the battle in political arenas in which formal institutions are established, whereas the conflicts of interest between different types of garment sellers in the final consumer market are characterized by competition.

The larger point I want to make is that the structure of the market and its institutions can be directly constructed by the collective efforts of the members of the market or indirectly if others impose regulations, such as through political means. In the following, I give other examples to show that collaboration between "competitors" is not rare in a market.

Splitting and Fusing Markets

Cohesion in markets is constituted by the actors' mutual orientation, but also by the values and culture of the market. Market changes can be an unintended consequence of actors orienting themselves towards one another due to competition, but also because of orchestrated activities, as mentioned in the previous section. This is also the case with the making of markets. Two or more markets may become one—for example, if two or more markets start to orient themselves more towards each other in the same way as actors do in "their own" markets.

This can also be discussed in relation to real markets. Contemporary garment markets are predominantly national. A national market may harbor ten to twenty larger chains of branded retailers that are in competition with each other (cf. White 2002). That markets are still predominantly national is evident from a visual analysis of the brands represented in the city centers of different cities. I have spent much time walking and observing the brands represented in the areas of cities where clothes are sold. In five cities—Cologne, Istanbul, London, New Delhi, and Stockholm—I did this in a more focused manner, such as by photographing exteriors of stores and their surroundings. One does not find the same brands in Cologne as in London, though some will be represented in both cities; yet others will be found in New York or Boston.

To enter a new market is not easy, and several Swedish firms have tried to establish themselves in markets that are culturally close to Sweden, such as Denmark and Germany, but failed, and were forced to withdraw due to losses. That some BGRs struggle when entering a new country may not only have to do with problems of fashion of course, but the fashions of different countries do contribute to the formation of national markets for fashion garments (cf. Bair and Gereffi 2001: 1895). The fact that advertisement and fashion magazines are still national, or local, rather than global also suggests it is too early to talk of a single European consumer market for fashion garments.

A BGR, as said, may have more than a thousand stores in several countries. This means some of the larger actors, such as H&M, Zara, Topshop, and the GAP, are not only operating in one or a few markets, but are beginning to orient towards each other on the European, and one may add, the global level. Their relative strengths, in terms of market share, may differ, however, and so may the identities of the same firm in the different markets. Thus, this pattern of competition suggests there may be a European fashion market in the making, characterized by rivalries for market share.

A prediction based on the market theory presented here suggests that a European market is likely to form when acquisitions and mergers of garment firms become prevalent across Europe. Indications of this process are becoming apparent in European consumer markets.

One market may also become two or more, which may be due to entrepreneurial actions or the split of one market into many. Over time, garment markets have become segmented, and one can therefore talk of differentiation of markets into a greater number of more or less autonomous markets. In all these processes, market cultures and identities are changed, and a new one may develop. The process can partly be controlled, but no collective identity is completely autonomous, which means no one is in control of the result.

Summary

I have analyzed a set of markets that stand in competitive relation to each other. I have also defined what a market is, and discussed competition within markets. The issue of competition and collaboration at the level of markets has so far not been taken up seriously in the economic sociological discussion of markets. Markets are made and changed in social processes. Change in a market can thus be due to its internal affairs, but other markets—which make up a large part of a market's environment— may also be the reason for change. Finally, the state may be a reason—for example, by introducing new laws. We have seen that change must be understood in relation to order, and many conditions must be in place before we can talk of order in any social formation, including markets. I will discuss this in more detail in the next chapter.

Markets exist in relation to other markets; cars are sold in one set of markets and garments in others. The market for affordable fashion is one fashion market. In other words, a market can only exist if it has been decided what is traded. The BGRs constitute a collective identity, positioned on one side of the market. This collective identity is constructed in relation to other collective identities of garment sellers. In this chapter, I have only mentioned the BGRs, focusing more on other types of garment sellers, such as the independent designer, the private store, and haute couture. This structure of collective identities (that is, different competing markets) is the immediate background, or context, of the BGRs' activities. The rules of the market determine what behavior is accepted in the market. Though all markets exist and are created based on people's lifeworlds, every market also needs rules that govern behavior. This can be determined by organized coordination, or it can emerge in a more or less spontaneous fashion due to interaction. The result is a culture, and possibly formal regulations, which may partly be decided by the market actors, and partly by the state.

In the next chapter, I focus on the firms that make up the collective identity of Branded Garment Retailers. These firms constitute one side of a market, and they are separated from other collective identities and markets. This will show how differentiation takes place within the collective of BGRs.

Chapter 2 _

Affordable Fashion

IDEALLY, WE SHOULD INVESTIGATE the historical development of the market in which the BGRs face final consumers. This would enable us to see how the different social constructions became entrenched—for example, how the garment firms gained their positions, and how it came about that the BGR market has grown more rapidly than the other garment markets I have described (cf. Braham 1997: 149–61). Here, I have a less ambitious goal, however: to explain the BGRs' consumer market by studying its components and how they are related to each other. Although the empirical research starts from the situation of order, we must look at the components that make up this order. To explain the partial order in a single market, as indicated in the previous chapter, one must look at the combined effects of value, social structure, and culture; one should not focus on one dimension alone (cf. Zelizer 1988: 627). We therefore need to look at what is valued—affordable fashion—as manifested in the material objects traded in the market, the social structure with named incumbents who hold the roles of buyers and sellers, and the culture of the market.

This chapter describes the fashion consumer market at a general level, not at the level of a concrete market, which would require an enormous amount of empirical material gathered over several years. The general presentation, based on empirical research by myself and others, stresses the theoretical notions that can be used to explain the large number of concrete markets of fashion garments.

The different fashion garment markets are made up of actors who hold one of two fixed roles: buyer or seller. The identities of those holding these roles are reflected in one another. Buyers are defined as *consumers* because they purchase their commodities and services without reselling what they buy.[1] When talking about markets, the focus can be in the selling direction or in the buying direction (sometimes called "upstream" and "downstream," cf. White 2002). Firms usually obtain their identities as sellers. White has theorized the identities of producers, but does not discuss the identities of consumers at all; instead he talks of "the mysterious consumer" (Leifer and White 1987: 92). To understand order in this market, one must analyze the social structure in terms of its two sides—retailers and consumers—and the product: fashion garments.

At a more general level, the question of order in markets should be discussed in relation to three prerequisites that must be met before a market can come into being. These three market prerequisites assume a taken-for-granted lifeworld (cf. Husserl [1954] 1970) made up of general culture, institutions, and values that is the bedrock of all kinds of social action and institutions.

1. *What the market is about.* The market differentiation discussed earlier implies that different markets are about different things. One can say that each market values one thing (Favereau, Biencourt, and Eymard-Duvenay 2002; Karpik Forthcoming). In other words, though garments are sold in all of them, they are different enough to constitute different markets.

2. *How things are done in the market.* The second prerequisite has to do with culture in the market, which determines its "rules of engagement" (White and Eccles 1987: 984). I define culture as beliefs, "tools," and behaviors—for instance, discourse and practice—appropriate to the setting. The culture of the market also covers the idea of "rules of exchange" (Fligstein and Mara-Drita 1996: 15; Smith 2007: 3). Culture, finally, is intimately linked with the narrative of the market (Mützel 2007). A market culture is made up of ideas about what a market is and how one normally behaves if one operates in a market—for example, as a buyer (cf. White 2002: 2). The culture of a market helps bring it into order, since it prescribes what can be done and what is not allowed, as well as any corresponding sanctions involved.

3. *The worth of the offer.* Given that there is a culture in a market so that it is clear what one can and cannot do, and so that actors know what is traded, the economic value of the good can, and must, be determined (Smith 1989). Economic value is usually expressed in terms of prices. Prices imply that products can be compared with other commodities and services.

I will show that these three prerequisites are met in different ways in the consumer market (discussed in this chapter), and in the producer market (discussed in chapters 4 and 5). The point is not that actors have to sit down to agree on this, but that these are essential elements of a market. This chapter includes a detailed discussion of fashion, but I will not differentiate between product categories, such as outdoor and underwear.

Identities of Branded Garment Retailers

Given their information and knowledge, BGRs try to control their identities, often by controlling their environment. But the environment is uncertain, and so are the identities that emerge out of this process (cf. White 1981, 2002). These control attempts, which often involve the control of individual ties, are embryos of order in a market. In these control processes, which take place in any fashion garment market, retailers carve out niches, which they essentially hold on to from year to year (or from season to season). This is to say that identities of branded garment retailers are formed in continuous processes.

However, BGRs are not in control of their identities, as their identities emerge from interaction and evaluation by consumers, in this case centered on "affordable fashion." This process presupposes a tentative social structure, so that one identity is stable only in relation to others. However, this interaction also brings the structure into being. In many cases, actors enter an already established market, in which case its structure, values, and culture are already taken for granted, as are the identities of the actors taking part in the market.

Let us begin by looking at structure, though one can only separate structure and value analytically. Radcliffe-Brown defines social *structure* as a "complex network of social relations" (1952: 190). The core of the definition is social relations, or "the behavior of a plurality of actors insofar as, in its meaningful content, the action of each takes account of the others and is oriented in these terms" (Weber [1921–22] 1978: 26; cf. Radcliffe-Brown 1952: 199). Actors (or incumbents, as they are sometimes called) hold positions in the structure. This is a condition for talking of identities, which means the incumbents share a role (cf. Biddle 1986) and a collective identity. It is not only a role structure, but a social structure with known incumbents; Marks and Spencer, Next, Topshop, and Debenhams have their respective identities in the market—all of which have been relatively stable over time.

Before turning to a detailed discussion of BGRs, we must describe how actors can generate and manage their identities in a market by means of their reflexive capacity. Identity is different from brand, a difference that will become clear after reading this book. Identity is a much more general notion, but as I have indicated—and will continue to show throughout the book—the theoretical notion of identity makes possible the analysis of different levels of actors as well as of "things," including the existential level, which brand does not.

I call this existential level of identity *reflexive identity*. It explains how actors, such as BGRs and consumers, behave in relation to who they think they are and what they want to become; it is thus inseparable from their interpretation (understood broadly enough to include practices) of the world they are in. Reflexive identity refers to actors' desire for an identity, which can be different from how they perceive their current identity (cf. Goffman [1963] 1968: 129ff). It is wrong to see this level as non-social, however; reflexive identity and the process of thinking about one's identity only become meaningful in relation to the identities of others (Quante 2007). The reflexive level is at the explanatory core of what actors do. Actors do what they do because of what they are and what they want to become. It is hence at the level of reflexive identity that one can talk of agency (cf. Emirbayer and Mische 1998), with reference to both individuals and organizations. Agency means that actors have the power to act, to try to change structures or values, to understand the environment they operate in, by reflecting and acting on the different options they perceive. In this way, actors can switch paths or even strike new paths. Actions must be seen in context, however; reasonable persons mediate their wish for an identity with who they are, as seen by others, which is to say that one cannot reduce reflexive identity to "free will."

However, in contrast to other forms of identity, reflexive identity represents actors' "free variation" of their beings, which also includes their potential. Though both organizations (Warde 1994: 878; cf. Lash 1994) and individuals have reflexive capacity, only individuals are "beings"— that is, are anxious, have existential concerns, and have intentionality (mental directedness). Humans' reflexive identity constitutes a fundamental phenomenological core of analysis. To maintain the central distinction between the reflexivity of collectives, such as firms, and individual human beings, the term "self" is reserved for the latter since the self cannot be replaced or represented by someone else; it is always "my" self.[2]

But how can one talk of reflexivity at the level of firms? Firms' and organizations' reflexiveness is different, not least because it involves many humans, each of whom has reflexive capacity. Reflexiveness is constructed in interaction by those employed by a firm (for example, board members). Some market researchers, most notably Fligstein (2001), acknowledge that what I call market order depends on the "conception of control" that firms may impose on markets. This conception of control, Fligstein argues, must be understood in relation to the internal struggle for "control" within firms. Alfred Marshall presented a similar idea when he argued that organization is the fourth factor of production (cf. Aspers 1999). There is also a large literature in organizational studies that talks about organizational identities (Hatch and Schultz 2004). To acknowledge the reflexive capacity of firms is also to argue that we need to view the firm as a unit of various actors who struggle and who are active partakers in the firm's identity formation (cf. Boltanski and Thèvenot 2006). I cannot expand upon the "inner life" of firms here, because this would require detailed information on how boards operate, and so on, an area to which it is notoriously difficult to gain access.

The final important aspect of reflexive identity is that it separates what we normally call human identities from the identities of things; in short, it separates humans from things. Though both humans and things can be said to exist, it is only humans who can ask and reflect about themselves

(Heidegger 1927 [2001]). Obviously, all other forms are contingent on human beings. This phenomenological perspective puts human beings at the center, and though it sees material objects as essential for understanding human beings, it rejects the ideas of, for example, Actor Network Theory that essentially speaks of "actants" (for example, Latour 1996) and fails to see that a social "ontology" is rooted in human being.

Differentiation between Retailers

Differentiation, as shown in the previous chapter, implies differences among things that have something in common, like different firms competing in the same market as sellers. The collective identity shared by all retailers makes it possible to develop clothes that are seen as fashionable in the eyes of consumers, based on the kind of input materials available, which is essentially the same for all firms sharing a collective identity. What makes a difference is how, in the broadest sense, firms make use of that in terms of the products (which indirectly includes marketing, design, and much more). It is, however, not obvious which aspect matters most in stabilizing and generating identities in the final consumer market.

All BGRs compete to sell fashion garments to customers; customers respond by either buying or not buying. This competition creates cohesion in the market. Many consumer markets, like fashion garment markets, are characterized by competition between firms that differentiate their products, by "branding," which Marshall (1920b: 300–2) observed long ago (cf. Chamberlin [1933] 1948). Entrepreneurs and firms with differentiated products (cf. Kirzner 1973: 137–38; Coase [1937] 1988: 37) try to carve out niches. By offering different products, they still operate in the same market and thus share a collective identity (White 1981). The product, however, is not homogenous but a variable (Chamberlin 1953). Product differentiation is a way of competing by other means than price. This niche form of competition, according to Schumpeter, is much more effective than price competition "as a bombardment is in comparison with forcing a door" (Schumpeter [1950] 1975: 84). This might best be described as rivalry, which should be contrasted with the classic "cutthroat competition" that focuses on price. In the past, when fashion was more standardized, it was also more price-oriented; as Gregory noted, "standardized [garment] models ... often lead to cutthroat competition" (Gregory 1948: 71). Other historical studies indicate that the final consumer markets for garments were most likely ordered according to the principle of standard (to be discussed next). Balkin's (1956) discussion of the production of raincoats is essentially not oriented to fashion, but to production, quality, and pricing. To avoid price competition, differentiation is preferable for many garment sellers.

How, then, do firms differentiate and generate identities in the garment market? Only through consistent identity management that extends over time can firms generate a coherent identity. It is important to realize that "consistency" may involve simply "doing nothing," which is another way of creating an identity—that is, keeping the firms' stores the way they are, and not making changes to, say, the logo is to repeat the decisions of the past (cf. White 1981) in order to maintain consistency. Thus, not changing is also a form of "management." The importance of identity management is underlined by this quotation from a representative of a garment retailer, "the important thing is that you are coherent—in everything you do." Thus, the way the firm presents itself over time and across markets and other contexts must appear as a coherent whole in the eyes of market actors, so a narrative of the firm can be created.

Without the construction of narratives there would be no firms, only a number of completely unconnected actions. Thus, if all firms constantly changed products and the type of clothes they sell, moved their stores, redesigned their logo, used different styles of advertising campaign, changed names and personnel, there could be no identities. Neither consumers nor producers would know what was going on. In fact, there would not be a garment market, only a bunch of actors. Narratives are essential for identities, and by controlling them, actors can manage their identities. The means of communication, of forming and controlling narratives, include text (e.g., information and prices), practices (e.g., what the staff does and the quality of the products), and visual material (the appearance of advertisements, for instance). Thus, the coherence of a firm's identity must be seen in relation to the identities of other firms, all of which share a collective identity.

Differentiation covers aspects that a firm can (largely) control, such as design (or more generally, aesthetic style), but also price level, advertising, and target customers. Other aspects exist that the firm cannot control, such as the general economic climate, turnover, profit, and of course, consumers' perceptions.

Order Out of Differentiation

So far I have described how firms differentiate, but have not gone into detail concerning how the different firms are ordered in relation to each other. Thus, in addition to difference, there must be a way of positioning BGRs in relation to each other. To speak of positions—in a phenomenological way rather than in terms of Cartesian space that only presupposes what is to be explained (Heidegger [1927] 2001: 88)—calls for a way of separating the actors. To be specific, a BGR has only "high" or "low" status, in relation to other BGRs, if there is a way of actually valuing or ranking them. To make these distinctions and rankings one must talk of both value and structure. Though it is important to separate value and social structure analytically (cf. Swedberg 2003: 238), they must be analyzed together. An individual may constitute a value, but a structured value can emerge only because of social interaction (see Joas 1997 for a discussion of the emergence of values, and Husserl [1913b] 1989 for a discussion of the constitution of values).

Can retailers sort things out among themselves, determining the dimension that should be used for the evaluation and ordering of the BGRs, namely the value of the market? This is not possible because the identity of the firm in this competitive market is determined not only by the BGRs, but by their competitors and the consumers. The BGRs differentiate according to the fashion/price mix, a value I call "affordable fashion." The consumers can say "yes" or "no" to what the BGRs offer in the market, and the more high-status the consumers that shop at a BGR, the more status they bestow on the retailer. The result of differentiation and consumers' evaluations and decisions is a rank order of the social structure of the BGRs based on status. The value is a result of this process, of which no one is in full control. It is thus not enough to talk of the retailers; one must also consider the consumers and the products, or in more theoretical terms, what is valued in the market. Only after these three dimensions have been discussed is it possible to understand order in this market. In the next section I deal with the consumers, and then I turn to the product and how it is priced.

Retailers' Customers

The number of branded garment retailers in, say, the British or Swedish markets is relatively small, perhaps ten to twenty, but the number of consumers can be counted in millions. To give a precise number would be possible, for example, using block modeling, but would only inscribe a false certainty in the world, and we would risk losing the phenomenological dimension that preserves the important role of complexity that the actors themselves experience in this market (cf. Heidegger [1927] 2001: 88). Furthermore, the phenomenological idea of markets is central to White's market model. Consumers participate in this market to buy clothes, though their purchasing power differs considerably. There is a large literature on consumption and consumer markets, particularly for clothes and fashion (for example, Hogg 2005; Crane 2000; Entwistle 2000; Meyer and Anderson 2000; Slater 1997; Featherstone 1991; Finkelstein 1996; Frenzen, Hirsch, and Zerrillo 1994; Craik 1993; Green

1994; Bourdieu, [1979] 1984; Douglas 1969; Simmel [1904] 1971; Foley 1893). This literature serves as the background of my analysis.

Branded garment retailers operating in final consumer markets have a good knowledge of consumer demand (cf. Griffin and Hauser 1993; Lengnick-Hall 1996), though the available information may be used even more effectively (Jacobs 2006). One way of knowing one's customers is to hire people who "design for themselves"; meaning, designers who have similar backgrounds and interests—in short, "habitus" (Bourdieu [1980] 1990)—to the customers (cf. Aspers forthcoming), or who can give them what they do not yet know that they want. To obtain a good knowledge of the consumers is the "tricky part," as one merchandiser put it. It is in relation to the consumers that BGRs orient their marketing and develop their brands (Lury 2005), or what I prefer to call identities. They may also divide their customers into different kinds of ideal-type consumers. Furthermore, the staff may treat various types of customers differently (Jungbauer-Gans and Kriwy 2005), to encourage certain customers to shop, but sometimes also to discourage others.

Ideal-type consumers have traditionally been based on age, but gradually lifestyle (which may include the supposed "mental age" of the customer) has become common. To identify, or sometimes generate, ideal-type consumers, several strategies are used, such as qualitative methods, including market research drawing on focus group interviews. Forecasting of consumer lifestyles is another method. The general strategy also includes setting up so-called "showroom" stores, which can be used by firms to test and monitor the effects of new products and strategies (Lury 2005: 190–93). These strategies can later be implemented in all the stores in a chain, such as Debenhams. A particular "brand," such as Redherring, can be used to gain information for the design and merchandising of less cutting-edge fashion brands offered by the BGR. Selling cutting-edge brands will also more likely attract young customers into stores, and as they grow older they may well continue shopping in the store, but buy "brands" directed to more mature customers. Some firms cater to children, or as one firm puts it, "[to] women between 30 to 50 with a family," which is a way of offering clothes to women and their children, since women still buy most of their children's clothes.

Market researchers even construct children as consumers (Cook 2000). This reflects the insight that children are aware of brands (Ross and Harradine 2004). BGRs make use of different ideal-type consumers, such as "young professionals" and "urban women," or "fashion for young and old, fashion that fits every occasion and suits every style," and even groups that are "style conscious, independent and addicted to fashion" (cf. Pettinger 2004). A BGR may, for example, define its goal in relation to an ideal-type consumer as "to cover the total demand for garments from all men who are concerned about quality and price." These statements relate to overarching policies and values such as to "offer great fashion at great prices." Thus, BGRs must construct ideal-type consumers or "virtual consumers" (Carrier and Miller 1998) based on more or less real actors. This is to say that the identities of the consumers are co-constructed by the BGRs, and represented in a polished and enhanced way in advertisements.

This discrepancy between "real" consumers and consumers as presented in advertisements is a reflection of what retailers think their customers want to be rather than what consumers think they are. Consequently, models in advertisements are often younger than the intended buyers of the clothes depicted. Fashion models are intended to reflect what ordinary consumers want to be (i.e., consumers' reflexive identity), and not what these consumers may be in the eyes of other consumers, which is their unique identity.

Buyers and designers working for BGRs have to internalize how these consumers think and act in order to know what they are likely to buy a few weeks or months later. It is, in other words, not the knowledge of the consumers' preferences that is of greatest interest (as the very idea of fashion is about changing preferences), but the ability of cultural intermediaries to "know," feel, and think what their customers would like to be (cf. Callon 1998). Fashion buyers can use this contextual knowledge (Aspers 2006b) about their consumers when they are buying garments for stores (Entwistle 2006). This often means they let their own preferences be proxies for their customers', so they buy what they like themselves. In this way, they operate as cultural intermediaries who affect what is in fashion.

Ideal-type consumers do not, so to speak, grow old. I view ideal-types as social categories whose positions are filled by different incumbents, who are replaced over time. In this way, although individuals are replaced, the social relationship between a producer and its typical "consumer" is more stable than the relations between particular individuals and BGRs. Naturally, ideal-types can disappear or emerge over an extended time (cf. Rich and Portis 1964). Retailers can operate with many different ideal-types and have many different fashion lines, such as H&M's "Collection of Style," which may be more expensive. Some of these are oriented to basic needs, and others can be of higher fashion profile and, as one firm declares, "available in smaller quantities for those who want to be first with the latest." The practical side of this is that firms restrict the number of garments produced and the period during which they are available. Limited edition (explicitly or implicitly) garments diminish the risk that customers will meet others wearing the same garments. Furthermore, some stores within a chain may target young consumers, whereas others are more for kids, men, or other consumer groups.

It is possible for BGRs to differentiate between consumers within a firm and within its stores. One representative of a BGR explained that her firm combined the selling of their own fashion line with garments from designer brands, which can be seen as a trend in European retailing (Howe 2003: 168). She also said that their own designed "brands" were cheaper than the brands they merely represented, which indicates that the retailer was trying to increase its status by association with more prestigious independent brands. It is nonetheless the case that consumers, in the eyes of the BGRs, are seen as more or less fashionable, or in other words, as having more or less status. In the next chapter, I discuss how firms, by means of advertisements (and marketing), not only try to manage their own identity, but also create their customers' identities. To understand how differentiation is carried out and how order comes about in this side of the market, we have to include the consumers and their perception of the market.

Consumption and Identity

From what I have said so far, it is clear that BGRs participate in the construction of the status order of different ideal-type consumers. How does this look from the other side—that is, from that of the consumers? The formation of the collective identities of consumers, such as skaters and hip-hoppers, can be related to consumption because the consumption of fashion is one way of generating, maintaining, and expressing collective identities (Crane 2000: 1–25; Entwistle 2000: 112–39; Falk and Campbell 1997).

Not only BGRs, but also consumers have reflexive identities. Consumer choice is a way of creating and reflecting on the self (Warde 1994: 882), which contributes to the development of actors' identities. Alan Warde expands on this:

> [P]eople define themselves through the messages they transmit to others through the goods and practices that they possess and display. They manipulate or manage appearances and thereby create and sustain "self-identity". In a world where there is an increasing number of commodities available to act as props in this process, identity becomes more than ever a matter of the personal selection of self-image. Increasingly, individuals are obliged to choose their identities. (Warde 1994: 878)

Most researchers today accept the following statement: "Persons confront moments of consumption neither as sovereign choosers nor as dupes" (Warde 2005: 146).[3] The collective identities of consumers result partly from consumption, seen broadly enough to include lifestyle (Slater 1997). Consumption of garments is thus not the only aspect of what makes consumers belong together and sometimes constitute a collective identity, but I shall focus on this aspect. Muggleton (2000), to take one example, has talked to people belonging to different subcultures, which is another way of labeling ideal-type consumers. Individual "members" of a subgroup orient themselves towards the collective identity of that group and the activities that define membership. The following excerpt from an interview illustrates how clothes are merely one aspect of this identification process. Muggleton (2000: 70) asked a Mod: "What do you have to do to be a proper Mod?" The answer, "Spend a lot more money on clothes, wear, I don't know, wear more of the right clothing and sort of listen exclusively to soul music, garage and things like that" shows how ideal-types normally integrate several dimensions. Clothes are particularly important because only they can signal people's group membership to those who do not know them personally. Goth is a stable subculture, with its own fashions. Clothes are a central component, as one Goth told Hodkinson: "To me it is about being able to dress how I feel—it is not about being miserable and dull" (2002: 48). To an outsider, the typical black garb of the Goth may be an example of a uniform rather than of fashion. This, seen from within, is not the case: "Goths ... had always worn considerable amounts of silver jewelry ... the main change that occurred by the 1990s was that piercings, for both genders, had also spread to lips, eyebrows, tongues and belly buttons" (Hodkinson 2002: 48). Hodkinson also observed the "gradual incorporation of particular aspects of dance-club fashions into Goth appearance" during his research (2002: 58). This shows that Goths too are directly involved in the fashion system. These examples of change could also be found in other subcultures.

Through the consumption of material commodities, it is possible to express different looks and to control one's identity. The commodities concerned are also affected by this interaction. Consumption, and not least the visual dimension, is a crucial and integral part of identity formation through fashion. Consumers can differentiate people, a process in which they relate themselves as individuals to their own group(s), that is, to what they want to be, while at the same time distancing (decoupling) themselves from other collective identities (what they do not want to be). One may say, with Simmel ([1907] 1978: 306–7), that there is a mutual dependency between what one owns and wears and who one is, or, in a more existential sense, between "having and being."

The situation of consumers resembles that of retailers; "horizontal" differentiation produces dissimilarities, but it does not create social order. In this case, order is related to fashion (or more concretely, fashionable items), and that some collective identities, or ideal-type actors, have a higher fashion profile than their peers in the eyes of consumers and others, which implies a higher position in the status rank order. This means one can talk of "vertical stratification" based on consumption, though it must also be seen in relation to horizontal differentiation, in terms of subcultures and anti-fashions. Thus, if one looks more closely at consumers, one is likely to find different ideal-type consumers who, so to speak, deviate so much from other consumers that they are in fact not included in this market; hence, neither consumers nor BGRs see them as relevant in this market. For instance, groups who do not wear "affordable fashion" because it is "mainstream" claim to stay outside fashion. In practice this is impossible, however (cf. Finkelstein 1996: 17), since any statement on fashion by definition automatically acknowledges its existence.

The rank order of those actually included in the market is related to consumer groups that have developed their own styles, and with reference to which the idea of horizontal differentiation is more apt. The idea that people are stratified in social and cultural groups is an insight that goes back to the sociological classics. At the top of the consumers' fashion ladder are typically royalty and celebrities, like sports players (and their wives and girlfriends, so-called WAGs), musicians, and movie stars, though they are less likely to wear clothes from BGRs. At the lower end, one finds children, the elderly, and others who are seldom seen as trendsetters. In this case, there is a correlation so that those who tend to spend more money also have more status, but it is unclear how strong the correlation is. This, alongside the characteristics of different groups and their role in the "fashion game," is common knowledge in the industry, at least among those working in marketing and design.

The status of the different consumer types is not merely a function of this market. Furthermore, ideal-types do not gain their position only through the consumption of garments. Music, activities, work roles, and many other dimensions, each of which is evaluated, play a major role in this process. Thus, one could and should—to enable a more detailed analysis—conduct an empirical study, similar to those carried out by the BGRs, also of ideal-type consumers. It is obviously possible to conduct a more detailed analysis also of how individuals gain unique identities, though this demands considerable empirical work. Here, however, I restrict the analysis to the argument that there is a status order of ideal-type consumers, without empirically studying specific ideal-type consumers.

Price and Garments

So far I have made the argument that retailers and consumers, respectively, are ordered in status ranks. These two orders are interdependent. I have, however, only indirectly discussed the commodity of this market. If the material characteristics of commodities determined the logic of markets, the production and consumption markets of garments would be almost identical; one would talk of a single market. The physical object, a garment item, would be sold, bought, and sold—much like stocks in exchange markets—and eventually purchased by someone who would then wear it. This is not the case, and it indicates that one cannot apply an approach that focuses on the material or "inherent" qualities of the product, though this is often the way in which fashion journalists present and "review" fashion garments. It suggests that, in this market, order is not primarily built around the material dimension of the commodity (say, a piece of fabric), but around its symbolic value. In fact, it is not the material commodity that is in focus, but the status orders that generate the commodity. Looking at it in this way is radically different from the goods-centered view that economists use.[4]

All garments have basic functions, such as protection and keeping their wearer warm. However, "quality"—measured, for example, in terms of the strength and colorfastness of clothes—does not determine the value of the product. It is moreover clear that consumers do not pay primarily for long-lasting fabrics. Many clothes are left in the wardrobe before they are worn out, or are recycled to developing countries, where they flood local markets. Niklas Luhmann offers an insight into this, suggesting why products are no longer purchased because of material need, "Under the conditions of industrial production it is surely more of an act of desperation than reason to buy something again" ([1996] 2000: 50), which according to him is largely due to advertisement.

I shall examine the role of prices in creating order, which involves investigating the relationship between the commodity and its price. This will also show how the third prerequisite, namely the worth of the offer, is met. Economic sociologists have studied prices only to a limited extent (Swedberg 2003: 129–30). A short and simple definition of *price* is an assigned numerical value of a good, service, or asset, for which it can be exchanged. It represents the economic value of goods. Prices, expressed in one form of money or another, are a means of comparison (cf. "money of account," Dodd 2005) for completely different things, such as an apple and 30 minutes in a tanning salon, and they are created by means of trade. Prices are constituted (become subjectively meaningful) in relation to traded garments, and in relation to other products. An individual may thus constitute the value a commodity has for her, and if it is on sale at a fair price and within her budget, she may buy the item. Therefore, a price is a social construction related to other social constructions, such as money (cf. Dodd 1994; Ingham 2004) and markets.

Prices are public and help to make markets transparent. They have a "personal" side, as they are interpreted, but also a "social" side, as the outcome of interactions. Wittgenstein connects the personal and the social level nicely: "The human gaze has a power of conferring value on things; but it makes them cost more too" (1980: 1e). Cost here refers to the so-called market prices that are quoted, and for which money and the items traded are exchanged on a regular basis in the market. Prices, in contrast to the merely "subjective" value attached to what is offered, are intersubjective constructions that may become more or less entrenched, depending on how much prices fluctuate in the particular market. Thus, a market cannot be sustained in the long run unless at least some trading takes place, which produces these prices. The social construction of prices is important for the subjective constitution of the value of the products.

But how shall we understand this value? If the physical characteristics of garments were the only thing that mattered, pricing would essentially be a function of the cost of the input materials, to which one could add the cost of labor and other costs (as Marx and his predecessors in economics argued). If products could easily be ranked according to this or another underlying value that measures the commodity, prices would follow.[5] This is not the case in the market for fashion garments.

I argue that price is a dimension that contributes to the construction of the commodity. Thus, price is not merely a reflection of the value, but also creates the economic value of the priced commodity. This is a similar argument to the one made by Veblen, namely that something—such as a commodity—may become valued because it is expensive (cf. Simmel [1907] 1978: 384; Velthuis 2005: 104).

Prices, however, are not merely the effects of status positions. They have meaning only in relation to something that is priced. Two prices, $500 and $700, are meaningless unless one knows what they refer to. However, in combination with identities of buyers and sellers, price may co-determine the meanings of commodities (cf. Bourdieu [1992] 1996: 115).

The case of garments illustrates an interesting point regarding the role of price. Essentially the same commodity—such as an almost standardized T-shirt—could be sold at a higher price by a BGR that has more status than by one that has less status. Status as a high fashion retailer can in this way be translated into higher prices (Podolny 1993, 2005; cf. Velthuis 2005: 8). In fact, prices in a pure ideal-type status market would simply be reflections of the actors' status. Thus, high-status sellers would set higher prices for their products. Does this mean it would be enough for an entrant in the garment market, regardless of what it produces, simply to set a high price and thereby position itself in a high-status niche of the market? No. It would just be an unknown firm selling very expensive clothes. Only a high-status firm can sell high-priced garments, and it is this status dimension that is largely left out of Veblen's, and other economists', product-focused discussion. By being present in a market, whether through marketing, being represented in the "right" stores, or because their garments are worn by the "right" consumers—all the activities that are tied together in a narrative—the firm is perceived as having high status by consumers and producers in the market.

How, then, do prices emerge in this final consumer market? The relative price level of real markets is a result of historical factors (White 1993: 163), and must be seen in relation to other markets.[6] A single BGR has a price policy, which means it prices its garments within a certain price bracket, and essentially sticks to it over time (cf. White 2002).

Prices are not only the consequence of calculations based on added costs and profits on the production price. Branded garment retailers set prices in the final consumer markets, and pricing is integrated in firms' market strategies. A high-price policy implies that the BGRs never sell garments in outlets, or never have them on sale. In this way, the "value" that comes with expensive products is not devalued by the fact they are on sale (discounted) two months later. Finally, it also makes it less likely that the regular customers will see "their" clothes being worn by people they do not want to be associated with, as exemplified by the appropriation of Burberry clothes by so-called "hoodies" and lower class youths known in the UK as "chavs" (Power and Hauge 2008). This is not a cynical observation; it merely describes a condition for maintaining identities. Some firms, as I was informed in the course of my research, would never allow their clothes to be discounted—they are withdrawn from their stores and destroyed. The very logic of fashion—"to be first with the latest"—means that access to fashionable items must be restricted to protect the identity of the firm. Price is one means of excluding larger groups of consumers and maintaining the exclusivity of the items as well as of the consumers. In the words of one shop owner, "[there are] people who do not care if a pair of trousers costs $600, if they have something extra." The other side of the coin is that there is no way consumers on a budget can consume the most exclusive brands.

If price were the only means of competition, this situation could not occur; firms with high prices would be forced out of business (cf. Bourdieu 1990: 89). Hence, some firms advertise at prices that cater to consumers who focus on cost, while other firms focus more on lifestyle and imaginary values—all of which ultimately must be translated into prices. This also suggests that some firms cannot compete at low prices, which would degrade their products (Velthuis 2005), since a low price may signal low quality (cf. Plattner 2000: 127–28) or low fashion. Even though prices affect the identity of a firm, they are not entrenched enough to define products in the markets I have studied. A clear indication that prices derive from status rather than the other way around is that firms cannot compete on price alone. A firm that sells knockdown versions of more expensive brands may not be profitable. This phenomenon is often recognizable in art markets (Plattner 2000; Beckert and Rössel 2004; Velthuis 2005). This must be contrasted with a standard market (discussed next) in which anyone who, for example, offers a stock (which by definition is identical to all other stocks) at a lower price will sell it before anyone offering it at a higher price.

Neither physical characteristics nor price, then, are the most entrenched features of this status market. More entrenched are the social structure of the identities of BGRs and their status, on the one hand, and ideal-type consumers in their status order, on the other. It is clear that price can be seen as an integral part of BGRs' identity management. To fully understand this, one must look beyond sellers and buyers in the market to the meaning endowment (i.e., the process in which commodities gain meaning) of fashion commodities and the logic of this process.

Fashion

Fashion has always interested sociologists and scholars from other fields. This is because, among other things, it has to do with change, typically of clothes of particular styles that succeed each other, thereby rendering other styles unfashionable. Fashion is a continuous process, often seen as taking place among the ranks of consumers, especially women. The scope of the phenomenon is large, and Alfred Marshall realized its economic importance long ago, declaring that "the rule of fashion is spreading, till it will soon have little ground left to conquer" (1920b: 809).

My main point regarding research on fashion is a critical one, namely that the literature is too focused on consumption and on the material dimension of clothes.[7] In this book, fashion is seen as a social process, which means viewing it similar to Simmel ([1904] 1971) and others like Blumer (1969) and Cannon (1998). In earlier times, fashion was made for the individual, and "fashion" was a factor in maintaining cohesion in the upper social strata. Simmel saw the class structure as stable, and essentially whatever the upper class was wearing came into fashion and was then diffused to the lower classes (cf. Veblen [1899] 1953). Street and subcultures have over time also become highly important as sources for new products and ideas in many cultural industries, including fashion

(Slater and Tonkiss 2001: 168–71; cf. Huat Chua 1992: 123–24). Craik (1993: xi, 217) calls this a "trickle-up" process, in contrast to the "trickle-down" variety described by Simmel (Crane 1999). What is missing in the sociology of fashion literature, and the fashion literature in general, is an account of the link between production, in which brands are created in markets and outside markets, and consumption (fashion, and fashion research, are discussed in more detail in Appendix V).

Despite all the research that has been carried out, fashion is mysterious to many academics and members of the fashion industry. One buyer told me: "One cannot put a finger on what exactly creates fashion, everything affects it." She then tried to qualify this statement: "The role of movies shouldn't be neglected. But also stylists and fashion magazines affect it a lot." An important step in explaining fashion is to connect the buyers with the products and the sellers. That the meaning of a thing is affected by the people who interact with them is not a new insight (cf. Heidegger [1927] 2001: 117–18). It can be seen in the seventeenth-century practice of the East India Company, which successfully introduced cotton into a British market previously dominated by wool. Its method, apparently based on detailed knowledge of the market, was to extend favors and services to "prominent and useful people; samples of Indian goods were distributed where they would attract attention and create fashionable demand" (Douglas 1969: 29). Thus, not all customers were seen as having equal worth in the eyes of the sellers, and some were targeted because they were assumed to influence other consumers. All this was done by sellers who knew that existing or potential consumers must be reached through the "right" people (Moor 2003: 46). Fashion, seen only from the side of the consumers, often begins among trendsetters and these trends later spread to other groups. A key idea, then, is that some consumers persuade others of the value of brands or certain commodities.

This idea of distinctions between groups is also expressed by Simmel's ([1904] 1971) "trickle down" theory of fashion, though he of course saw distinctions as being created within a class structure rather than among icons, trendsetters, and reference groups (cf. Merton 1968). One can also identify distinctions at the level of individuals (Thompson and Haytko 1997). Thus, much has happened since the pioneering days of the East India Company in the 1660s; income distribution has become more equal and "prominent and useful people," "opinion leaders," and "fashion leaders" (Blumer 1968: 343) may be found not only in the vicinity of the royal family or the upper class, but also in the gay population, among celebrities, or in clubs in Los Angeles or Manchester (cf. McCracken 1988: 80–81; Agins 2000: 39). The role of celebrities in particular has increased over time (cf. Blumer 1968:343; Agrawal and Kamakura

1995; McCracken 1989; Marshall 1997). This was noted by the head of one buying department, who said, "these days, trends travel extremely quickly all over the world. People immediately notice when icons like Beckham or Madonna are wearing something new." This is in line with the argument put forward by Marshall (1997: 194–95), namely that a celebrity "who moves into marketing other products is selling her capital as a kind of brand loyalty to the advertising company." However, many fans and regular consumers follow these celebrities, and mimic what they do regardless of marketing. This means celebrities form a group of actors who affect fashion in a way that BGRs cannot predict. What they can do is adapt to the consequences by producing copies of the designer clothes that some celebrities wear. Contemporary trends are also more circular, and ideas are picked up and used from both the "top" and the "bottom." This makes it harder to tell who initiated a trend. It is perhaps not the full story that people such as David Beckham, the wives of sports stars, Madonna, or other kinds of celebrities invent fashion trends, but they certainly contribute to the diffusion of them.

Making Fashion

Fashion garments are created with reference to BGRs and ideal-type consumers (cf. McCracken 1988: 71ff; Beckert and Rössel 2004). The constitution and construction of a commodity are the result of who sells it and wears it (which is related to their status), as well as its relations to other commodities as perceived by the actors in the market (cf. McCracken 1988: 74; Bourdieu [1979] 1984; Slater 2002: 71–72; Callon, Méadel, and Rabeharisoa 2002; Baudrillard [1976] 1993: 88). Thus, a certain brand of garment—or even a certain type of branded garment—is awarded high status by consumers and producers because it has edge and is seen as "cool" or "mochino" (cf. Auty and Elliot 1998). Thus, items seen as in fashion by a smaller but influential group of consumers may have an impact on what is fashionable in larger consumer groups, too. The meaning of a product depends on who its wearers are as well as who produced it. This is because the meanings of the rank orders of wearers and retailers (brands) are more entrenched—more taken for granted as social constructions—than the product. It is this social structure that makes up the "backbone," or rather the most entrenched social construction of this partial order. Therefore, it can be said that this order is ordered according to the social structure.

Because they have reflexive capacity, consumers who want to distinguish themselves may start consuming garments that are not in fashion. By doing this, they add new meaning to the commodity and, depending on their status, may or may not make fashion. This helps us understand why the wearing of unfashionable items by fashion leaders does not render such people unfashionable. The reason is that actors whose identity involves defining fashion—that is, who have status in the market—have the power to make the unfashionable fashionable. In the right circumstances, unfashionable items can be used to make distinctions, thereby entrenching their identity and position.

In contrast, if such people started to wear clothes that were already in fashion, they could no longer maintain their position and control their identities. In other words, only those ideal-types who are seen as fashion-oriented, and thus having high status, can define fashion. This process, in which consumers are aware of brands and orient their purchases to certain brands and not others, is governed by "significant others."

Two examples will clearly show how fashion is created in relation to status. The first shows how a firm, Airwalk, successfully launched its brand of sneakers (Gladwell 2000: 193–215). Airwalk was originally used only by skateboarders, who constitute an ideal-type consumer. The firm producing the shoes sponsored skate events, and by broadening its customer base so that also surfers and mountain bikers were included, it became "cool" (Gladwell 2000: 194). Because of successful research and marketing based on advertising campaigns, the firm managed to use its cool "edge" to attract mainstream consumers. The products were segmented so that the most expensive shoes were sold in certain stores, and mainly bought by the core group of consumers, considered the "coolest" consumers (those with the most status).

It was the firm's deliberate strategy to seek out trendsetters and "early adopters" (of fashion, music, or other things, cf. Rogers 2003). Only when enough of these so-called early adopters start to use a certain brand can it become a trend. To create a fashion, the firm launched campaigns that tied together a number of trends with momentum, albeit with only a few followers. In this way, the firm created a trend (cf. Gladwell 2000: 208–13). When a trend gets going, it may become self-propelling. This is the case when regular consumers start buying things because people they know, or see in the streets, wear them.

A firm is likely to hold on to its core ideal-type consumers as long as they feel that the firm retains the identity that made them buy its products in the first place. When this is no longer the case—perhaps because the firm's products can no longer be used to maintain distinctions—those who initially gave them meaning will abandon them. Then, the firm is left with its less cool customers. However, since the commodity has now lost its edge, this group may also stop buying. So how can something be cool if the cool people have stopped wearing it (cf. Kawamura 2006)?

No one side can determine a fashion trend, but the last example described is a largely producer-driven fashion trend. Other trends are consumer-driven. Gladwell (2000: 3–5) exemplifies how products that have been out of fashion for a long time can come back into fashion due to strategic choices among small consumer groups that turn something that is anything but cool into a cool product by starting to wear it again.

The existence of trends, and their logic, is, of course, not new. Bourdieu ([1992] 1996: 252–56) describes the rise, peak, and decline of a trend. He argues that there is an avant-garde, composed of those who define what is in fashion, which later is followed by other consumers who consecrate the process, terminating with the product becoming *déclassé*. This life cycle resembles the general idea expressed by fashion theory, but it is a process in which the firm lacks control, which Bourdieu ([1992] 1996: 254–55) has described:

> [J]ust like Carven [a French fashion house] in the 1960s, they have little by little brought together a composite clientele made up of elegant but ageing women who remain faithful to the perfumes of their yesteryears and of young but less wealthy women who discover these outmoded products when they are out of fashion, so in the same way (because differences in the matter of economic and cultural capital are translated into temporal differences in access to rare goods), a formerly highly distinctive product which is disseminated (hence making itself less select) simultaneously loses the new clients who are the most concerned about the distinction and will witness its initial clientele age and the social quality of its public decline. ([1992] 1996: 254–55)

This indicates that the commodity becomes something because of its wearers; in itself it is nothing. It is just a "material" peg upon which meaning rests. The material part of a garment is taken for granted, and can therefore function as a "peg" for fashion. This is not to deny the role of materiality. It is only to say that it is rather the social context that determines materiality, not the other way around (cf. Heidegger [1927] 2001).

In sum, a certain type of garment is more likely to come into vogue if enough people—enough of the right people, that is: typically consumers with high status, in which ethnicity, gender, age, and lifestyle are important components—begin to use it. This effect is more likely if the commodities are sold by high-fashion (high-status) sellers. BGRs are seldom fashion leaders, but because of their superior logistics, they can quickly respond to new ideas and come up with their own versions of fashion, which they offer customers.

Fashion and Power

One conclusion from the discussion so far is that though fashion trends are difficult to predict, they are possible to change. Actors on both sides of the market—producers and consumers—have some power to change current patterns. They also have "power" to affect each other's identities. The activities of market actors, which are based on their interpretations of what happens in related contexts, are largely what make fashion what it is. Actors on both sides can, for example, couple and decouple—that is, shift among those they "interact" and "collaborate" with in the market—thereby affecting what is in fashion. Actors' market identities are affected because of changes in the status hierarchy (cf. Podolny 1993, 2005). Garment sellers, retailers, and others come up with new products, put things on display, advertise them, and create brands. However, only because of consumers' choices, and trend-setters' choices in particular— the concrete manifestation of the evaluation—will certain garments come to be in fashion and others will not (cf. Beaudoin, Lachance, and Robitaille 2003). Certain brands may also be affected by their wearers, over whom the sellers have no control. When Radovan Karadzic, wanted for war crimes in the Balkans, was finally caught and shown in media photos around the world, he was wearing a particular brand of shirt. A representative of the firm in question stated: "it is a pity that the logo can be seen, but we cannot decide who buys our products." The same applies to entire consumer groups, not just individuals.

Fashion is an effect of interaction between actors, and the field of fashion lacks a command center with the power to decide what shall be in vogue. In other words, no one controls fashion. However, larger players—typically independent design houses, fashion magazines, retailers, and branded marketers with more status—usually have more to say than others about the development of fashion (cf. Entwistle 2000: 220–36), as well as about the "rules" of interaction in the market (cf. Bourdieu [1992] 1996: 254–55). The power to influence fashion is a function of size and status, or, more concretely, of identity, represented by position in the social structure. In the following, I will give several examples of the collective capacity for action possessed by actors in this industry. Fashion, in sum, is neither "planned obsolescence promoted by retailers" (Law, Zhang, and Leung 2004: 362)—an idea which assumes that consumers lack reflexive capacity—nor the result of trickle down among consumers (Simmel [1904] 1971), which views producers as automata issuing garments they have no idea whether the consumer will buy.

Identity Management

Actors are not fettered to positions in the structure of the market, nor is the structure set in stone. Nevertheless, it is easier for an actor to change his or her position, via identity change in the structure, than to change the market, its value, or the culture.

An employee who is dissatisfied with a firm may move to another firm. A consumer who does not like a certain firm's clothes can stop buying and shop elsewhere. This is a consequence of the freedom of choice that markets represent for actors. A retailer that wants to make a move in the market must change its identity. To change identity is never easy, though in principle it is possible. I will here briefly discuss how it can be done (cf. Kotler 2004).

In the discussion, I will treat BGRs as a unit, and not look inside the firms to see how different departments may have different goals (as discussed by Fligstein [2001], but above all by Boltanski and Thévenot [2006]). Large firms usually hire consultants to help them with many things, and specialists in different departments within firms perform complicated analyses and tasks. Within fashion companies, and in relation to them, many actors act as intermediaries. These people affect fashion and are essentially what make up a fashion firm. Joanne Entwistle's (2006) study of fashion buyers is the best example of one such category, namely fashion buyers. I have not studied this in detail, and will therefore talk about it only briefly. The point I want to make is that though external intermediaries may influence the decisions firms make, and though they can take part in identity management, they are hired and exchanged at the behest of the BGR, not the other way around. Large consulting firms may, however, not only be passive, but also set organizational trends and be proactive.

Identity management, or impression management (Goffman [1963] 1968), can be described as a strategy to get closer to, or maintain, reflexive identity—that is, the identity a firm wishes to have, or keep, in a market. Actors strive to manage their behavior to form identities. Power resources at the level of individual actors imply that they can manage their identities. Power may, for example, be due to status, financial capital, the resources of political associations, and of course sheer violence. Power depends mainly on what is culturally allowed in the market. This means that the context conditions the power. One cannot directly translate power resources into action, nor does one have to exercise them to get an effect (Korpi 1985).

Change is costly, and it is difficult to know whether a strategic move in the market will be profitable or not. Only if power is used in an environment in which uncertainty can be translated into risk is it possible to make rationally calculated decisions. However, the fashion industry makes these calculations difficult (cf. Knight 1921).[8] This has partly to do with the fact that a BGR cannot control how its identity manifests itself in the eyes of consumers. The uncertainty (cf. Godart 2009) is ultimately because there is no standard of fashion—as there is in the market for crude oil or gold—to which BGRs and others can orient themselves, and which would render them "good" or "bad" before they enter the market.

Market inertia has to do with entrenched social constructions, and change must often include as many dimensions as possible of those that form the identity of firms. The location of stores, their manufacturers, the staff, the customers, the design department, the buying department, and the advertising must be changed, in addition to the products. To change all this will in all likelihood require a change in the culture of the firm. A firm, provided it has the financial resources, in principle has control over these matters. By altering them, a firm may move within the social structure—meaning, it may try to change its market niche, an issue that will also be discussed in the next chapter.

However, if the customers do not accept these ideas (if they do not buy the garments), the firm has spent its money in vain. Finally, its competitors (cf. White 2002) can clearly observe the movements of a firm trying to change its market niche. If other firms, and their market niches, are under threat, they will most likely launch counterstrikes. Hence, not only is it unclear what the customers will do, it is unclear what competing firms will do. Though as actors in the market with long experience, firms can make qualified guesses concerning what other actors may do. Through connections and friendships, which may be stronger bonds than firm loyalties, individuals may gain information about what is going on. Gossip is another word for this.

It may in some cases actually be easier to enter another market than to change identity in the market in which the actor's identity is constructed, which explains the stability of markets (cf. Burt 1988). Furthermore, entrance into a market such as the fashion garment market is an important decision. It is central that the firm entering a market identifies a niche it can successfully occupy. Thus, a strategic move into a market, to take a concrete example, is made with an existing or indented niche or market identity "in mind." To attain this goal, the firm must direct its move so the identity becomes what the firm is aiming at—that is, to let the reflexive and the unique identities become one and the same.

The Culture of the Market

Not everything can be done in a market. Behavior and activities in markets must be related to what is permissible, which refers to the second prerequisite of a market. The culture of a market is based on the lifeworld that markets are both part of and, more fundamentally, embedded in. But a specific market culture is also determined by informal institutions, and on the decided formal institutions, though it is often a combination. This prerequisite may be met more or less spontaneously in any existing market. For those who enter a market, it means they must relate to what the market culture allows. Each market has a history and is likely to have its own culture ("this is how we do it here"), which is known and practiced within it.

I define *culture* as beliefs, "tools," and behaviors—such as discourse and practice—appropriate to the setting. It is a form of implicit and explicit knowledge that actors use in interactions with each other (cf. Knorr-Cetina 1999; Swidler 1986). This definition includes the notion of institution (cf. Martin 1968: 101), so that formal institutions that are the result of organized coordination, such as the law, are conceptualized as "culture." More specifically, institutions grow out of culture, they cannot just "appear"; and imported institutions are often interpreted locally. Tradition or informal institutions that have emerged in an evolutionary process may be as important for markets as formal (deliberately decided) institutions. Culture "informs" actors concerning what one can and cannot do. This means culture is connected to direct or indirect sanctions, and ultimately to values. Culture can be seen as a "large concept" (Ogburn 1937: 161), and one can talk, for example, of scientific culture, but also of national cultures, and even of cultures as civilizations (Heidegger [1919] 1987: 129–35). Thus, there are general cultural dimensions that are valid across—and in fact underpin—many markets, as well as non-markets. Morality is included in culture, and only certain things are accepted as legitimate in market exchange (Zelizer 1981). Capitalism is the cultural "ethos" in many markets, each with a different set of rules concerning how to behave. I shall return to this topic in the last chapter of the book. I talk of partial culture of a specific social setting like a market. A partial culture is rooted in the lifeworld, and may include the same formal and informal institutions that one also finds in other partial cultures. To this extent, it is similar to the partial culture of other markets and non-markets. Thus, some formal institutions, such as tax law and labor law, apply to all firms in a market, and though these of course matter, they cannot explain why there are different orders in different markets.

I focus on partial cultures in markets, in the form of institutions valid in many markets, but also those that are valid in only a single market. The *partial culture* of settings includes the logic and type of gossip, the language used, the special meaning of the terms used, and the history of a market. It is thus intimately linked to the narrative of the market, and is important in making the market what it is (cf. Fligstein's notion "conception of control," in Fligstein 2001: 18). My definition of culture enables us to separate out what I will focus on next: the culture of the settings of the market, from the general culture. It makes it possible to analyze partial cultures, as well as the specific cultures of single markets. In sum, culture refers to how to do things and how they are done, while value refers to what it is all about, a view not shared by all researchers.[9]

Contracts, ways of payment, and many other things are examples of institutions that govern behavior in a market. Simmel argues that competition in a market is restricted by what I call the cultural limitation of the means of competition that are accepted in this market (Simmel [1908] 1983: 227). This limitation is also due to the morality to which people adhere, which is to say that the partial market culture is rooted in the lifeworld. For instance, culture includes whether and how customers may try clothes on in stores, and whether they are likely to return them to their correct place in the store or leave this to the sales personnel. Cultural bonds between BGRs and consumers may differ between markets. Some firms offer their customers loyalty cards. If consumers accept them, this results in a more stable consumption pattern. These and other things contribute to bring order into this market. The culture of a market contributes to the partial order of the market. But seen in the light of my evidence, it is not the most important component in understanding contemporary-fashion consumer markets. This does not mean culture is of no importance; it merely means that the culture in this market is largely the same as in many other final consumer markets.

Status Order

Culture alone cannot explain order in the fashion consumer market in which BGRs operate, though it increases predictability in the market. Order in this market is constructed according to the principle of status (cf. Aspers 2008; 2009). I introduced this earlier, but we are now in a position to discuss it in more detail. Both sides of the market are ordered according to this principle in the market whose underlying value is "affordable fashion." The social structure is the most entrenched construction in the market—that is, more taken for granted than the value that underlies the market for affordable fashion (which, so to speak, changes with the fashion). This means that actors' performances—what they do or produce—is determined according to their status position. In a status market it matters who one is, and what is produced is a function of who made it (the name of the producer) and who is wearing it. This market attracts actors, BGRs, and consumers who are interested in either providing or purchasing affordable fashion. The market structure is made up of two different roles, each of which is oriented both to its own side and to the other. It is this social structure with named branded garment retailers that is entrenched. While the incumbents differ between countries, one may speak of national fashion markets in which the BGRs operate.

It may appear strange that the orders of the identities of garment sellers and the ideal-type consumers are considered stable, but the important point is that these orders are at least more entrenched than the value of the commodity (the fashion garment), which changes much more frequently. This is the explanation of how the first prerequisite—what the market is about—is met. That is, though the value of the market remains "fashion garments," its manifestation in products (or what this means) changes quickly, which means that one cannot predict how the market operates based on knowing what is traded. Thus, what some call the "path dependency" of the market cannot be connected to the product or any technological standard because the order is derived from the social structure. This idea of status as an ordering in markets is central in this chapter. In the following, I analyze a market in which the situation is the opposite—that is, there is a standard for evaluating the actors in the market, and their identities are a function of what they do in accordance with this more entrenched standard.

In a status market, a commodity essentially gets its meaning with reference to observable patterns of interaction between the commodity and its wearers. Actors perceive and interpret the commodities, as well as the observable interaction patterns in the market. Through this interaction, retailers and consumers form their identities, as well as the identities of the garments they wear. The meaning and value of products, as constructed in the market in the eyes of the consumers, come more from their social ties (White 2002), position, and status in the respective status order, and less from, say, the types of fabrics used. Consequently, the frequently used notion of "objective" quality (cf. Podolny 1993: 833; Marshall 1920b: 56–57, 799–803) cannot be central in the discussion of status markets. High-street firms and brands exchange status with one another, whereas retailers with less status and "non-brands" mutually reinforce their lack of status.[10] This is a form of "communication" between actors and things, as well as between actors and between things, all of which gain new meanings or entrench old ones in the process. This is to say that what we observe is, of course, conditioned by many humans (Heidegger [1927] 2001).

Summary

In this chapter, I have analyzed the final consumer market for fashion garments, concentrating on branded garment retailers. In this market, actors have fixed roles, either as sellers of garments or as consumers. The firms hold on to market niches, represented by their fashion/price mixture. The consumers' side is stratified in terms of different ideal-type consumers at different levels of fashion. When the two sides interact, the market is like a mirror in which actors on each side can see themselves through the activities of the other. It is only when the two sides and the commodity—in practice its value—are analyzed together that order in this market can be understood. The products are differentiated, an aspect that makes this kind of market different from the neoclassical economic model. I have shown that the three market prerequisite of order in markets—what is traded, how it is done, and the generation of prices—are to be understood in relation to status. What is traded is an effect of the social structure, and prices on garments are a function of status orders in this structure. Finally, the culture that emerges manifests how things are done in the market.

Identities and order in this status market are co-constructed, though not according to a script that can easily be changed. Many aspects that define the ways consumers and BGRs interact, and how BGRs interact with each other, can be described in terms of culture. The constitution of BGRs' identities, as consumers view them, can be achieved in different ways. Because of this, meanings differ slightly between the participants in the market. However, the two sides that come together in the final consumer market are perceived in ways that are shared by those taking part in the market. Consequently, the meanings—the social constructions—become entrenched parts of the social world because actors orient themselves to them. This process of construction cannot be separated from an actor's constitution of meaning.[11] I have argued that the perception of identities is essentially the same among all participants in a market, particularly those on the same side of the market.

From the analysis in this chapter, we can conclude that the market's organization is not explained by the fact that branded garment retailers are in the market to make money. This market is not the result of a single decision; no one has determined that the market should be organized as it is. Different states have provided institutional frameworks, but they have not organized the garment markets. The market is rather a consequence of actors interpreting the world in different ways, having different goals, and also positioning themselves by using different strategies in the course of various struggles.

This chapter has not explained how many of the social constructions that are seen as entrenched—such as the status ranks of the BGRs—come to be so. In other words, if the book ended here we would be left with the explanation that fashion is merely the result of decisions made by consumer groups to buy or not to buy what the different retailers offer. In fact, this chapter assumes that the orders of both sides are stable social constructions, and it treats at least the BGRs' identities as a result of this market alone. This is only part of the picture. We need to explain how the identities of the BGRs become stable, what social constructions make up these orders, and in what processes they are constructed. This will show how markets are embedded in other markets, but also non-economic partial orders.

Chapter 3 ----------------------------------

Entrenching Identities

THE PURPOSE OF THIS CHAPTER is to analyze how the identities of those on one side of this market—the branded garment retailers—become entrenched. An identity can in principle be generated in a market if a firm's activities acquire coherence over time by means of a narrative. The identity that an actor acquires in one particular partial order in which they are evaluated I call *discrete identity*. This suggests that a BGR can have several discrete identities. But this is exactly the point. BGRs share a collective identity in terms of which they differentiate amongst themselves in terms of different unique identities.

What I term *discrete identity* is made up of several discrete identities, as seen from the perspective of actors in one particular market. BGRs gain their unique identities in the eyes of the consumers, not only as a result of their products, but also, for example, depending on how they advertise and how they design their stores. The unique identity of a BGR is a unit in the eyes of the consumers and the empirical starting point of the analysis. Analyzing discrete identities involves something like a phenomenological deconstruction of the perceived unit (cf. Husserl [1913a] 1962: 237–40), which is to say that the notion of discrete identity is more analytic than that of unique identity. The starting point, to repeat, is thus the phenomenology of markets that departs from the practices and intentionality of the actors.

The question, then, is how BGRs' identities are affected when they take part—and thereby become evaluated—in many different markets and non-markets. In some markets, retailers can use their power to direct, manage, and thereby exercise some control over what I call discrete identities. In other markets or non-economic evaluations, discrete identities are formed by retailers because BGRs are included without having a chance to control or affect either the principle of evaluation or how their "performance" is perceived. Nonetheless, all these situations, from the consumers' perspective, affect the unique identity of a BGR. Hence, only activities in situations that consumers know about, either directly by observation or interaction, or indirectly via media reports, have a chance of affecting a BGR's unique identity. It follows that it is in the interest of BGRs to conceal or inform customers about their various activities in order to manage their identities.

In this chapter, I seek to analyze, or take apart, unique identities in the final consumer market in order to understand some of the social construction, which ultimately determines the rank order of the BGRs. I analyze four ways in which BGRs are evaluated, each of which contributes to the formation of unique identities in the final consumer market. One may, in other words, say that these dimensions are what make up the BGRs' identities in the final consumer market. I begin with how BGRs can control their identities through the design of their stores. Then, I discuss advertisements. This section is followed by a discussion of editorial fashion. Finally, I analyze the role of ethical production of garments in the perception of BGRs' unique identities in the eyes of consumers. On this basis, it will be possible to see how different partial orders are embedded in each other, but also how the identities of BGRs are the result of several interrelated activities in different partial orders.

Final consumers can observe how different BGRs perform in relation to each other in the cases discussed. In all the cases I explore, I focus on what the BGRs do and how the consumers can interpret this. At the end of the chapter, I discuss the different forms of identities and their relations. To analyze the unique identity of BGRs and study the different discrete identities they comprise is a way of studying order as a consequence of interrelated economic and non-economic evaluations.

Performance Control

Performance control must be understood in light of the relationship between the structural conditions of actors' identities and their reflexivity. The reflexivity enables them to react and form strategies that may involve attempts to change their collective, discrete, and ultimately their unique identity, which can include attempts to change the environment of the organization (Ahrne and Brunsson 2008: 49ff). A firm can act strategically to try to hold on to, or change, its identity, which is to say that control may be about either stability or change. Though it may have control of its activities, as indicated, the firm can never know what their consequences will be, nor how they will be perceived by the final consumers or any other of its different audiences (Ginzel et al. [1993] 2004). I shall now analyze important aspects of the reality facing BGRs, in which they have to manage and control their identities. Studying performance control is also a way of coming to understand how markets are connected. Thus, what happens in one market may depend on, as well as affect, what is occurring in other markets. Though some markets are more autonomous than others, there is no first "unmoved mover"—as assumed in Aristotelian physics, for example—and no simple causal analysis is possible. We should rather look at this as a process of reciprocal constitution.

Store Design

Store design is one way in which branded garment retailers can affect their customers (Corrigan 1997: 66–80). The design of stores, is, however, also part of what consumers judge, and in this section I analyze the construction of discrete identities of "store design," which is one component of the unique identities that BGRs seek to establish as a result of final consumers' interactions and evaluations in markets. In other words, BGRs act and consumers comprise the audience that evaluates them. The value underlying consumers' evaluations is how well or badly the store is designed. This evaluation must be understood as a status order. This reference to status should be understood to mean that the social structure made up of the rank orders of BGRs and of ideal-type consumers is more entrenched than the value (the design of the fashion store) that is constructed by means of the interaction, though it is more likely that it is the perceptions of the consumers that matter. This is not an economic evaluation, because no money is exchanged. However, the design of the store has economic consequences due to its effects on consumers' decisions. It is obvious that such design comes with costs for the BGRs, but the point here is that the evaluation of the store design on the part of consumers does not involve money. The importance of store design is evident from, for example, business magazines for garment industry insiders, in which lighting, fixtures, and much more are analyzed and presented in detail. These all have the purpose of increasing sales figures, but should be understood in light of the firm's identity.

BGRs' market identities—their unique identities in the eyes of consumers—are reflected in the stores. In other words, their identities explain why their stores look as they do (cf. Birtwistle and Shearer 2001). At the same time, store design contributes to these identities. The identities are constructed when consumers perceive stores. Though all stores may appear similar from a distance, this is not the case if one looks more closely. I have made a systematic study of stores, and from my own observations it is clear that first impressions have a major impact on how one perceives them. This first impression includes the colors, the light, staff, smell—for example, the perfume worn by the staff—music, and, of course, the witnessed experience of other customers.

Garment stores in developed countries differ considerably—for instance, there are discount outlets and factory outlets. In developing countries especially, we find stores that sell substandard garments, as well as shops that could be called "oversupply" stores. During fieldwork in Turkey, I entered a small department store in Istanbul that was divided into several floors. In contrast to, say, Selfridges (Entwistle 2006), these stores have no names, and the price tags, in Turkish lira, are handwritten, sometimes over the "original" tags in euros, pounds, or whatever other currency is in use in the country for which the clothes were originally produced. In New Delhi, it was common to see large piles of clothes on sale in the streets, coming directly from local factories. These were being sold in this manner either because they could not export them or, more likely, because of the overproduction that is common to make up for substandard garments.

Street mongers, who sell leftover substandard clothes or copies, are positioned at the bottom of the sales order, but they are nevertheless part of the industry. They operate, quite literally, at the corners of the business—that is, street corners. In Istanbul, Turkey, I observed people selling garments in the street on a number of occasions. One field note recorded a man with a black plastic bag, standing on a street corner holding up a jacket adorned with a Lacoste label. It was obvious this was not a real Lacoste jacket.

The importance of evaluating BGRs' stores became evident to me when I took some pictures in a larger BGR outlet. After taking two pictures, I heard an announcement over the store's public address system and very soon a security guard informed me that it was "strictly forbidden" to take pictures inside the store. Clearly, firms want to make it more difficult for competing firms to study and copy their store design concept. It cannot be to stop visitors from taking pictures of the clothes—in many countries, it is a routine matter to buy an item and then return it the next day, providing ample time to analyze garments in much greater detail than from a picture. In such circumstances, it is also possible to measure the garment and construct a pattern that can be used to produce copies. But to acquire a full knowledge of store design is more difficult.

I have so far talked about the store as if it was the unit of analysis. In practice, however, it is also possible to analyze the components that make up the store's discrete identity. Several dimensions matter in consumers' evaluations of BGR stores. One such dimension is how the staff serve the customers. Pettinger (2004) has studied how firms treat their customers. She labels her two firms "Distinction" and "Cheap Chic," and shows they have different service policies. In addition, store personnel, who represent the retailer with their physical appearance and the clothes they wear, form part of the identity management strategy. This may involve some kind of uniform, a dress code, or individual styles that nonetheless are rather similar. A BGR can achieve this, for example, by allowing, or requiring, the staff to select from the stock of clothes of the store (Kawamura 2006). Thus, firms look for people who "could fit the shop, who had a similar fashion style as the shop they would be working in." This is important because "sales assistants prepare the store as a branded environment" (Hauge 2007, III: 17). At the same time, the staff cannot be "too fashionable" and thereby "intimidate" the customers (Hauge 2007, III: 17). In some British stores, sales staff may even be "policed" so that the store as a whole gives the right impression (Pettinger 2004: 178). Moreover, fashion is partly about feeling attractive, and firms prefer to present "attractive faces" and presumably "attractive bodies" to their customers.

Depending on the location of the store, both its customers and its staff may have different origins, sizes, and preferences, which affect the sales figures of the different garments of a fashion line. Differences in demand between areas are also reflected in sales figures. Using so-called electronic point-of-purchase information, a BGR's head office can observe how many, in exactly what colors and sizes, and in what combinations, clothes are selling in different stores. Such information enables firms to relocate garments between stores to maximize sales.

One consequence is that individual stores of the same BGR can differ from one another. The design of an individual store may be adapted to the local market—that is, a particular country—in terms of lighting, number of staff, and how sales personnel interact with customers, as well as the store's degree and type of security, and many other dimensions. This is a form of micromarketing, aimed at the local community (Halepete, Hathcote, and Peters 2005). Some stores are designed to be more high-end than others, and these are called "flagships," often located on high street, such as Oxford Street in London. These stores offer the most recent and advanced fashion lines the firms have to offer. These may be located in areas that are best described as "test sites of fashion." London is one example, but Stockholm is also an important place for this purpose.

A particular item may be in a store only a few weeks or at most a few months. To increase turnover it is important for a BGR to have, as one BGR representative put it, "more regular visits from our customers." To achieve this, the firm cannot have "empty fixtures." To make sure the store does not stagnate, the staff regularly and frequently redecorate the store, or at least switch the clothes on their mannequins. The redressing of the mannequins, which can be seen as proxies for real models (Evans 2005), in store windows is often done in the morning or before the stores are open, which I have observed during fieldwork in shopping areas. In this way, one actually sees the change of fashion. Redecoration is an easy but also highly visible way of signaling change. (Figure 3.1 shows this task being performed by a member of staff in a store in London.)

Store windows are important for attracting customers. Normally, firms use not price but the clothes displayed in the windows to attract customers. BGRs do, of course, have sales, when the windows are covered, often with big red banners advertising the sale (see figure 3.2). Moreover, customers normally know the price level of a BGR, which means they "know" what prices to expect in the stores they enter.

Figure 3.1. Woman redressing a mannequin at 10:30 in London, near Oxford Street.

It is clear that BGRs view their stores as important for their image. One head of a major chain explained to me that stores are an integral part of the identity management of the BGR she works for: "We are currently working on the platform of the brand [which is directed] to the customer, towards the buying department and towards the staff in our stores." This indicates that identity management is directed not only to those who work with customers, but also to those who work with the garment manufacturers producing the clothes.

Store design is predominantly visual in impact; most customers will get an idea of what kind of store they have entered just from its general design. In a communication to investors, one BGR expresses how they view this issue: "We ensure that our products are presented for sale in cool, contemporary surroundings by knowledgeable and friendly staff who are in tune with our customers." Figures 3.3–3.6 depict different types of stores, their design, and a glimpse of the area where the stores are located. They are included to show the design differences between different forms of collective identities. Such differences can be huge, but we often take them for granted. They are crucial in forming the identities of "ready-to-wear" and "BGR design." The template describes the pictures in more detail.

Figure 3.2. Final Sale (Sweden) banners; red with white text.

Not only is the interior of the store important, but also the location. One CEO said in a newspaper interview, "Twenty meters difference in the location of a store can be the wrong location." Location in this sense is not only a matter of physical space; location is something that these firms actively contribute to by their presence or absence. It is, in this light, no surprise that many chains have their stores in close proximity to one another. Oxford Street in London stands out as a particularly salient example: BGRs and other garment sellers even have several stores located close to each other in this—very long—street.

Another important consideration is the nature of the other firms located in the same area. Figures 3.7 and 3.8 show "branded" garment stores. The differences comprise not only the interiors of these stores, but also their locality in different contexts of purchase (in practice, neighborhood). Both pictures are from London, but taken in two different areas: The figure 3.7 picture was taken in a residential area with a large proportion of immigrants, Finsbury Park, while the one in figure 3.8 was taken on Oxford Street. These two contexts of purchase endow the garments and the brands with different meanings.

Some shopping malls and main thoroughfares are packed with fashion stores. The physical construction of the buildings, the locations and style of the stores—all these things are social constructions, but entrenched to various degrees. The design of stores is usually the same over several seasons. It is of course not "objective" time (in terms of months) that matters most, but rather how often customers visit stores and how often they are redecorated. The most central theoretical aspect is that the customer, who buys clothes from the chain, perhaps from the very same store, perceives

Figure 3.3

Figure 3.4

Figure 3.5

Figure 3.6

the store as a more entrenched social construction than the commodity. Consumers, in short, have the perception that they will find some new clothes rather than a new store—still less that it has moved—when they shop.

What does this mean in practice? I walked the Hohe Straße in Cologne almost every day for several months, on the way to or from work, usually outside store opening hours, often window-shopping. This is a typical example of a shopping street that one finds in many city centers. The street is a pedestrian zone, and garment and shoe stores make up a large proportion of the retailers. I grew familiar with the locations of the stores and the brand names, so much so I started taking them for granted. The clothes in the windows, however, were replaced quite often, at least more often than the mannequins and even their postures. The point is that though the stores, their price structure, their location, and—to speak in more theoretical terms—their status position remained largely the same, the garments put out within the framework of this social structure do change. This supports my claim that it is the social structure made up of BGRs in a status order that is the most entrenched social construction of this market, and what orders it, rather than the products per se.

It does, of course, happen that stores are relocated, close, and open. Before a store opens, or while it is being refurbished, it is common that the outside of the store is covered with a large picture to advertise the opening (see figure 3.9).

In the following, I will discuss advertisements as a means of identity management. It is, however, by no means necessary for a firm to advertise. The Spanish firm Zara has decided not to advertise. Instead, it uses its own stores, and its store windows, as means of "advertising." We have already looked at this as an important means of "giving off" a visual expression of identity. To a small brand, the cost of advertisement is often too high. It is also seldom the case that advertisement is in keeping with an identity of being "new and upcoming." The head of a small designer brand said in a magazine, "We want people to feel that they are smart when they buy [name of the firm]." This means the expansion of this brand is accomplished without "advertisement and aggressive PR."

Figures 3.3–3.6. The pictures of these four stores show various ways in which garments are sold. The first (3.3) is from a typical BGR store (Oxford Circus in London), the second (3.4) is of a small store in Germany (Bonn) that explicitly states it is selling fashion—usually a sign that this is not what they sell—and the third (3.5) is from a high-end ready-to-wear store in London (Knightsbridge). The last one (3.6) is taken in Istanbul to show how garments also are sold in Istanbul. Pictures taken 2003–2006. Notice the different contexts, i.e., the socio-spatial surrounding in which the stores are located, and in which they gain meaning.

Figures 3.7 and 3.8. Examples of stores. The top picture shows a local shop close to Finsbury Park underground station in London, while the bottom picture is from the shopping area close to London's Oxford Street. (Both photographs taken in May 2006.)

Figure 3.9. Waiting for the store to open (London, May 2006).

Instead, the owners of the firm hope "that our brand will evoke interest, so that people will check it out for themselves." To use only its own stores is of course another way of practicing identity management.

A final, but probably quite important aspect is that the store is only appropriately "designed" when it has customers. That is, the customers, and the way they look, their age, and the kind of clothes they wear, are important signals to other customers of what kind of store it is. Thus, the customers also become part of the interior of a store, and this interaction becomes part of what is evaluated. Because it can be hard to conclude from observation where the people you meet in different public arenas have bought their clothes, people may be informed by observing the customers in the stores, the branding on the clothing itself, as well as the labeled shopping bags that customers are carrying. This process may not be entirely reflexive, but I argue that combinations of this possible constitution of meaning help people to form impressions of different BGRs, as well as of other sellers.

From observation, it is clear that some BGRs try to have fewer items on display, thereby looking more like high-status brand stores. A firm must, given the cost of storage space, make a trade-off between the number of items sold and their price; the fewer the items they display and sell, the higher the price must be. This is a trivial statement in a way, but it must be understood in relation to the store's identity.

I have already argued that store design is one way in which BGRs become different from other collective identities, including other garment sellers. But they also differentiate amongst each other by means of store design. What is valued is fashionable store design. Consumers evaluate the BGRs, and some BGRs' stores are seen as fashionable. Some BGRs get high "marks," and are seen as high fashion, while others get low marks. BGRs are of course not left in the dark concerning how to design their stores, as I have shown. BGRs can observe their competitors, as well as the stores of high-fashion firms, and orient their design accordingly. They cannot, however, design their stores for the same customers as, say Hugo Boss, or any other brand name with high status. The reason is that regular Hugo Boss customers are less likely even to enter their stores, while their own traditional customers are not likely to be interested in Hugo Boss items.

This evaluation process is largely parallel to the one I described earlier, namely consumption. But from an analytic point of view it is possible to create different status orders, some of which are non-economic. In other words, a BGR may be better at designing its stores than producing affordable fashion, and vice versa. The point is that the design of stores affects the unique identity of BGRs. It is one dimension of BGRs' identities.

I shall now look at another dimension, or another discrete identity that is part of BGRs' unique identities: advertisement.

Advertisement

BGRs produce advertisements and customers evaluate them in a way that resembles how their stores are evaluated. These two roles—advertisers and audience—are stable, and it is the BGRs who make the first step by making their ads "public," followed by their evaluation according to how fashionable they are. This is an evaluation in which actors are ordered according to status, which means actors on both sides define "good advertisements" rather than the other way around. Structure, of course, also comes out of this process.

BGRs and their customers do not exchange money when the latter evaluate what the former produce in this way—that is, the customers do not have to pay, nor are they paid to receive these advertisements. Thus, the discrete identities that the BGRs acquire through advertising campaigns are part of what makes up their unique identity in the final consumer market. These identities are the result of consumer evaluation. In this section, I shall study not only this evaluation, but also the market in which BGRs select advertising agencies to produce the campaigns, which is another way of connecting different partial orders. I will—to say something about how values emerge—also discuss how these agencies create order among themselves. I begin by discussing what makes it a unique evaluation process.

Fashion, as we have already made clear, is not primarily about text or language. This is one reason why it is so difficult to *talk* about fashion; fashion without the visual aspect is nonsense. In fact, it is easy to observe the interaction between retailers' and brand identities, on the one hand, and ideal-type consumers on the other. One can observe this interaction in magazines, which usually have text that informs people about the different garments included in the picture. It is moreover possible to recognize the brands on clothes, on billboards, on TV, and in the street, or elsewhere, where one sees the small wash tags and labels. Thus, being around certain people or being in the places they frequent can provide information about current fashion. The visual dimension reaches further than this. Consequently, such things as fashion pictures, advertisements, and the shopping bags carried by customers are also important in the construction of fashion. This is so because they help construct identities, and ultimately the market (cf. Luhmann [1996] 2000: 50).

Advertisement is a public form of visual identity management (McCracken 1988: 79). It is a way in which BGRs try to frame the product for consumers (cf. Slater 2005: 62; Moeran 1996). Why do firms advertise? Niklas Luhmann also raises this question, "After truth comes advertising. Advertising is one of the most puzzling phenomena within the mass media as a whole. How can well-to-do members of society be so stupid as to spend large amounts of money on advertising in order to confirm their belief in the stupidity of others?" ([1996] 2000: 44). One answer is that advertisement informs customers about products. Luhmann ([1996] 2000: 44) also makes the interesting point that advertising "plays with an open hand," by which he means that it, or its sender, does not conceal its aim or its interest.

The information that advertisement provides, however, is not about the quality of the products—that is, something that could be evaluated independently of the buyer and seller. According to Luhmann ([1996] 2000), advertising is more about exposing what is offered than informing about what is produced. Thus, if it was possible to judge the value of garments independently of the identity of those who produce them, there would be little need for advertisements; information concerning the existence of the products would suffice. Prices would be determined on this basis. Quality, of course, is always one dimension considered by customers. No firm could survive in the market selling shoddy goods that fall apart after the first wash. My point, however, is that quality is not the central value in a fashion market. Advertisements must convince consumers to buy, and the means are not primarily "quality" in the sense of information about how long-lasting the commodities are, but "fashion."

Advertisements directed towards customers are especially important in situations of uncertainty. The lack of entrenched social constructions for evaluations—in practice a standard for evaluating the quality (cf. Marshall 1920b: 257) of garments—increases uncertainty. Thus, if no tables of values (Nietzsche [1882] 1960: §335) or "standards" exist that can inform people about what is good, and if no clear social strata can be identified from which good taste "trickles down" (cf. Luhmann [1996] 2000: 47), advertising is one factor that brings order by suggesting what ought to be valued. Advertising is promoting garments (cf. Goffman 1979), but it is also a statement by the firm concerning what fashion should look like. This means that advertisements, through interpretations by actors in the field, help to construct fashion. One may therefore speak of advertisement as one way to "overcome" what is unclear about the products or about what the items on sale "are."

Advertisement has a second purpose, besides controlling uncertainty. Advertising campaigns enable BGRs to differentiate their market identity from those of other firms (cf. Moeran 2004: 40–41; Ruggerone 2006). The identities of BGRs are maintained by the narrative that they establish with the "help" of advertisements produced over time; but it becomes a narrative only if it is perceived as such by journalists, fashion photographers, fashion editors, and others, as well as, of course, the consumers, who observe and evaluate what firms do. A BGR, in order to control its identity, needs to present a coherent visual "output" over time. An identity may be perceived as distorted if what it gives off in terms of visual expression is not coherent with the rest of its identity. To further their aims, firms advertise in ways that make their identity correspond to the targeted consumer groups, so that the consumers feel "this is for me" (cf. Moeran 2004; Pettinger 2004: 166). To control its identity, a BGR's advertising campaigns are constructed not only in relation to its own identity but also in relation to the campaigns of its competitors, since they observe each other (White 1981). However, firms, though strong rivals, usually do not directly communicate in advertisements by explicitly criticizing each other.

A firm seeking to reproduce its identity and its market niche, one may assume, would create a campaign that visually represents it. The easiest way to be consistent would be simply to reproduce the same campaign as last season, and let the same models wear the new line of garments.[1] This is not what happens, because fashion campaigns too must be in fashion; they too are part of fashion, which is to say that they call for change. The retailer not only must identify the fashion line that is attractive to its consumers, but also find a visual presentation of the clothes that are in fashion.

Several additional dimensions contribute to the visual style of BGRs, and I will describe a few of them here.[2] It is well known that models are geared to certain careers depending on their look (Aspers 2006a: 50; cf. Entwistle 2002). The consequence is that some models are seen as "cutting edge" and will be used only by fashion sellers with a high profile, whereas other, more "natural" or "traditional" beauties will be used by different firms. The styling, makeup, and age of the models are other dimensions that can be used for differentiation. The way the pictures are taken also matters. In some cases, the pictures show the clothes in detail, whereas in others the clothes are not really seen. Some advertisements include prices, usually when prices are lower (cf. Aspers 2006a).

The context in which the ads appear is an important dimension that contributes to a BGR's identity. If the pictures appear in the context of youth magazines, it may be difficult to attract customers who are older. Thus, to see identity as something that explains means that mature consumers, who are comfortable in themselves, do not want to look like young teenagers, since this is not what they are nor want to become. In other words, the opportunities consumers face must be related to who they are and who they want to be.

Moreover, if a low-status retailer advertises in a high-status fashion magazine, the money may be wasted since regular readers of the magazine would never consider buying such clothes, and the regular customers of this BGR will not see the advertisement. Furthermore, high-status magazines are likely to turn down requests from low-status garment sellers who want to advertise. They do this to protect their identity and to safeguard their stock of high-status advertisers (who may stop advertising in the magazine if it also includes advertisements from low-status firms). Another advertising strategy is so-called product placement, which means that firms pay to have their products "appear naturally" or as if not advertised in films and books. Advertising costs are often substantial, and this is one reason why firms that change their identities may have to spend even larger sums on advertisements. BGRs can, in other words, develop and maintain a "style" not only in terms of the design of garments and stores, but also their advertisements. Even though firms' advertisements must change over time, a new campaign usually "refers" to the style of the BGR's past campaigns in order to maintain its identity. This reproduction of identities (cf. White 1981), also in the form of advertisement, is one reason for the stability of market order.

Of central importance is the fact that BGRs' advertisements are interpreted and evaluated by consumers. They are "aesthetic" evaluations. Some BGRs' advertisements will be seen as cutting edge, others as traditional, but these evaluations do not involve any reference to the money spent on the campaigns. Some BGRs are seen as fashion producers and so they are awarded more status by customers, who differentiate between

advertisement campaigns. This evaluation by consumers leaves few manifest traces. The reason is that the consumers who evaluate the ads are not
in direct contact with the BGRs, and because this evaluation is less likely
to be made in a reflexive and calculated way. Today, retailers sometimes
test their ads on potential customers. It is nonetheless hard to ascertain
how much the pictures contribute to the sales figures, since advertising is
only part of the entire "offer," which of course also includes the perceived
quality, price, and design of the garments that the market is judging. It is,
consequently, difficult for BGRs to be sure in advance whether their campaigns will be successful or not. One reason for this is, as Luhmann says,
that "[a]dvertisement cannot determine what its addressees will think,
feel or desire" ([1996] 2000: 48). Some have even suggested that advertisers cannot judge the value of advertising as a form of marketing that
directly increases sales, and that it may to a large extent instead be seen
as boosting the morale of its staff, and above all be designed to "build the
brand" and "create conditions for selling products." What I propose here
is only that the key notion in a status market, such as the one for fashion
garments, is identity, and it is vain to expect the clothes to sell without an
identity. Though it is hard to judge the value of a single campaign, there
is potentially positive value in terms of identity formation by advertising,
which, of course, may be turned into increased sales.

It is in situations like these, when the BGRs cannot judge the value of
their output, that the worth of intermediaries increases. I will therefore
also include the market of advertising services in the analysis. This is a
market in which firms, such as branded garment retailers, pay advertising
agencies to arrange advertising campaigns that are seen on billboards,
TV, in magazines, and elsewhere. This is a market with fixed roles, in
which buyers (BGRs) and sellers (advertising agencies) meet and produce
fashion campaigns. The research on advertising agencies is substantial
(for example, Aspers 2006a: 115–25; Corrigan 1997; Moeran 1996,
2004, 2005; Nixon 1996), and it serves as a background for discussing
the market in which BGRs operate as buyers. This is a status market, and
it is essentially the advertising agencies that have status, for which BGRs
pay. Though firms usually have a marketing department, they seldom do
the advertising campaigns themselves (Moeran 2004). This is instead the
task of the advertising agencies they hire, which is typical of an organization in the production chain of creative industries (Hirsch [1977] 1992).
The garment firm, however, always has the final say on whether to run a
campaign or not.

The marketing department of a BGR comes up with a basic idea, decides on the budget, and makes the decision on which agency to use based
on the offers received, after a more or less public call. The choice of which
agency to work with is based on the proposed ideas concerning how the

campaign should be run, its content, slogan, and visual presentation. The BGR may also specify features of the campaign, such as the number of pictures and the number of commercials.

An agency must often refer to past campaigns. So, even though each campaign has the intention of bringing something new to the market, it must, as already mentioned, do so by considering the past visual narrative of the firm—meaning, its identity. Advertising agencies may also suggest how the identities of firms should be changed, which means they often actively take part in the reflexive process of BGRs (even researchers can do this—cf. Moeran 2005).

Advertising agencies are not in direct contact with their target audience: the final consumers of the advertisements. As a consequence, they may know little about the specific customers of a BGR, though agencies too can do market research to find out more. The fact that it is sometimes difficult to evaluate the advertising agency's contribution to rising or falling sales protects them to some extent from external evaluation.[3] On what basis, then, do BGRs make decisions on which agency to choose?

The order based on status positions of advertising agencies compensate for the lack of a standard of evaluation. Agencies' positions in the status hierarchy guide BGRs in seeking out firms to run their campaigns. The knowledge BGRs have of advertising agencies is based on gossip and observations of their status order. The value "fashion advertisements" is not entrenched in this market. This indicates that the social structure (the rank orders or status distribution) of the advertising firms is more entrenched than the value. One must remember that this does not imply that the status order is an extremely well entrenched rank order, just that it is more entrenched than the value of "good" advertisements. This essentially means that high-status actors make good advertisements. But how is it that some advertising agencies are seen as "good" when there is no standard or yardstick to tell the good campaigns from the bad ones?

I will here take a further step and briefly analyze the status order of advertising agencies to see how it is constructed. The identities of advertising agencies are largely the result of an evaluation process carried out by bearers of the same collective identity. Hence, the advertising agencies decide among themselves what are good and bad advertisements. This means that a value generated by this particular evaluation is made only by advertising agencies, ordered according to the principle of status. This value is largely symbolic and refers to the "inverted economy" (cf. Bourdieu [1992] 1996) of aesthetics and art, of which advertising is part.

One practical way of distributing status is to arrange competitions and give winners awards. This means that actors, representing firms, take turns to acting as judges of which campaigns are the best. Typically, previous winners make up the jury. The awards may not primarily recognize the economic importance of campaigns; it is better to see this industry as creating a value of artistic creativity. In view of the fact that advertising agencies as a collective identity are fairly autonomous, in the sense that it does not depend much on what others do, the status orders and the values (in the form of "good" advertising campaigns) that come out of nothing, as it were, can also be used to create order in other situations and markets. What is constructed when the advertising agencies come together—such as social structures that are accredited with determining the value of good advertising—will be social constructions that are taken for granted in other circumstances as well, such as the market for advertising services, in which they can serve as building blocks. The partial culture of this evaluation reflects the autonomy of advertising agencies, and one can observe the culture in the way people dress and talk (cf. Nixon 1996). To learn to behave, talk, and dress as a "creative actor" is different from becoming a businessperson.

The internal orientation generates a status order of identities that also becomes known outside the industry. Only individuals get awards. Agencies are credited only indirectly. Mostly insiders, like art directors and others working at these agencies, know the names of the people concerned and where they work, but their clients often do not know this. Thus, a firm may have high status in the eyes of the buyers—for example, BGRs—or other outsiders, even though its "stars" have already moved on to other firms (Aspers 2006a).

When the advertising industry distributes status among its members, money is not involved. It nonetheless has economic effects because those who are endowed with status are more likely to get jobs, and their agencies are more likely to get assignments. This means that the symbolic credit gained in an evaluation can, to some extent, be converted into money in another sphere, such as in a market (Bourdieu [1992] 1996).

In this section, we have seen how different partial orders, markets and non-markets, in which evaluation takes place are interdependent and how they generate values and order that later function as constructions that become useful tools for the creation of order in yet other evaluations, as in markets.[4] Some social constructions—for example, advertising campaigns—must be understood in relation to the way BGRs and advertising agencies come together. Moreover, what is a good advertisement is decided independently not only by the advertising agencies' customers, the BGRs, but even more so by the final consumers.

Do BGRs' representatives see the evaluation processes I have discussed in this chapter as separate from each other? The following quotation from an operating officer of a British firm shows this is the case: "We create the reputation of our brands through marketing, quality product design and the image of our stores. It is the combination of these three things that makes [our brand] what it is." BGRs have control over what advertisements they produce, but not how they are perceived. So what happens in situations where they have less control over how they are evaluated?

Editorial Fashion

Magazines produce editorial fashion stories built around photographs. Fashion magazines choose photographers, stylists, and others to take the pictures, which include clothes (cf. Aspers 2006a). The social structure of magazines is ordered according to status since the value of fashion is less entrenched than the status ranks of ideal-type consumers and fashion magazines. It is the magazines that evaluate BGRs, mainly by the decision to use or not use BGRs' clothes in their editorial fashion stories. Everyone who reads these magazines can observe this, which makes the evaluation public. The effect on fashion of this evaluation is largely a result of its public accessibility, and eventually the consumers orient themselves to it. The BGRs and other garment producers, hence, are not directly involved in this evaluation. This means the evaluation should be seen in contrast to advertising, in which firms can pay to have their garments shown. Moreover, editorial fashion pictures are different from advertising fashion pictures because the latter must make sure the customer—in the end the BGR—is pleased. In advertisements, the BGRs can control at least what they emit, though not the effect. In editorial fashion stories, BGRs can control neither what is put out nor its effects.

The structure, practice, and visual appearances in this market contribute to the construction of ideal-type consumers, and each magazine has an ideal-type reader, which further helps structure both consumers and garment firms. The logic of this market is similar to that of the final consumer market for garments. In this market, too, there is a distribution of status, so that larger and better-known magazines, together with smaller and more avant-garde periodicals, have more status and impact on fashion than, say, magazines for young teenagers or older women.

The consumption of fashion magazines is a way of creating distinctions (cf. Bourdieu ([1979] 1984; see also Corrigan 1997: 81–96), both directly, as a sign of who you are and want to be (and thus as an extension of reflexive identity outside of the individual's mind), but also indirectly, because these magazines inform people about fashion, thus functioning as a source for many consumers in determining what to buy.

Editorial fashion is important for the development of fashion and the construction of the identities of different garment producers. The role of pictures is, of course, central in this process. Editorial fashion affords freedom to the actors involved in producing the pictures. The result is a fashion story—of about eight pages—that is published in the magazine. It is a visual genre, though text is of course part of the message, with conventions of its own, like journalism (cf. Becker 2000).

It is the task of the fashion editor to combine clothes from different brands. She has, in principle, a very large selection of clothes available for the stories, but in reality she is restricted by the identity of the magazine. This identity relates to competing magazines. Each magazine has an identity it must control, which means it has customers who "expect" something from it, and which makes it different from other magazines. The knowledge the editor needs in the process of creating and maintaining the identity of a magazine is sometimes labeled "gut feeling."[5]

It is either the fashion editor of the magazine or an external stylist who decides which clothes are to be included in the stories. To simplify a little, in this evaluation many actors, each of whom represents a collective identity, come together and produce a fashion story (cf. Becker 1974). The actors involved in the collective production are the fashion editor, the makeup artists, the hair stylist, the photographer, the models, and a number of assistants, all of whom are operating in markets.

How are clothes selected for a fashion story? The clothes included in a story are usually a mixture of designer wear, including clothes from ready-to-wear firms; some items from BGRs and also private garments belonging to the designer may appear in the pictures, though this depends on the identity of the magazine. The problem of selection is connected to the production process. There is a time lag from the decision of the editor, who makes the call concerning which photographer will do a story and what clothes are to be included, until the story is printed. The fashion editor can keep up to date with the most recent fashion, for example, by going to the show rooms of independent designers. In addition, BGRs, of course, have garments in the pipeline. This "wholesale" and marketing side of the industry is inaccessible to the average customer.

It may appear that only the magazine can direct its identity, by choosing certain garments and not choosing others. However, it is not always easy for the fashion editor or other staff to access clothes for a fashion story. Garment firms of all kinds may control their own identity by not granting access to their test collection to every editor. Only editors and stylists working for the magazines in which the firm would like to see their clothes featured will be invited to use the clothes from the show room. At the high-fashion end of the fashion publication industry, there is even a struggle to be the first to have access to a specific garment. There may in some cases be only one example of a particular garment in the world, and magazines will compete to be the first to publish a picture of it. It happens that items "disappear" when garments are sent around to the different magazines, not only because they are valuable to the fashion editors and others, but also because it is can be a competitive advantage to restrict rivals' access to these rare pieces.

The problem of access to fashion garments can be serious for fashion editors representing magazines that have very young readers, like teenagers, or other kinds of readers with less status. Hence, large international magazines, such as British *Vogue*, do not have a problem getting hold of the latest garments, but for a small magazine in a small market like that of Sweden, this may be impossible. The fashion editor, however, can also buy clothes in stores, use them in a story, and then return them.

Another alternative open to the editor is to try to construct fashion by transcending the current fashion—for example, by including items that are not "in," such as secondhand clothes. This is one way for the magazine, as well as the individual fashion editor, to generate unique identities within the framework of the collective identity of fashion magazines. This possibility is mainly restricted to the high-status magazines (cf. Aspers 2006a).

But why do firms selling fashion not want to show their clothes in magazines for free? Why do they want, in effect, to limit the exposure of their garments, which is likely to limit the number of people who get to know about them and ultimately purchase the clothes? This tendency to concentrate their exposure is prevalent among garment sellers, but above all among high-status design houses. The reason for this is that firms try to control their identities, and also that one cannot be "all things to all people" (that is, sell to everyone). A status production market, as already discussed, implies that each firm creates and often holds on to a position—and a corresponding niche—in the market. In the process of evaluating the clothes, in which magazines decide to include or exclude particular items, the clothes, and more importantly the BGRs, are endowed with meaning by means of this interaction—or lack of it—as perceived by final consumers.

One can also argue that garment producers pay—or "bribe"—magazines and fashion editors to use their garments as they advertise in some magazines, but not in others. There is often an overlap between the advertising firms and not only BGRs, but even more so other garment firms, and the clothes presented in editorials. However, this should not be seen solely from an economic point of view. There is often a correspondence between the interests of the fashion editor and the clothes she likes to show, the readers, and the clothes of the firms that advertise in her magazine. Thus, the unique identity of a magazine, in this case seen from the point of view of the readers, is made up of many things, such as its fashion profile and what it writes about. It is also made up of the firms advertising in it. Firms that advertise are endowed with meaning by the consumers who see the ads.

What means are available to BGRs to control how their identities appear in magazines? A BGR tries to control its identity by making fashion journalists—that is, fashion editors—aware of, and write about, their fashion lines. In this way, they hope their garments will be shown. In reality, one seldom sees garments from BGRs in the more influential magazines. One editor of a smaller fashion magazine explains that "*Elle* [in contrast to her magazine] makes fashion stories and constantly uses exclusive brands like Gucci and Prada ... dresses that can cost US$ 1100." However, *Elle* does not combine such dresses with a bag from a BGR that costs US$ 15. The most common way for BGRs to try to exercise control, as mentioned earlier, is through selected advertisements in certain magazines, which is a means of putting pressure on the fashion editors of these magazines to also use their clothes in editorials. Magazines and their fashion editors can be influenced in other ways. Gifts, as well as paid trips to fashion shows, in which editors are "ranked"—"bribed" or "rewarded"—by being given better ("front-row") seats, or punished with worse seats, for a fashion show (with more or less status) are other means that sometimes can be used to influence fashion journalists.

Clothes from BGRs that we never see in the fashion stories of magazines do not, so to speak, represent fashion; these clothes may be out of fashion or copies of fashionable brands. Both BGRs and magazines have status ranks. High-status magazines may endow BGRs with status, but if BGRs' garments—that have almost no status at all—appear in certain magazines, it may threaten their identity. The outcome is that high-status magazines mainly try to show high-status brands (and hence not BGRs' garments). This reciprocal relationship is typical of a social structure in which status is the ordering principle.

The main source of the power wielded by magazines is the influence exerted on consumers by their evaluations of fashion garments. Fashion editors are in principle independent of the BGRs. BGRs and other garment sellers are evaluated by the fashion magazines. Thus, if a less known or low-status BGR sends an example of every garment they produce to every magazine in the world, few magazines will consider them for their fashion stories. This illustrates the idea that this non-economic evaluation made by fashion editors is able to endow BGRs with status. There is, of course, no law that says fashion editors' judgments must be accepted, but fashion decisions come out of this evaluation if consumers and others, such as designers, pay attention to them. Editorial fashion thus helps distinguish the different collective identities (discussed in chapter 1) of fashion producers from each other.

In relation to activities in which its identity is formed, though essentially out of its control, a BGR's situation is stable as long as the editorial fashion stories in which its clothes are included reflect the identity towards which it is striving. In this way, editorial fashion stories serve only to entrench the firm's identity. It is only if there is a discrepancy between the two—meaning, the discrete identity of a BGR as it emerges from the evaluation of editorial fashion, and its reflexive identity—that a firm may perceive it is under threat. Though any discrepancy (either more or less status) can be seen as a threat, more status is usually advantageous for the firm. The status acquired by a firm whose products are shown may become an economic benefit—for example, it in effect reduces the sums that must be spent on, say, advertisements (cf. Podolny 2005).

Fashion magazines would not be required to act as judges if it were obvious in the consumer market what is good and what is not. The lack of a standard of what is good (and bad) in the final consumer market for garments opens up opportunities for magazines as sources of information—such as concerning the different kinds of clothes available and their prices—but also for the evaluation of garments. This symbolic interaction, an objective social construction expressed in pictures, is part of what is used by consumers when they interpret what a BGR is.[6] Thus, as mediators, magazines contribute to order in the fashion garment market. In addition to their direct effects on different actors, fashion magazines, as I indicated in figure I.1, are important for presenting and thereby generating fashion (cf. Moeran 2006).

But other mediators also judge fashion. More or less professional fashion blogs constitute a similar kind of evaluation (Hauge 2007, III: 16), which has grown in importance. By writing a blog, actors may start to promote their own styles and judge garments. In this way, they resemble fashion editors. Bloggers, however, lack the resources of magazines, but may be even more independent (which is the form of capital they can draw on). Garment firms, consequently, try to influence bloggers to write about their garments. Firms may even send their garments to bloggers or give them front-row seats at fashion shows. There are also indications from other industries that firms pay people to chat and to blog about specific products. Bloggers have also admitted that this can happen, but few firms would admit that they try to affect bloggers, or that they hire people to act as normal consumers in chat rooms and other Internet arenas, but with the secret task of promoting products.

Ethical Production

The final component I will discuss that affects the unique identity of BGRs concerns ethics. BGRs are also evaluated according to how ethically they operate as producers of garments. The actors who "take part" in this—NGOs (non-governmental organizations) and BGRs—have fixed roles, as evaluators and evaluated. There is also a standard that serves as both a reference and a scale of evaluation of "ethical production." This is often combined with environmental standards, which I do not analyze here.[7] The main issue in the ethical discussion of the garment industry is the working conditions of those producing the garments in developing countries. These workers are not employed directly by the BGRs, but by their suppliers. It is nonetheless argued by final consumers and others in the developed world that the BGRs are ethically responsible for such working conditions. Hence, the ethical discussion connects the final consumers in developed countries and the workers in developing countries via the BGRs.

That the evaluation of how ethical BGRs are takes place in a social structure that is ordered by standards rather than by status means that the value underlying the evaluation is more entrenched than the firms being evaluated (the BGRs). In other words, the evaluation of firms does not depend on who they are, but what they do, or how well they meet the ethical standards that have come to be taken for granted. The underlying value is the basis for the rank order of BGRs that emerges out of this evaluation. This does not mean that the value (the standard) is set in stone, only that it is a more entrenched social construction than the social structure of named firms and ideal-type consumers, and it in turn "orders" the social structure. Both the firms and the value can be easy to change; status and standard have only relative strength—they are not entrenched in an absolute sense.

The notion of standard implies a scale, whether ordinal or cardinal. Value constitutes a scale, not a dualism (cf. Biggart and Beamish 2003). In this case, there may be differentiated products or activities that are evaluated according to the scale, which producers meet to different degrees because their offers are differentiated (cf. White 1992: 29; White 2002: 78–79). Market participants know the underlying standard, and it is therefore possible for actors to identify the "quality" of what they produce according to the scale.[8]

The culture of the social structure that gradually emerges and later becomes established in the evaluation process is reflected, for instance, in the way firms set up internal units and employ people to monitor Codes of Conduct (COCs) and communicate them to customers and manufacturers. COCs are presented in documents, which essentially must be public to be credible. BGRs are today expected to have a COC. However, it is not according to their own COC that they are evaluated, but according to the standards that NGOs have developed.

One important aspect of this evaluation is that the BGRs are included in the evaluation, but without the possibility of saying "no" (Zuckerman et al. 2003; cf. Powell 1997). In such cases, actors cannot control their identity, and one can speak of passive identity formation. The BGRs must react to the NGO standard, though they lack direct power to influence the evaluated aspects. This evaluation does not directly involve money, though it may have economic consequences.

What are the consequences of this evaluation? These days, when consumers decide what garments to buy, quality and fashion are, for many, not the sole determinants. In recent times, ethics has become part of the evaluation of firms, and hence a factor that at least some consumers consider when they buy clothes.

Ethics, in simple terms, is defined as "a set of rules of conduct, or 'moral code'" (Abelson and Nielsen 1967: 81). Ethical ideas emerged among consumers, became articulated, and later became standards. These have developed into particular demands, representing an organized response, putting pressure on retailers to implement codes of conduct (see Aspers 2006c for more details). NGOs have organized the voices of consumers and developed standards that are used for evaluating BGRs. These are also important for making consumers aware of the situation facing people in developing countries.

What are consumers demanding? One common demand is to organize business in a fair or ethical way. But what does this mean? The following is a definition of fair trade taken from an organization that organizes many of the organizations articulating ethical demands, the International Fair Trade Association (IFAT):

> Fair trade is a trading partnership based on dialogue, transparency and respect, that seeks greater equity in international trade. It contributes to sustainable development by offering better trading conditions to, and securing the rights of, marginalized producers and workers—especially in the South.[9]

The ethical claims and values expressed reflect a teleological, in contrast to a deontological, ethics. Deontological theories are characterized by duties that actors are committed to follow, no matter what the consequences are, which means that some acts are obligatory from an ethical point of view, regardless of their consequences. Kant takes a strong deontological position, but there are of course "softer" versions as well—for example, Etzioni (1988). Teleological ethics, by contrast, involve seeking what is good (which may vary with the circumstances). The practical consequences of teleological ethics in the garment industry are not clear. Does "humane working conditions," for example, include air-conditioning if the air temperature in the factory is more than 25 degrees Celsius? Or should it be 30 degrees, or even 35 degrees?

To monitor how values are reflected in practice, on the shop floor of factories, and to make it possible for firms to orient their behavior to these ethical demands, organizations have been forced to "transpose" teleological ethics into deontological ethics. Consequently, the standard resulting from this transposition consists of a mixture of teleological ethics and a soft form of deontological ethics.

Because BGRs and other sellers do not determine the standards that NGOs have developed, they have responded by developing COCs, which are generally documents of about five to ten pages. These codes may include references to ILO principles. A COC may also include various aid programs that the firm has committed itself to, as well as ethical principles.[10] The BGRs monitor how these codes are implemented. Such control is not always extensive, but it is likely to be better than among smaller importers. To obtain knowledge about working conditions, for example, is much harder for a small buyer who visits the production country only a few times a year. One buyer working for a small importer informed me that he "doesn't know how many factories his supplier owns." Though he can always visit factories if he wants to, he is not in a position to know whether they are "set up" for his visits.

A code of conduct aims at communication in two directions: final consumers and manufacturers. In the following, I present a few concrete examples taken from retailers' COCs. They should be contrasted with the COCs endorsed by fair trade organizations. The most obvious difference is that retailers' COCs are more concrete—for example, "Normal working hours must not exceed 48 hours a week," and "Weekly working time must not exceed the legal limit." The COC may also be included as a clause in contracts with suppliers. This means that the buyer requires access to factories. This is an excerpt from a proposed contract between buyers and their manufacturers, so that the latter can enforce their COC:

> We, as buyer (or any party appointed by us), reserve the right to carry out random inspection at any place of production at any time.... Upon our, the buyers', request the supplier undertakes to provide a list with complete information of the locations of the production units, factories and subcontractors, which are used for the production of ordered goods.

The construction of codes is such that they can be easily monitored. They are also unambiguous and relatively easy to communicate to manufacturers as well as to consumers. It may also be advantageous for the buyer to have these clauses. Clauses on working conditions, such as clean and safe factories, are of course good for the workers, but they also have the advantage for retailers that packing can be done without the risk of stains from the workers' hands on the garments. Installing air conditioning may yield the same result.

BGRs and others with garment suppliers are scrutinized and evaluated according to the standards of ethical behavior established by NGOs. Though there are variations among NGOs, the ILO (the International

Labour Organization set up by the UN) standards are often seen as the baseline.[11] The practical implication of these standards is that firms are evaluated and ranked according to how ethical or unethical they are. In this sense, firms cannot directly affect how they are evaluated or the underlying values that determine whether they are "good" or "bad." The BGRs are included in this evaluation process through reports that have a public impact when journalists write about them.

There is, of course, also a potential threat for retailers who do not comply with their own COC. They may face bad publicity, eventually losing customers, and perhaps becoming a less attractive employer. Thus, economic transactions as seen by economic theory, in which every contract is made voluntarily and by independent actors, is here reframed by consumer power so that the BGR is also responsible for the contractor. Retailers, if they implement their COCs consistently, can become moral actors or virtuous corporate citizens. Not only may this constitute an advantage in itself, but it could also lead to good publicity and even to more customers.

The ethical and the economic evaluations are of course integrated, but a particular manufacturer's production becomes an issue only if people come to know that it breaches the ethical code of conduct, either its own or the one that NGOs are using. In the past, this did not constitute a separate evaluation, but was constructed by consumer demands.

Relations of Identities

Before concluding this chapter, I would like to show how the different levels of identities are related. The empirical approach, to repeat, involves analyzing, or taking apart, the unique identities of BGRs as seen by final consumers, in order to understand the logic of the constitution of meaning at the individual level and the construction of meaning at the intersubjective level of the final consumer market. BGRs acquire discrete identities by means of the evaluations discussed in this chapter. These four kinds of evaluation—store design, advertisements, editorial fashion, and ethical production—come together, in the eyes of consumers, to form unique identities.

I have discussed four examples of discrete identities, all of which are important for BGRs, but it is not a complete list. What can one say more generally and theoretically about which discrete identities may play a role in the formation of unique identities? Only the activities (discrete identities) that are known (cf. Simmel 1964: 334), and seen as relevant (cf. Schütz 1962: 14–15) to the consumers—namely the audience carrying out the evaluation—matters in the formation of unique identities.

TABLE 3.1.
Four levels of identity with examples at the level of individuals and organizations. The examples of individuals are included to show the generality of the four levels.

Level of identity	Clarification	Example (person)	Example (organization)
Collective	An identity shared by many	All members of an exchange market	An organization of organizations (a Meta-organization)
Discrete	Identities in an evaluation from the perspective of one market	A designer's innovative capacity, as seen by the customers	A firm's ethical behavior in a market as seen by the customers
Unique	The combination of discrete identities seen from one market	The identity of a designer as perceived by fashion journalists	The firm's "identity" as perceived by consumers
Reflexive	Internal desire (being)	What an individual wants to be	A firm's target position in a market

Consumers who buy fashion garments, for example, seldom know how the different firms are "doing" in the labor market. This means that a BGR's identity may be seen differently depending on the perspective of the consumer. In other words, evaluation and identity formation have a large phenomenological element; they are based not only on the actors' values, but also of course on what they know.

The notion of discrete identity is a way of handling the complexity of identities that actors may hold in connection with different evaluations; hence to understand a unique identity, one must sometimes focus on the discrete identities that make it up. Thus, it is clear that the "synthesis" of BGRs' unique identities conducted by actors in the final consumer market is the empirical entry point, since it comprises the phenomenological perception of actors. The unique identity of a BGR is the phenomenological core, which analytically is made up of the different valued and known discrete identities of the actor in the eyes of participants in the final consumer market for fashion garments. In other words, the identity of a BGR is the result of a narrative constructed from their different activities in the eyes of consumers. The unique identity may, or may not, be what the BGR aims for in the market. To repeat myself, what the firm wants to be I call its reflexive identity.

The similarity of the BGRs justifies the assertion of a collective identity. Within the framework of what makes them similar, variation is of course possible and BGRs have some room to maneuver (cf. Simmel [1922] 1955: 147). However, the collective identity also restricts what its members can do to maintain their "membership." In this book, I use four levels of identity (see table 3.1), and the definition given above of identity (a perceived similarity bound by a narrative pegged on a "thing–event") applies to all of them.

Summary

In this chapter, I have shown that one partial order that exists over time, and which produces evaluations and discrete identities—namely the market for affordable fashion—depends on several evaluations. This is to say that these partial orders are embedded in each other. I have also mentioned that different media can relay and inform actors in one market, or other evaluations in which the BGRs are included.

The concrete point of departure is the unique identities generated in the final consumer market for fashion garments. A BGR has the power to control what it produces, but that does not mean it can control how consumers perceive its activities. This, in other words, is to say that it does not have full control of its identity. Consumers do not perceive BGRs as separate atoms, but always in relation to other BGRs' identities. BGRs also "take part" or, more correctly, become included in other evaluations of their activities and products. An evaluation process of discrete identities can also be open so that everyone can decide whether they want to take part in it or not, as in the case of advertising, but also closed so that only some are involved and in control of what happens, as in the case of editorial fashion (cf. Weber [1921–22] 1978: 43–46, 341–44; Swedberg 1998).

The unique identity is a result of the activities of firms that are evaluated, and of how they are evaluated. The BGRs as individual firms may find it very difficult to control this. As a collective—for example, by forming an organization—they may strengthen their power and act "politically" to impose regulations, standards, or, more generally, institutions for their own benefit. This is a way of trying to determine what is evaluated and, of course, how it is done. Potentially, this is a way of closing or expanding the market. It may also involve some actors being excluded or others being included.

Advertising and design—including location and staff—are means that the BGRs can use to differentiate themselves, as well as to affect how consumers perceive them. One can also view these strategies in a more general light. The strategy is not simply to sell more. Turnover in a status market is achieved in relation to the niche and the corresponding identity of the firm. The strategy is to act in accordance with one's identity, which for some means restricting volume (cf. White 2002; cf. Podolny 2005).

Uncertainty in this final consumer market is considerable. The order that nonetheless exists is based on status, and made up of the rank orders of the two roles that incumbents hold permanently, sellers (BGRs) and buyers (consumers). The status order is a social structure, which is a relatively entrenched social construction. I have stressed the importance of including the visual dimension to make it possible to understand how meanings are constructed and entrenched. I have argued that we must use an interpretative approach, taking the actors' perspective as a starting point. This means, in concrete terms, that not only the clothes, but also the "interaction of garments" as observed by actors influences the identity of the firm. This is an important aspect to consider if we want to understand fashion: objects acquire their meaning from the context in which they appear. This meaning, to repeat, is not something that reads like a text—for example, that a researcher sitting in his or her armchair (Barthes [1967] 1990) can discern by conducting a semiotic reading of "signs"; it must be studied empirically based on actors' interpretations and activities (cf. Moeran 1996: 30). Don Slater eloquently expresses the difficulty facing semiotics in giving a reasonable account of meaning, markets, and objects: "Markets are in fact routinely institutionalized, and are even stabilized, around enduring definitions of products, whereas the semiotic reduction would assume that—as sign value—goods can be redefined at will" (2002: 73).

In the final consumer market, there are of course laws governing, say, the return of items to the shop, which regulate relations between BGRs and their consumers. However, it is always open to firms to make their policy more generous. The aggregation of such activities makes up the culture of each of the markets and non-markets in which BGRs are evaluated. The culture that is developed is thus part of the order.

This market is a *social* construction, and hence there are similarities in the ways in which actors perceive these different evaluations. In other words, actors share essentially the same view on values and the market, its culture and structure (cf. Favereau, Biencourt, and Eymard-Duvernay 2002: 220). The actors do not, of course, know each other or have an identical view. In the strictest sense, each actor has his or her own intentional content, his or her own constitution of meaning, but these are similar enough to enable coordination through the individual to create order. Hayek (1973) makes a similar point, namely that coordination and order are the result of many actions, though no one may have an identical view of the situation. Moreover, the cognitive capacity problem that White (for example, 1981, 2002) speaks of—that there are only a handful or 15 or so producers in a market—suggests that there is also market cohesion due to cognitive capacities. It is, however, the combined effect of actors having different identities in each of the partial orders that they operate (which puts them in different situations) and the fact that they perceive reality in slightly different ways, which triggers them to act and propel change in the market.

The order—shown in the way actors know what to do and the fact that their expectations of others are largely reaffirmed by their actions—is maintained chiefly by the similarity of the meaning structure of actors. This structure is the ground of their interpretation and actions, and ultimately the world in which actors operate. Their expectations are oriented to this structure, but it is also this structure that they use when acting, and they reinforce it by using it. Later I shall analyze order in the production market, which is the origin of the garments sold in the consumer market.

Theoretically, this chapter has argued two substantive points. The first is that markets can be ordered according to either status or standard. I have concentrated here on status, but in the next two chapters I shall discuss standard markets in greater detail. The second point concerns the analysis of how identities in markets, conceptualized in terms of unique identities, are formed and must be seen in relation to the different discrete identities that make them up.

Chapter 4 _____

Branded Garment Retailers in the Production Market

THE PURPOSE OF THIS CHAPTER is to analyze the market in which BGRs operate as buyers of garments and in which garment manufacturers operate as sellers. Thus, when BGRs turn around to act as buyers in the producer market for garments, they face manufacturers. Our analysis therefore concerns how BGRs operate in a business-to-business market—that is, one in which they face other firms. I continue the strategy of the last three chapters and discuss interrelated evaluations, zooming in on the production market from the perspective of the buyers. The analysis therefore includes not only BGRs but also garment manufacturers. In chapter 5, I look at this market from the perspective of the latter.

Today, hardly any retailers have their production chain in-house, though some firms assemble parts of garments in their home country (for example, Zara), or have some production close to the main headquarters. Instead, firms located in designated "production countries" produce the majority of the garments sold. Production countries, on condition that they meet basic requirements of political stability and infrastructure, are chosen mostly because of low wage costs, which is a crucial factor in this labor-intensive industry.

A central question that we must address is how there can be order in this global market; this cannot be separated from the question of whether there is one or more markets. The focus of this chapter, from a theoretical point of view, is to analyze order in a standard-oriented market. This is to say that the principle of order, in contrast to the final consumer market, is a standard. The production market for garments is separated into two fixed roles: an actor is either a buyer or a seller (which in this case is synonymous with a manufacturer).[1]

A few remarks on this market were included in the introduction. This chapter will go into more detail, and we will trace how the demands of the consumer market are transformed into demands in terms of fashion production. We shall begin by discussing the design process to see how the demands that BGRs face in the final consumer market affect how they act in this producer market. Next, we turn to the interface "upstream" in the production process, and to the question of how BGRs' relations to their manufacturers are created and maintained. This leads to the issue of BGRs' evaluation of their suppliers, which brings us to global competition between the latter. Another, and perhaps less known, side of this global market is also discussed, namely how BGRs compete with each other for the best suppliers. The chapter, moreover, includes an analysis of what is actually traded in this market. Three issues are raised that are relevant at the level of theory. First, the chapter shows how markets are interconnected—I show how the consumer market has strong repercussions in this market. The second is the argument that this market is ordered according to what is traded in the market, namely the standard "contract" of producing garments. The third theoretical contribution is the detailed analysis of the contract, which captures what is actually sold in the market.

Design and Fashion

What does the production process of clothes for BGRs look like? The following rather mechanical description by a buyer informs us how a typical firm operates from the perspective of the BGRs:

> First the designer makes a sketch, and a pattern with a list of the sizes of the fabrics that must be cut, and then the buyers make what we call a "quotation sheet." Then we determine which market is suitable to produce this garment. Then we send this quotation sheet to different suppliers in different countries. Then we get prices and offers in return, and after this we make a decision [on which firm will produce it]. Sometimes we carry out tests [to find out] which factory will do this garment for the best price, and then we order.

Though this description is informative in many ways, it also raises questions. What is the role of design? Is design carried out only by the BGRs' design departments? How are relations maintained between buyers and suppliers? Should one describe them as arms-length relations? These are among the empirical questions that this chapter addresses.

Before discussing the production side of fashion, it is worth clarifying the demands imposed on production by the final consumer market. One BGR representative explained how one must tune in production in the garment industry with consumer demand: "[in] the fashion business, it is more important [than in other markets] that you have the goods at the right time; you have to be quick to catch the train, and if you are late the goods don't sell." Thus, firms must be "first with the latest" in order to be attractive to consumers who want to be first with the latest.

The rate of change in fashion has increased over time. This means that short lead-times have become a crucial competitive advantage between

BGRs. Lead-time is the time from the decision to put a garment into production to its appearance in the stores. Today, some firms have lead-times as short as two to three weeks (cf. Bonacich and Appelbaum 2000: 29; Tokatli, Wrigley and Kizilgün 2008). BGRs can achieve this so-called "fast fashion" (Barnes and Lea-Greenwood 2006; Tokatli 2007) by securing or buying fabrics for their suppliers, as well as booking production capacity in advance, or by having their factories close to the market. To react to the market, BGRs must maintain flexibility concerning what to produce. The main demand on BGRs as "producers" of fashion garments is to be quick and fashionable. Next, I discuss the organization of the production process in light of the demands of the consumer market.

The Design Process

The design process is of great importance to the BGRs, and is shrouded in secrecy.[2] It is in this process that BGRs develop and perpetuate their garment design style, which is important for their identities. A *style* is a multidimensional self-referential picture system produced and extended over time (Aspers 2006a: 75). It is only when a style is given aesthetic "credit" by the audience or reviewers who have the right to label styles as "aesthetic" that it can be part of a firm's market identity. Before this happens, there is no way to rank styles; they are just different. A style is seen only in relation to other styles. That BGRs have specific styles is also important in understanding their design process, since they need to create unique niches (White 1981) in the consumer market. It is moreover the identity of the firm that specifies what clothes the designer should make—that is, trousers, skirts, shirts—as well as the product mix. Negotiations between actors with different competencies are common in the development of fashion lines (Mora 2006).

The restrictions that the identity of the BGR imposes on the work of designers should be contrasted with what an "independent" designer can do. A designer explains what any designer ideally prefers: "You must have your own idea of fashion design; your own vision," which means, she says, "[that] you can choose the fabrics – something you cannot do with ready made garments." This is another way of saying that the designer wants to enter the process at its beginning, or in the words of one designer: "You want to start with a blank sheet of paper and develop a product that is 'your own.'"

At first appearances, designers have tremendous opportunities. They can draw on thousands of years of dress history and use materials from all over the world that are available in an almost indefinite number of colors. They can combine all these different things in individual garments as well as in the fashion line of the "season." However, the fashion design process is constrained by the identity of the BGR.

Fashion used to be divided into seasons. However, "seasons," with a beginning and an end, have gradually become rather imprecise as a description of the logic of this industry. It is nonetheless still used by the people in the industry to structure time collectively—for example, to give structure to the calendar of fairs (cf. Skov 2006). It also helps to structure and ultimately bring order to this industry, which facilitates the determination of trends (cf. Blumer 1969).

Planning must start long before the clothes appear in stores (from a few weeks up to about 15 months for designs for upcoming seasons). The working process usually begins with design. Many things inspire fashion designers, and they utilize information from fairs, catwalk shows, local street fashion, films, and music videos (cf. Slater and Tonkiss 2001: 176–81; McRobbie 1998). They may also use trend analysts (Davis 1992: 129) and trend forecasters (Giertz-Mårtensson 2006). Thus, while no one can predict upcoming fashion trends (cf. Abernathy et al. 1999: 88–106), different fairs (Skov 2006) – some with trend seminars that "inform" people about upcoming fashion trends – keep manufacturers and others up to date in the business. Magazines, including the abovementioned fashion magazines, and gossip are additional means of at least acquiring a broad idea of what colors and fabrics are most likely be in vogue.

The head of a design department of a BGR, who travels abroad, explains in a newspaper interview how she goes "second hand shopping" and visits "the trendy parts of cities." She buys clothes to be used in the working process of developing new designs for her firm. But not only clothes are used to further the design. "Art exhibitions" and "spend[ing] time in a café, just watching people" are also ways to understand and create fashion. Fashion design development is about what will be in fashion in the future, and this designer explains how she tries to imagine what it will look like: "When I am on the underground, or a bus, I sometimes look at people, trying to think what they would like in their wardrobe next year."

Trend firms, like WGSN that offers trendspotting services on the Web for those firms that are willing to pay for it, have become increasingly important in the fashion industry. To avoid chaos, trend firms not only "discover" trends, but also create them by means of "political coordination." A lesser known association such as the International Intercolor Committee comes together to discuss colors every six months, and one can purchase trend analyses for seasons up to two years in advance. A person working for one member-firm describes how their "forecast is based on the collaboration of an international network of specialists

and the keen following and analyzing of international fairs and events."
How is this coordination done in practice? In one interview, I talked to
an informant with knowledge about this committee, which has member
organizations and forums from about 25 different countries. They come
together a few times a year "to determine the color trends of two years
later for that season." So, for example, "in June [2003] they go for …
spring/summer 2005." This means that the color trends for spring and
summer 2005 are "determined in Paris at the beginning of June [2003]."
How are the trends "determined"? Each group that comes to the meetings in Paris has earlier sent their own proposal concerning color trends,
and the committee makes a collective decision from among them. This
means that the committee "come[s] up with one color trend, which they
all adopt for two years later." My analysis suggests that fashion is not
only "performed" (Callon 1998), but also fashioned. It is, however, hard
to assess the impact of this kind of performativity on fashion.

The larger picture—the basics in terms of colors and fabrics—is more
or less fixed in advance. One may say that the degree to which fashion
can vary narrows the nearer the industry gets to a "season." Thus, more
than one year in advance the colors and fabrics that will be in vogue
are discernible; these trends are given labels, such as "Arty Nomad" and
"Culture Mix."

The information that exists about upcoming fashion is largely "free."
It can be found in industry magazines as well as in fashion magazines,
which feature editorials, but above all pictures from catwalks. There is,
in addition, a large supply of pictures on the Internet.[3] The problem is
that such information exists in abundance. Actors may therefore pay to
have information collected that is more or less tailored to their purposes.
This includes paying for trend analysts' views and analyses of what they
think will be in vogue. This is a growing industry, and it should be seen
as a combination of an interpretation of the world and the prediction of
future developments on the one hand, and performance of these ideas
on the other. But not even the best trend analysts know what will be in
vogue. One can, however, assume that a design department that wants
to justify what it does design-wise will hire several trend analysts. In this
way, no one can be blamed for mistakes. The crucial issue, however, is
not information but knowledge concerning how to interpret it and select
what is relevant.

The fashion line of a BGR is an interpretation of general fashion trends.
The head of a buyer department explains how her firm reacts to a trend:
"We have a frame that is [name of the firm]'s style … we have a foundation, and if there is an Asian trend, then we handle it so that it fits into our
style." The aesthetic frame of a fashion trend or a season is represented

on a so-called "mood board," which includes colors, the style, and some pictures of clothes, perhaps from catwalks, and it mirrors the firm's market identity. This means that BGR designers have only a limited aesthetic freedom; their designs must be in line with the aesthetic identity of the BGR's previous season, as well as with consumer trends, which means tying together fashion lines over time. Creativity is thus directed by the identity of the firm as perceived in the final consumer market.

This is another way in which aesthetic identity is controlled. In other words, the design must refer to the firm's previous ways of interpreting trends so it does not distance itself from its present customers, yet at the same time gains new ones. This is an important reason why individual designers may not be of great importance in a design team that can involve 50 or more people. There are obviously designers who are seen as more or less "good," if designers draw up a rank order among themselves. Still, to lose a member of staff to a competing firm may not be a very big issue. The reason, in contrast to more free forms of design, is that every designer has to comply with the identity of the firm and its designs. One informant working for the buying department at a BGR says that "in the past one was a bit worried if people shifted from one firm to another, that the person took secrets along, but today there are not that many secrets anymore." Though a designer who leaves will take some information, as well as his or her skills, along, she can only inform the competitor about what her former employers are up to. When she is working for a new firm, she and her new colleagues nonetheless must design in a way that is in accordance with the identity of this firm. To a firm, it may be of greater importance to have constant updates on what its competitors are designing than to recruit a top designer from a competitor to gain the information, unless they plan to change their general approach to design.

Designers use mood boards to create a fashion line based on a few underlying ideas, which in designers' words simply mean that "we are working on a concept." One head of a design department describes a slightly different strategy. She says, "I as a designer sit down together with the buyer and make sketches," which only indicates that also in this industry there is some variation within the larger picture. The following is a short description of the process as provided by a designer: "we collect samples and ideas, and then we make the fabrics, and of course the colors that we will use; fabrics, designs, we collect all of this, and then we develop it for the tailors, so that they can start making things that can be seen ... for everyone." The story that follows, told by the head of a women's wear chain, shows the process of collective production of a fashion line within a firm. It indicates how they are inspired and how this relates to the decisions they make.

The designers are the key actors in the startup of the process. They go to fashion and fabrics fairs, [and] we buy trend books, produced by different trend scouts, and the designers attend many trend seminars. Obviously, they also check out international fashion shows, and what the big fashion designer names are doing. Out of this, the designers make what we call a "trend board." This includes the trends we are going to work under the next season; it is like a source of inspiration with different pictures, colors, fabrics, that feel right for this season, and from this we start.

Others have described similar production processes in fashion.[4] Thus, a large part of the designer's job at top-end firms is to transform and include general trends in production lines to attract customers. Designers increasingly do this in a way that resembles the logic of art rather than the logic of craft (Becker 1978; cf. Gronow 1997: 108). Furthermore, the production process of this industry resembles that of the art world (cf. Becker 1982) or technological production (for example, Latour 1996: 79, 86), with many people working together to produce under certain material and economic restrictions.

Fashion designers are not autonomous geniuses who design while detached from society, colleagues, and restraints. On the contrary, they depend on many other actors. It is because of this dependency on others, including non-artistic actors such as economists, marketers, merchandisers, buyers, and consultants, that fashion designers' work can be described as a collective effort (cf. Becker 1974). They also get information from their buyers, suppliers, and garment manufacturers. Fashion designers at the BGRs, then, are certainly not free to design "art"; they are rather involved in a form of aesthetic creative work (Aspers 2006b). It is more important, as a representative of a BGR said, that they can "translate the catwalk trends into commercial [name of firm] products." The designers are also, I was informed, "involved in designing specs, mood boards, trend research," and more generally trying to support others in the design process.

I have argued that the price level of the firm is a reflection of its status position in the consumer market, which determines how much a garment may cost in the store. Firms have a good knowledge of how much their consumers are willing to pay for, say, wool trousers, in their stores. Hence, it is price in the final consumer market that determines the production costs, rather than the other way around. Also, the sum a BGR spends on the design and production of garments is fairly fixed. A BGR's price level is about the same as the previous season, given its rather entrenched market identity, and it is the task of its designers to develop an attractive fashion line within that framework. The fashion line is also based on last season's sales figures and a guess concerning what demand will be. Thus, every season is evaluated and as one buyer told me, if a firm decides to "grow in shirts" because of indications that the merchandiser has picked up, or because of an assumed change in fashion, the firm may have to decrease the number of T-shirts. It is not the task of the designer to determine how many shirts will be made; but the shirt must be designed no matter whether 2,000 or 120,000 shirts are manufactured. It is more the task of the merchandiser and the buyer to keep these things under control.

To have a fashion line that is a sign of the market identity of a BGR is not to determine everything before a season. BGRs can also have a small budget for buying garments from importers and agents close to the season so as to be on top of the fashion trend, but often only to fill out their fashion lines (cf. Lane and Probert 2006: 51; cf. Entwistle 2006). This is in line with studies reporting that research and development by globally active firms often takes place close to their main office (Hirst and Thompson 1999: 91). If they rely too much on outside designers, it is harder to maintain an identity in the market. In other words, using the same personnel, who know the aesthetic style of the BGR, results in consistency concerning how its fashion line looks; it is part of the corporate culture. This culture makes a firm a unit in the eyes of its employees, which is thought to enhance its performance (cf. Sørensen 2002).

Firms can of course change their orders as the season develops, and through the advanced feedback system (using point-of-sale information) they see what their customers buy and what is not doing well in the stores (Abernathy et al. 1999: 1). Through this information, and also loyalty cards, firms can find out much about their customers (cf. Marzo-Navarro, Pedraja-Iglesias, and Rivera-Torres 2004), and thereby adapt to changes in the market. Moreover, the firm can decide the final details, such as how to cut and drape a skirt, when it has knowledge of market demand. To facilitate this, they may move production closer to the consumer markets. This means that a BGR can, to some extent, react to changes in the market, both to what competitors are doing, but more fundamentally to the interests and behavior of its consumers. However, it is very difficult to change the larger framework, and most changes come with added costs. This means that the general ideas governing the fashion line must be decided in advance; not everything can remain flexible.

Despite updated information from consultants, planning, and close contact with other actors in the industry, things may go wrong for the BGRs. By the time the designers have made up their minds, the buyers have placed orders with manufacturers and the items have been produced, shipped, and are in the shops, fashion may be different from what had been predicted a few months previous. The weather conditions prevailing during a season also matter; a short spring, for example, diminishes the possibility of selling garments from the spring season. This means that the clothes will not be sold or must be sold at discount prices.

Fashion must be understood in relation to a coordination process of producers that is partly the result of collaboration and partly the result of competition. One outcome of the process is that fashion alternatives gradually diminish the closer the "season" comes.

Finding Manufacturers

So far, I have described processes that take place inside the firm, and between firms, both of which are oriented to the final consumers. I will now turn to the buying side of fashion. This side is of course also oriented to the final consumers, but the direct relations between buyers and merchandisers mean that firms take part in a market that from a material perspective is upstream in the production chain, but from the perspective of the meaning production of fashion is downstream.

How do BGRs identify business partners in this market? That is, how are relationships created across the market, say, between the buyers (BGRs) and the sellers (manufacturers)? More sellers than buyers exist, and a large BGR may have hundreds of firms producing garments, accessories, and shoes for them. Though the world abounds with several hundred thousand garment manufacturers, only a small portion of them are considered by a single buyer. It is mainly the task of the BGRs' merchandisers to locate manufacturers around the globe, though buyers may also be involved in this task. Branded garment retailers can buy garments through agents, buying houses, or direct from manufacturers. I shall concentrate on the latter.

Risk and Knowledge in a Global Arena

The garment industry has been global longer than most industries, and today the garments sold by European and American BGRs are likely to be produced by a firm that is detached from the consumer market, and often located in another country or even continent. The BGRs must handle the large number of potential manufacturers all over the world in a strategic way, and not all manufacturers are potential business partners. One typical comment from a buyer exemplifies the reasoning involved: "We want to spread the risk, and the possibilities." He elaborated on what he sees as the comparative advantages of different production countries: "jackets are best made in China, and they have the most competitive manufacturers … and Bangladesh is the most competitive [production country] for T-shirts and shirts." This kind of account of countries and their capacities is well known to manufacturers. Manufacturers claim that they are able to deliver many kinds of garments, and in interviews and informal communications they often assert that Western buyers are conservative, and that they have preconceptions concerning what kind of garment can be produced in a specific country. Buyers' "knowledge" can draw on experience or on rumors and gossip. One must realize that the search costs involved in finding the perfect manufacturer are substantial. However, it is of course buyers' beliefs, justified or not, that shape the actions of those working at the main offices of BGRs.

The process of selecting potential new manufacturers starts from crude assessments of countries and ends with an analysis of individual firms; a process in which the firm's experience of its present manufacturers is of course crucial. Thus, the national level is always present; a larger retailer does not want to concentrate all of its production in one country. This involves too much risk. The risks can be of a political or economic nature. One senior buyer expresses the established perceptions in the industry, namely that the fashion level, the price level, and "of course, political instability" (cf. Kettis 2004) become important for larger buyers when selecting countries, "so that one doesn't get too dependent on one single market." Consequently, other reasons exist for not concentrating production than risk management or aesthetic production (Hirsch [1977] 1992). Observed relationships cannot be understood in their complexity using the rather narrow transaction–cost approach (for example, Williamson 1981). Flexibility, at least for larger purchasers, must be maintained at the national level, but also at the level of regions and firms within regions. The need to maintain flexibility and at the same time diminish the risks are the reasons why BGRs may hesitate to run and own plants, especially in foreign countries.

To have plants means to tie up money in certain regions, which may or may not be a good location in the medium or long run. It would perhaps be possible to increase quality if the BGRs had their own factories, but the cost is obvious. The flexibility of using the advantages that different countries and regions offer, in terms of infrastructure, political stability, and production costs, would diminish. Not only are these aspects difficult to foresee, but so too is the demand for future fashions and fabrics, of which different countries and industrial districts may be more or less good providers. Under "industrial district" I include relations to suppliers that provide input material and other kinds of resources, such as labor and transport, that a factory depends on. A further reason is that the firm does not have to learn to handle the often less predictable and sometimes corrupt bureaucracies that are common in many production countries. One Indian, now working for a European buyer, explains this in more detail:

For a multinational company ... it is very difficult to understand the labor laws, and stuff like that. And manufacturing business in the subcontinent—forget India. It is not the easiest of businesses. It has high levels of corruption ... and other kinds of stuff which keeps happening.... So it is always better to have a trading outfit so that you do clean business.

It is within this smaller frame—which excludes entire countries and even continents from the possibility of getting orders—that a BGR operates and evaluates manufacturing firms. Larger retailers may locate so-called buying offices in the countries of operation on which they decide to concentrate. Smaller importers do not have enough business to have a buying office. A buying—or liaison—office represents the BGR in the country concerned. These offices may also be opened to test a new production country, and later closed if business is not good. To have buying offices, instead of traveling buyers and people who control the quality, and who try to find good business partners, is partly a way of cutting costs, but it is also a way of acquiring local knowledge of the market. It is, as one BGR representative said, the local employees who "know the market, they can communicate, they know the language, and this is crucial."

One problem is that actors on the two sides of the market often live in different worlds, and have different views on fashion, so it's here that local employees can become mediators. One consequence is that communication becomes more difficult the less standardized the topic of discussion is. Fashion, like many other aesthetic topics, is difficult to talk about in abstract terms, but pictures too demand interpretation. The problems are aggravated in this case because, for many actors, English is not their mother tongue. The language of business, however, *is* English. This is obvious, of course, in British garment chains, but it is also true in Swedish garment chains. For example, because the information comes in English from Sweden, it is then easier for a Turkish employee to "add something in English, and then forward it directly to the supplier." As this Turkish employee explained, "So if you ... translate the phrase, he [the manufacturer] is even more confused." Sometimes language is a big problem. Though actors may understand a particular language, and though it is the central means of communication, the meaning of fashion cannot be expressed by language alone, because, say, a small change to a dress could be, I was told, "totally misunderstood."

Buying offices are mostly staffed by locals. They serve as a training ground for people working within the organization who need experience. People who are sent out from the main office may talk to staff members who have experience in the destination country, and practical business culture seminars can also be part of the preparations before a firm sends its staff out from the main office.

A closer look at these buying offices suggests that this side of the BGRs is predominantly technical, and does not directly concern fashion—this became evident in an interview with the head of a buying office. I asked how she kept herself updated on fashion trends. She said she used websites such as "Apparel online" and "Clothes online." She also gets information from suppliers and from the main office. She seldom attends trend seminars or similar kinds of meetings. Instead, she reads about them in magazines. This may at first glance seem to be quite a passive strategy, but her task is not primarily to be responsible for fashion, but for the production of clothes. This means she orients herself to questions of delivery and quality control (so the goods are packed correctly, stitched in the right way, and have the right colors).

The concentration on production represents a clear example of division of labor on a global level in the fashion industry. Moreover, though buyers and designers must have a detailed knowledge of fashion and design history, this is not the case for a representative of the buying office of a BGR. They may instead come from a production background, and they may have attended courses in merchandising and gained work experience. Another head of a buying office explained to me that "merchandising is one thing which a person can do quite easily … but if you do not have a production background it is very difficult to make buyers understand what you are trying to convey." Given there are few producers in, for example, Western Europe, the number of people with practical experience of garment production is correspondingly narrow.

The members of staff at buying offices are thus experts on the production of garments in the country they work in, but not fashion experts. They are also experts in relations between actors from their country of origin and those from the buyer country. The focus on countries also affects the need for buyers—and the BGR's buying organization—to specialize. I asked the head of a buying office that caters to many markets whether the merchandisers he employed specialized in one market—for instance, the Spanish market. He replied, "Yes, I would say yes. We have kept it so, in textiles we have merchandisers who take care of the Scandinavian market and those taking care of Italy and Spain." He also added, "In home textiles, which is not a very big area for us, we have one merchandiser who caters to all countries." This means that a buying office or a buyer may work with a few suppliers with "more than ten years, fifteen years [of experience]," as one buyer explained. These suppliers have "learned" to trade with these countries. I found that fashion is the reason for the long-lasting relationship. One buyer explained that "fashion is more important, because you can't teach every one and because they have to go to [our stores] and … see what [name of the BGR] wants." This means it is better if the suppliers can offer suitable items, but only as long as they are in the BGR's price range.

As representatives of the buyer's side, it is the task of the buying office to find suitable manufacturers. Finding manufacturers is not difficult, but finding good ones is. Besides the knowledge of local manufacturers that the staff of the buying office possesses, they receive many company profiles from manufacturers. One head of a buying office says, "I get ten company profiles per day. Until you have visited them, you don't know what's good or what's bad about them; what their infrastructure is like." These profiles are often quite simple. They do not normally include production prices or details about production. Manufacturers, however, describe the size of the plant and its capacity, the number and kind, including the brand, of the machines. They also include references to former and present customers (buyers).

According to those I have talked to, most of the profiles are from firms that are not appropriate for the buyer, which means that BGRs "send them the reply that at the moment we are not interested in any expansion," but if they are still of interest to the buyers, they look for "suppliers working with our countries," and then they begin to "look into these profiles, and contact them … and begin to evaluate them, and we take it from there."

Neither buyers nor sellers are willing to "put all their eggs in one basket." This is another reason why a BGR has many suppliers. BGRs try to identify manufacturers that have production units for their runs. A representative of an Indian buying office explains this: "I am not looking for a very big factory. Bigger factories in India are about 500 machines, and they work for American labels. I was working for [name of BGR] and we started at 40,000 and would run to 400,000 [pieces]. I mean the factory would be doing that for the next six months. Here [his present BGR] they start at 5,000 pieces and go to 12–14,000." In order to be important to each other, small vendors hook up with small purchasers, and larger players seek each other out. Moreover, the identity of a BGR in the final consumer market thus has repercussions for what kind of manufacturers the firm seeks out. A BGR with a lower fashion profile may have a lower turnaround time (the time between making a decision to having an item in the stores until the stock of garments is on sale) of ten months, whereas other BGRs with a higher fashion profile may have only a few weeks. Given their identity in the consumer market, different strategies are open to the BGRs in the producer market for garments. One buyer says there are two strategies: "either you buy big, or you buy big lead time, and then [have a long] turnaround time, with very high markups." In this case, the garments stay in the stores for months. The other alternative is to have a very high turnaround ratio, which means the clothes are in the stores for only a short period, from only a couple a weeks to a month. To have the clothes in the stores for a long time may be a more or less bad business strategy, but it is never a good option from a cash-flow perspective. However, the costs increase in proportion to interest rate increases.

Regardless of the identity of the BGR and the degree of fashion, the primary task of a buying office is to handle the day-to-day business with local manufacturers. A major task is to make sure that the products are delivered on time and that the quality is correct.

Building Relationships

A BGR invests time and resources in trying out different manufacturers, but is unlikely to drop the price for a batch and thereby make a small profit in the short run. It is not individual contracts that matter; it is more important to develop business relationships, often to the benefit of both sides. Thus, firms in this industry seem to prefer long-term relationships (cf. Lane and Probert 2006; Uzzi 1997). One consequence is that actions are embedded (Granovetter 1985) in social relations that cut across the market. As I will show, however, they are fundamentally contingent on the competitive market. One may say there is a "give and take" that brackets the competition, but a relationship cannot be sustained over time if only one side is giving and the other is taking, since both parties know "what the market has to offer." This finding is in line with what Uzzi (1997) reports. In his study of the garment sector in New York, he identifies two forms of exchange: arm's-length ties ("market relationships") and embedded ties ("close or special relationships"). What do these relations look like, and what strategies do BGRs use?

A large buyer may need plenty of manufacturers, located in different countries, to produce its fashion lines. Furthermore, a small buyer may hesitate to contact a large manufacturer because if the vendor is under pressure from his larger clients it is more likely that smaller purchasers will be squeezed out from its production line. Buyers develop strategies to cope with this situation. The following summarizes a typical strategy among larger buyers (buyers who operate in several countries and with lots of stores): "My game plan is usually that I have 15, 20, or 25 percent of the manufacturer's business. So that I am important to him, and he is important to me. It is a both-ways [relationship], that we both understand and respect. And that's what I mean by partnership." In this way, the buyer has power to enforce demands. He emphasized this: "You have to be important [as a buyer]. Tomorrow you go to an exporter and want 5,000 pieces and he turns around the day after and says 'I don't wanna do your order!' What do you do then?" Situations may also arise in which the buyer must decide and even put pressure on a supplier to obtain the goods, threatening to pull out and cancel all the orders.

The same person also informed me they had previously used the same suppliers as a much larger competing BGR, but that this was not a good strategy. He explained the dilemma: "You don't want all your vendors [manufacturers] doing garments for [name of the competing BGR]; at times this firm gets first priority, so you get squeezed out." This indicates that a smaller buyer can also be harmed indirectly in the production market by a competing firm in the final consumer market. In this case, it would mean that the goods of the smaller buyer arrive in the stores later, thereby preventing it from being "first with the latest." As representatives of a BGR, buying office staff try to "track down manufacturers." This usually means they also check out suppliers to see if they are taking on large orders from competing firms.

These examples clarify a central point of this chapter, namely that buyers primarily view manufacturers as production units that offer capacity to produce garments on time, at a certain quality and price, from a design that the BGR provides. This does not mean manufacturers do not provide any fashion input. In addition to the general demands made by a buyer on its supplier, it is an advantage if a supplier knows something about the buyer's final consumer market. A buyer explains that good suppliers know the fashion in the final consumer market and that "they are aware of the do's and don'ts of that country." This also includes basic knowledge of "what kind of things you run in summer, [and] what kind of things you run in winter." Some buyers may provide their manufacturers with quite detailed information—for example, about one kind of skirt—without giving away information on their whole fashion line, or the whole market, since this is part of the buyer's core field of knowledge (Schmitz and Knorringa 2000: 201–2). With more of this kind of knowledge a supplier is in a better position to offer what their buyers demand. As explained by a buyer: "based on the new forecasts of colors, they combine the colors, and they give us a range [of different samples] suitable for this market." This type of fashion input is possible only if the supplier has learned some basics from the buyer concerning what is suitable in the final consumer market; a knowledge that often takes a long time to develop.

In order to increase the input from their manufacturers, BGR designers inform them about the fashion lines they are working on, or at least the main trends, so the suppliers know "this is the way we are heading." However, this may not always include details or the whole picture. I asked one buyer about this: "Do you inform your manufacturers about trends?" She responded, "No, not very much, what we do is to inform them before a season, so they understand what trends we are looking for, but no, we do not give trend information, [it is more like] 'now we're looking for silk' [in a certain type of garment]."

Fashion is often communicated using pictures, and I asked another buyers' side representative if they also "hand over pictures [to their suppliers]."

> A: Sometimes we show them, but we never give them [the pictures], of course. They are not able to understand. They have to see them, but....
>
> Q: They are not allowed to keep them?
>
> A: Yes, exactly. Then they would just go away and make the garments on their own account [selling counterfeits].

This indicates there are limits to how much information, and under what conditions, buyers give to their suppliers.

The broader picture is that manufacturers are not central when it comes to fashion input for the BGRs' fashion lines. One buyer says that manufacturers' collections complement their own fashion lines. She continued: "It is their collection, but if you like something, you nonetheless change it a bit ... you seldom buy directly from a supplier" (cf. Creamer 2000; Collins 2000).

The kind of relations that emerge between buyers and sellers are predominantly not arm's-length ties and do not concern prices alone; it may even involve what people in the field call "teamwork." This means manufacturers can learn from buyers—for example, about the final consumer market—but also what fairs they should attend. Buyers may also ask their manufacturers to attend certain fairs, "so that they can meet," and the suppliers can use the "knowledge" they may gain from these fairs. It is, as I was told, "part of merchandising [to keep] ... them [the manufacturers] updated." Thus, to learn from buyers also includes, as explained by one head of a buying office, manufacturers "knowing our requirements."

Learning develops over time, and many interviewees stressed the long-term perspective. One buyer put it like this: "It is important to us to have a tight collaboration with the suppliers," which she contrasted with the strategy of squeezing suppliers. She said, "We are not interested in 'using' suppliers; both sides should make money, and the product must sell as far as possible." She explained what this collaboration might include: "We try to involve the suppliers as much as possible in the process so that they know why we are doing [what we do]." The time and cost involved in building up relationships with manufacturers means it is valuable to both parties; it is a kind of social capital.

The manufacturer can help the retailer with many things. A buyer may, for example, need more garments than originally ordered. If the manufacturer can produce these garments, the retailer can return this favor

another time, when the manufacturer has a problem. A head of a buying
office explained the relationship that the BGR has with the manufacturers: "It is a very stressful job, where you do a balancing act between the
buyers and the sellers, because the vendor is also a partner in the business." This relationship also means "that there are times when you tell the
exporter [manufacturer]: 'Do it, we'll make it up to you later.' So it is a
give and take; it is a partnership." He then stresses the important role he
thinks the manufacturers play: "I mean, if I don't have a good exporter, I
cannot deliver the right product, the right quality, at the right time [to the
main office]." To hear from BGRs that some manufacturers have "been
with us for ten years" is not a surprise, due to the explained benefits.
The business relationship, which to some extent can be described as a
give-and-take relationship similar to a network structure, however, is always embedded in market competition. But the market is bracketed in
the short run for the benefit of giving and returning favors that build trust
and create a bond to the benefit of both parties in the long run.

It happens, of course, that one side will terminate the business partnership. Seen from the perspective of a buyer this can occur for many
reasons. One buyer explained: "Sometimes we have problems with the
production, I mean, it can be production quality or some organizational
problems, so that it affects the quality, or … sometimes it is just the price."
Thus, an initial price can be good, but then later on they find better alternatives. This means that "it is very competitive" for the manufacturers, and also for those who are part of the business network. The direct
power that BGRs have in business relations comes from how much the
manufacturer depends on the buyer, and the indirect power comes from
the competitive situation in the market.

Evaluating Manufacturers

How does a BGR decide which manufacturers to work with? By answer-
ing this question, we shall acquire further clarity concerning how BGRs
see manufacturers and what they expect from them. A BGR screens the
company profiles (discussed earlier) to identify those manufacturers of
interest. Most companies are rejected after a quick glance at their profiles. Profiles that are of at least potential interest may be filed for later
use. Others are rejected later on in the control process. The manufacturers that are of immediate interest might receive a test order of little
economic and strategic value to the BGR. If the manufacturer delivers
this order to the standard the buyer demands, the manufacturer can get
a larger order, and from this the relationship may grow. The relationship
that grows out of this test phase is initially built on trust. In this process,

the two parties learn from each other, and the manufacturer must adapt to the demands of the buyer rather than the other way around.

A representative of the buyers' side describes how he evaluates manufacturers he finds interesting:

> Either I check the references ... or I say, "Ok, let's go and check the guy out, in terms of compliance. If compliance is very very strong for us ... we have a girl who does compliance for us, [who is] very very strict ... I [then] enter the factory, and first thing I check if compliance is ok, then you start talking. If the compliance is not ok, then you just walk out—"forget it." [laughs]

If a manufacturer is of interest, the buyers' representative starts by looking at the manufacturer's collection and bookings, and how financially strong it is. An insider's knowledge of the industry, often based on far-reaching personal networks, is an important asset. This is so because the large number of factories, even in certain areas of countries like Turkey and India, and even more so in China, makes it impossible to keep track of them.

Though the role of design is included in the equation when a new relationship is built up with a manufacturer, it matters less than the more standardized aspects related to establishing, maintaining, and evaluating a relationship. Failure to meet these requirements may even result in the termination of the relationship.

In order to keep in touch with the market, a large buyer may be active and "one always checks out new suppliers, and tries to add one supplier each year." In this way, BGRs also keep an eye on those that are already being used; one representative of a BGR says that, "we [continue to] evaluate them [even] if we know them." Each relationship is evaluated by both sides, and large buyers have so many vendors that they can easily judge each of them in light of the others, as well as in light of the business proposals they get from other vendors from all over the world. This makes possible a comparison that may lead to changes in their portfolio of business partners. One may here speak of an internal market with those suppliers they have worked with for many years, but these suppliers are also benchmarked against the external or open market.

The large number of different garments that a large BGR needs means that a core supplier may produce more than one order at a time. A BGR normally has a limited number of manufacturers that actually compete for an order, such as 20,000 red skirts made of cotton. Which manufacturer eventually gets the order can be a collective decision that involves the buyer and staff at buying offices. Given that a supplier can deliver on time and at the required quality level, which the BGR knows from past interactions, it is price that matters. Given a delivery date, price is a function of production and transport (including administration costs). Though labor costs are higher in, say, Turkey than in India or China, the cost of shipping garments by air can level the costs somewhat. Exchange rates also play a role in cost calculations. This means that in the final round a few manufacturers, possibly drawn from different markets, have the opportunity to compete for the order on price. Assuming that all comply with the requirements, the manufacturer offering the lowest overall price will get the order.

Competition among Retailers

The competition we have observed between BGRs in the consumer market is also present in the production market. As discussed in chapter 2, firms that sell garments essentially to the same customers compete with each other in the consumer market.[5] They tend to have similar price structures, "quality," and level of fashion. For international or global companies, competition can take place in one or more markets. If BGRs come from the same country, they tend to be even more similar—in terms of how the firms view, for example, fashion, codes of conduct, and business culture. All this translates into demands on the manufacturer that can be quite similar for several competing firms from the same country.

Competition in the production market is directed "upstream"—that is, it is the buyers who compete for the "best" manufacturers. One may see this as a switch from a downstream orientation ("push") to an upstream orientation ("pull"), as described by White (2002: 177–78). This indicates it is a supply-driven market. What garment-buying firms a manufacturer is working with is a useful signal to other buyers. If a buyer has met similar or slightly higher demands from another buyer—for instance, regarding packing or a code of conduct—it is likely it may be of interest also to other BGRs that have similar or less strict demands. BGRs are also looking for manufacturers with previous experience of working with other BGRs from their market. This is a way of facilitating business while these manufacturers know the kinds of demands and the culture of this market. One buyer even says that this experience is "a selection criterion that we work with." It is then clear that BGRs do not want to inform their competitors about "their" manufacturers, or in the words of a BGR representative, "it is extremely important in terms of competitive advantage ... so the stock of suppliers is not something that one talks about; one doesn't want to give one's best suppliers to anyone."

The competition between buyers in the final consumer market means that many BGRs demand almost the same garments from their manufacturers. Strong competition emerges in certain consumer markets, which are often coterminous with particular countries. The result is that this competition is reflected "upstream" in the production chain, when BGRs compete for manufacturers and try to find out what their competitors have up their sleeves.

A manufacturer is likely to specialize due to the type of machines the factory has and the skills of the workforce, which further increases the likelihood that two competitors who use the same supplier will order similar kinds of products. This sometimes leads to pirating. One buyer explains that one must insist on this issue in talks with manufacturers: "One is always careful to tell them that if we buy this specific product, then they cannot sell it ... to anyone else in our market." The control of BGRs' identities in the consumer market is translated into demands on manufacturers in the production market.

Not only BGRs, but also manufacturers may specialize in different markets, which supports the idea that there are different final consumer markets. This specialization is expressed by one head of a buying office, who previously worked for a German company: "but [now I am with this company] I am not using a single manufacturer from that time, because they do not cater to our market at all." Specialization is important not only because of the different logistics of the final consumer markets, but also because of the different ways of doing business in different cultures. Another factor is that firms may operate with different price levels. This also suggests that actors want to find actors on the other side of the market whom they "understand," and who understand their conditions.

BGRs can to some extent profile themselves in relation to manufacturers—meaning, they try to make themselves popular. One head of a buying office told me it is not because her firm pays more than other firms that it is popular among the manufacturers, but because it is "honest," as she puts it. Another firm had a competitive strategy in the producer market: "our payments are on time, we make proper enquiries, I mean, everything is done properly." One reason for this strategy was that "larger buyers have both the possibility and the danger of being perceived by the market on the basis of rumors."

Acquiring Information

The fiercest competitors in the consumer market are eager for information about each other. The producer market is potentially a way for the BGRs to get to know more about their competitors, but it is also a way of unintentionally giving away information. This mutual orientation among BGRs and its consequences are easy to observe. One example is that larger buyers may use their power over their suppliers to demand that they do not work for their competitors. In this way, they try to control their production sites so they do not leak information to competitors. This strategy, as was explained to me, has a downside, at least for firms that need this kind of information about their competitors, as the following statement makes clear: "the biggest disadvantage with that [strategy] is that you actually don't know what your competition is like, and what the market is doing. So you lose out on that."

The BGRs are interested in their competitors, and it may be an advantage to keep track of them. The contracts that BGRs sign with manufacturers give them virtually free access to the factory floor in order to visit factories without notice, to monitor production, and to check quality and the implementation of the code of conduct. I have personally observed a representative from a large buyer walking around freely in factories, touching, checking, and controlling the garments, as well as the production units. This control may also include manufacturers' bookkeeping and the wages they pay their workers. It is obvious these representatives are able to observe not only the quality of the garments the manufacturer produces for them, but also the stock of other BGRs' production that the manufacturer has. This means they have the opportunity to discover whether the supplier is selling identical, or similar, items to the BGR's competitors in the consumer market. I also asked whether information could be gained this way on, say, what leading BGRs such as Zara and H&M are doing. In the words of one representative: "Yes, yes, of course. And you see them [the garment samples] immediately in the showroom anyway."

To some BGRs, it is not a problem to have the same suppliers as their competitors. To others, it is a positive advantage, and to others still it is a disadvantage. I asked a small buyer with no buying office if it was not an advantage to have a manufacturer that "informs" him about his competitors. He replied that if he tries to get this information, "I have to assume that everyone else does the same." This was his main reason for using manufacturers with no connections to his competitors. He also added that it is "rare" that one "can get this kind of information, on what kind of fashion is being produced." He said that "if it doesn't hurt their relations to other buyers"—for example, if the two buyers operate on very different markets—"they may inform me that 'this is what their collection looks like,' but they are usually strict about this, and do not share information, especially [if it is] from the same season." Clothes from previous seasons are usually shown since they, in the strictest sense, no longer represent "fashion." This general information he got instead from "trend institutes and by looking in shops … and seeing what the brands are up to."

It is likely that the staff from the buying offices acquire knowledge of their competitors, as one person working for a buying office explains: "if

I go to a supplier, maybe one of our competitors has been there before," and they may "show me the drawings of the design." This, she says, "is not really right, [but] of course, I have a look. [laughs]" This is also a reason why she is less willing to "give [out information] from our side," as already discussed. If BGRs get hold of information concerning what a competitor is up to, they may alter their fashion line—for example, by making minor changes to the cut in order to meet the fashion of the competitor. One should interpret this kind of information in light of the long-term relationships of this industry. The exchange of information and the learning process in which buyers and manufacturers engage is a way for actors "to grow old together," as Schütz says. It is thus not the information about the manufacturers' fashion lines that appears to be of most interest to BGRs, but the fashion lines of competing firms.

I have already shown that manufacturers are involved in the design process because of the information they get from the buyers, a phenomenon which seems to increase—for instance, in the supply chain of Marks and Spencer (Tokatli, Wrigley and Kizilgün 2008). I also asked whether information about design developments could be picked up from the manufacturers. Such information is not primarily textual, but visual and perhaps tactile (in terms of fabrics, cf. Entwistle 2006:712). Thus, the tasks of the buying office may also include picking up trends from local manufacturers and designers. This, one buying office employee told me, also means she sends pictures of fashion garments back to the main office. To know better what to look for, since it is impossible to send everything, designers at the main office may let the staff at the buying office—or at least the heads—know what they should be looking for.

A further example of how buying offices may obtain information comes from someone I interviewed who worked for a BGR that operates in several European countries. He showed me how he had got hold of highly "secret" information, sent to him in an e-mail by a friend who was also working in this industry, concerning how one leading European BGR informed its suppliers of the most recent trend and the manufacturers' "take" on this trend. He said, "Just to show you … [searching his computer for the file]. [This] is the whole story of Zara, how they operate with one of the vendors.… . This is basically how Zara does it … this is how it comes in packages, what they usually send." He says this while both of us are looking at the screen. The document we have in front of us is essentially a series of pictures, with some supporting text that explains at what the manufacturer should look. He continues, pointing to another picture that shows the interpretation of the manufacturer, "this is how the vendor [that Zara is using] conceptualizes the embroideries. The buyers actually click on photographs and make a few changes, and they [the manufacturers] make a snap of the garment [that they have made], and then get back to them." The BGRs respond by asking for a few changes and then they send it back. He shows me additional pictures and explains their role: "These are all the samples made by the manufacturers; if you look at this embroidery—if you saw the last one [yes]—they are very similar." The result of this "design-process" is a product that is quite similar to the one shown on the catwalk that a photographer captures, and which later spreads across the globe.[6] In this process, the manufacturer "usually makes 30–40 samples," and from these buyers may pick up "about six styles."

This or even less sensitive information about the interaction between manufacturers and purchasers is not known to everyone in the market, quite the contrary. Few know which manufacturers, and what plants, a certain BGR uses. BGRs are unwilling to give this kind of information away because it would give competitors an advantage if they wanted to "spy." Avoiding attention from journalists may be another reason.

We can conclude that finding out where a rival retailer produces is certainly not easy for a small purchaser, especially if they do not have a strong presence in the production country. Firms with slightly lower status in particular can gain from knowing more about their competitors. Such information is a means of ensuring that one does not deviate too much in terms of trends and design. Market leaders in fashion markets have less to gain from sharing their suppliers with competitors of lower status. It is competitors with higher status in the final consumer market that are targeted "because these guys are the market, the trend leaders."

Market Leaders

What is a trend leader, or better, a market leader? To many retailers, market leaders are not simply those designer firms that present their garments on the catwalks in Paris, New York, or any other larger fashion hub, but other branded retailers that have more status in the final consumer market. Fashion leaders help bring order into the final consumer market, not least because firms with less status observe them, and orient themselves not only to their fashion, but also to their way of selling and buying fashion. The following extract from an interview with a designer working for a Turkish manufacturing firm indicates that certain firms are "fashion leaders." His problem is to "predict" fashion trends. I ask him how he gets information on what to design. "When you say that you get information, is it that you get pictures from the catwalk or is it drawings…?" He replied, "It's a booklet which is gathered from all the shops and companies in the market." He says that one is involved in a "kind of prediction game." He then expanded on this: "I mean, there are trendsetter companies as you know, like Diesel. You have to follow these guys to catch all the trends." This means that the firms he is working for also try to make predictions about what Diesel is going to do next season. It is based on this guesswork that the firms come up with a booklet "which shows the guidelines of the trend for the season." He also says that he tries to follow the information that the firm sends him. To know about these actors is a precondition for understanding the market. Actors with less status try to find out coming fashions and the trends that are under way and already in development from those with more status. This reflects their conformity and corresponding lack of possibilities to move outside their market niches (cf. Phillips and Zuckerman 2001: 389). This kind of information is often concentrated and rather easily accessible in "global cities" (cf. Sassen 2001), but less easy to obtain in more remote areas. Information is spread through gossip in networks and through formal channels such as industry magazines. Some manufacturers may also show buyers the contracts they have with other buyers, and in this way information is spread across the market.

This idea of market leaders refers to the position that BGRs hold in the consumer market. This means the status order of the consumer market in which BGRs and other garment sellers are ranked according to level of fashion also has implications in the producer market. The importance of this status rank, however, is not so strong that it dominates the logic of the producer market. The producer market is a standard-market, but to show this one must look more closely at the product of the market.

The Product

In the status market of garments discussed in chapter 2, the meaning of the product, fashion garments, is determined by those who buy and sell it. From a technical point of view, it is clear that what is traded in the production market is the same garment that BGRs sell in their stores; there is a material peg, or identity (cf. Husserl [1922] 1992: 117–18) as regards the commodity. Material identity means that the item of clothing produced—for example, in Dhaka—is displayed twelve weeks later in a store in Manchester. However, this is not the most relevant aspect for the meaning of the product. Phenomenologically, it may well be that the object produced is different from what is sold in the consumer market.[7] Furthermore, if one looks even more closely, the deals are not primarily about clothes. What, then, are they about? How can we understand the cultural commodity that fashion garments represent in the garment

production market? The product is defined in contracts and in price negotiations between buyers from BGRs and manufacturers. In the next
section, I first discuss the product from the formal standpoint, namely as
a contract, including price, and then return to the issue of defining the
product in this B2B market.

Negotiation, Contract, and Trust

All market transactions can be viewed as formal or informal. This, however, will not help us understand markets. The mutual evaluation process
of the business relationship can result in a "contract" between the BGR
and a manufacturer. The contract is a frame in which many transactions
are handled over an extended period.

It is perhaps already clear that the relations I have examined are not
based on formal contracts, but on more informal interaction. It is likely
this is partly a tradition in Sweden and the UK, compared with the more
formal and contract-oriented buyers in, for example, Germany (Lane and
Probert 2006) and the United States. Many buyers have no interest in
having contracts, since it is unclear how many orders a single manufacturer will get in the future or how large they will be.

What are the consequences of a contract? It summarizes many of the
demands that buyers make on manufacturers. I have already mentioned
that larger garment buyers have contracts that allow them to monitor
manufacturers both before and during the production process. This mon-
itoring includes financial, legal, technical, and social aspects. The contract
is written so that many rights are on the buyer's side, and the code of
conduct's demands are simply one set of requirements. One buying office head explained to me what this means, asserting that codes should
increase transparency. The manufacturers, she said, have to understand
and adapt to these demands. They cannot, she continued, merely say "no
problem" when one demands that there should be a fire extinguisher, or
that they have to take down a wall. "They can't just think that we won't
check this later. They have to realize that honesty pays off in the long
run." She concludes by saying that "they have to realize that they can't
promise to do a full job, and then be pleased if they get away with doing
half of it."

It can, of course, happen that one side violates the contract. The consequence is usually that the other side takes a loss. To pursue legal action, from the perspective of the buyer, in a culture with which they are
unfamiliar, and in which contracts and the legal system are less established and work less well, is unlikely to be economically efficient. This
strengthens the point that it is wrong to conceptualize market interaction
primarily as contractual.

Losses, however, must be minimized, and long-lasting relationships are perhaps the strongest remedy. This works in respect of other kinds of problems buyers may face. Uncertainty arising due to weak legal systems is a further reason why buyers want to diversify their portfolio of vendors. That, chronologically, trust comes before contracts is not a new insight in economic sociology, as Durkheim ([1893] 1984) made clear. It is a familiar idea that contracts may, in reality, play a limited role in practical business life. This means one does not need to settle disputes in courts (cf. Macaulay 1963: 61). The *lex mercatoria*—that is, the spontaneously developed convention of settling disputes between international transaction partners outside of national courts—is instead the backbone of international trade (Volckart and Mangels 1999). Word of mouth among people in the business can do a similar job to contracts in terms of control (Macaulay 1963: 64). Trust is, of course, important in any business. It is even more important in countries in which the legal system is underdeveloped and weak, which is often the case in garment-producing countries. Finally, the role of flexibility in the production process epitomizes the need for long-term relationships in the market, which ultimately are built on trust. Generally speaking, my research on this issue supports the findings of Uzzi (1997) and Macaulay (1963). In the next section, I turn to an issue of economic sociology, focusing on the "product" in detail, and from a phenomenological perspective that stresses the role of meaning (Aspers 2006a).

Price/Quality/Delivery

I have already mentioned that BGRs evaluate their manufacturers. I shall now discuss the principles they employ in their business negotiations. Buyers use, I was told, "a certain number of basic criteria" to evaluate manufacturers. If a manufacturer cannot meet these criteria, no deal will be struck. The three dimensions of price, quality, and delivery make up the standard that is used for this evaluation, as existing research asserts (Thaver and Wilcock 2006). Thus, to understand the "product" one must look more carefully at the process of buying the right to produce garments. The main point here is that the product is essentially demanded by the buyer (cf. Gereffi 1999: 38), and it is the task of the manufacturer to produce it. Garment manufacturers do not usually have stocks of garments, though they may have a fashion line that shows what they are capable of doing.

The standard of this market essentially implies that a buyer can order a number of clothes at a certain price and have them delivered on time at a certain quality by the manufacturer. It is a standard market because the standard is more entrenched than the identities of the actors. In other words, the standard remains even though the buyers and the manufacturers may change.

What is the role of price? One buyer explains what the manufacturers must have in order to be of interest: "They must be able to handle the volumes, and obviously, the right price level and of course that we think they have a certain level of quality that is important to us." The price level is often seen as an absolute test, which is true also in many other industries, including dyeing and tanning. There will be no deal if the manufacturer cannot meet the price level the buyer demands.

In contrast to knowledge of fashion in the final consumer market (which is a status market), knowledge of production prices is widespread. Prices, usually set in U.S. dollars, are normally fixed. As explained by one buyer, "Prices are not a problem; they can be one or a few cents higher or lower." In addition, the buyer, who in this case talks of changing prices in terms of a "stock exchange," also knows the costs of all input material. Large purchasers can even basically set the price. They do this so that the manufacturer's markup allows for a reasonable profit and meets the standard of production the purchaser demands. In other words, buyers may allow vendors enough profit that they can reinvest to maintain, and even improve, quality. I asked whether this effectively means that a larger buyer determines the profit margin, and received the following reply: "Indirectly, we do."

One may even say, as discussed earlier, that the prices are decided in the consumer market. Thus, pricing in the final market is the starting point, as explained by a buyer working for a larger BGR: "We have a price strategy, our outdoor wear shall be within this cost range, and our trousers shall be from this to that level. This one knows as a buyer, and one must adapt the quality and the manufacturers to this cost level." Though prices are fixed, they are still a major issue. Given the price the buyer can pay, there is always room for some negotiation on the design input.

Quality is the second component in the standard to which both buyers and manufacturers orient themselves. It is hard to determine if the quality level of the factory is sufficient, and that is why a test order may be a first step. However, sometimes a quick glance at the factory shows that "conditions are really poor, and then one cannot [use this supplier]; one, so to say, walks out of the place immediately." The effect is likely to be the same, I was told by a buyer, if a buyer is talking to the head of the manufacturer and realizes that the latter "only knows five words of English."

In order to maintain high-quality production, and above all, to control it, which of course is a way of controlling what the firm "emits" in the final consumer market, buyers may demand that their manufacturers do not subcontract. A manufacturer must of course buy fabrics, which sometimes the BGR can help them out with, but a BGR may be reluctant to allow them to hire jobbers, or to outsource production to factories that the BGR has no direct relations with. Jobbers are people who are contracted to run the factory and above all hire people to do the job; they are associated with poor working conditions (cf. Bonacich and Appelbaum 2000: 28).

Production quality is perhaps the least entrenched dimension of the standard. Quality is not measured according to a technological scale of reference and evaluation. It is rather a matter of the degree of compliance with the BGRs' demands on the part of manufacturers. One buyer explains what quality can mean in practice: "'Touch' is such a fuzzy question but it can be so incredibly important in our industry. Sometimes one simply wants the stitching to look a bit old. To get someone to understand this … that this is really attractive … can be very hard." The standard is by no means set in stone or always easy to express. Quality also means consistency, namely that there is no variation—for example, in colors and sizes—between the items that manufacturers produce. Quality in this market—and this is the important message—is not about the fashion content.

Out of the three dimensions that make up the standard, it is delivery that is hardest to be sure of in advance. That is, only by testing the supplier can a buyer know whether the promise to deliver the right goods on time will be met. One buyer explains the importance of delivering on time: "Ultimately, the name of the fashion game is to have the right goods at the right time, and if you are late, goods don't sell." Fashion garments, one may say, are to a large extent perishable (Weil et al. 1995: 190), and this is discernible in the production market.

I have shown that each of these three dimensions—price, quality, and delivery—is important. Does this mean, however, that the buyers see them in combination? I asked a buyer what she thought characterizes a good manufacturer. She replied: "A good vendor is [one who] has good products, the right price, secure delivery, and communicates well. Then it may be that the vendor has design input. But the first four are the most important." "Communicating well" is a matter of being sensitive to the interests of the buyer. The value of this market—what it centers on—is this standard. Ethical production is also important, but this is less of an issue to insiders. They know that some of the discussions that take place in Western countries, such as the size of the restrooms and the like, are not the most vital questions for the workers in the garment industry. To support their family, to have access to schools, and other more basic issues are often more urgent problems. The ethical issue, in other words, is treated in a different manner in the producer market for garments (cf. Aspers 2006c). Nonetheless, to take part in this market is to orient oneself to this standard. As will become clear in the next chapter, this market matters a great deal more to the identities of the manufacturers than to the BGRs.

The Service of Producing Garments

We can now summarize what the "product" of this market is. The value of the market is a standard consisting of a price/quality/delivery contract, which the purchasers essentially determine (cf. Callon, Meadel, and Rabeharisoa 2002: 197–201). The contract between purchaser and manufacturer is not primarily about the physical products—meaning, the garment. Instead, it is more correct to view it as a service contract. Manufacturers in this market acquire their identities in relation to how well they meet the standard.

One condition for talking about a standard market is that people actually know the standard and can, and do, orient themselves to it. An implicit condition of a standard market (Aspers 2009) is that information on the product is easy to find, and that one can judge whether one is capable of meeting the standard without directly interacting with the other side.

That this is a standard market acquires further evidence from the way BGRs arrange their relations with their manufacturers. Flexibility and shortening the time span from idea to sale are ways of increasing the fashion level of a BGR. A shorter lead-time can be accomplished by keeping many options open until very late. Feedback from the customers (what they buy and what they do not buy) can be used when deciding what to produce, how much to produce, and in what colors. BGRs can, in fact, acquire the right to the production of batches of clothes in the future, a practice that bears some resemblance to futures in financial markets (although these "garment rights" cannot be resold in a market). A futures contract is an agreement between a buyer and a seller to receive and deliver, at a future date, a specified amount of a product at a predetermined price. This means, in the case of garments, that purchasers book production capacity in advance, which is then filled—or occasionally not filled due to a change of fashion—with certain design content once the retailer knows what the fashion is going to be. This flexibility means the firm can meet changing consumer preferences. Thus, what the BGRs pay for is not, in a phenomenological sense, the physical object, but rather the right to have something produced according to the standard. This finding emerges via the phenomenological approach, which does not assume naïve realism and suggests that the "goods" gain new meaning as they travel from one partial order (market) to another, each with its own value and social structure. This suggests that the two markets, the consumer market and the production market, and are not only adjacent, but also embedded in each other. Furthermore, the same actors (the BGRs), take part in both, but in different roles.

Standards create a form of stability and predictability in the market (Storper 1997: 109). Simmel agrees, having observed a tendency that I have expressed theoretically as between status and standard markets. Simmel says that markets from "older branches of modern productive industry" are easier to survey; they are foreseeable, which means "production can be more accurately regulated." He continues: "Only pure articles of fashion seem to prove an exception" (Simmel [1904] 1971: 319); a statement that finds support in contemporary fashion markets.

Retailers' Identities

In what way does this market affect the identities of the branded garment retailers? I showed in chapter 3 that a BGR's relations with manufacturers matter from an ethical point of view. However, many final consumers do not care much which manufacturers BGRs are using. They do not, for example, know the difference between the thousands of manufacturers operating in Turkey and other production countries, and few seem to care about this, even though today it is common that each garment is clearly labeled to indicate the country of origin—for example, "Made in Bangladesh." Consumers do care, however, about price, fashion, and what they see as quality. These are also central items of information for investors evaluating the performance of BGRs.

Summary

In this chapter, we discussed a market in which actors hold permanent roles as either buyers or sellers, ordered according to a standard. I have shown that this partial order is ordered by the value, namely the price/quality/delivery contract. Empirically, one will find traces of status also in this market, but it is not the ordering principle. The standard (value) in this market is the service provided in terms of price/quality/delivery, not fashion. Thus, though the product obviously is a material commodity, which is later sold in the stores, it is constituted by cost, quality, and correct delivery at the agreed time.

I have suggested that the BGRs create the standard, though I have not really discussed how this happens. The standard is a value for evaluating firms. It expresses buyers' demands. BGRs, nonetheless, try to build long-term relationships with their buyers, but to keep up with the market, BGRs also need arm's-length relations and quoted prices in order to make a comparison. A larger buyer, however, uses several hundred suppliers all over the world, and this may be enough to institute "internal competition" among its suppliers to reap the benefits of the market. As I will show in chapter 5, buyers may also use their knowledge of markets as a discursive strategy in discussions and negotiations with their manufacturers.

It may seem paradoxical to develop long-term relationships in standard markets with more or less fixed prices. However, the profit that a buyer can make by switching suppliers is limited compared to the risks involved. There is a risk that a new supplier, though it may produce at a lower price, will not deliver. It may be more efficient to build a relationship on trust and cooperation than on price alone. To maintain relations with its suppliers it is necessary for the BGR to keep buying from them and to inform them if they charge too much.

Both sides orient themselves primarily to the standard of the market, and not to their respective identities (buyers and sellers). In the view of the BGRs, the more or less similar manufacturers that exist in abundance in many countries of the world are essentially interchangeable. This is also the case historically; production units have moved across the world at a faster pace than, for example, the identities and brands sold in the final consumer markets. In chapter 5, I shall analyze this market from the perspective of the manufacturers. I will discuss the role of culture in this market, and stress the global dimension.

Two general findings of this chapter are important for economic sociology. The first is our account of how markets are embedded in each other (White 2002). The second is the focus on the product, which is often taken for granted in the economic sociology of markets. These two points are related. Only when we understand that markets are embedded, and that they can be ordered in different ways, is it also possible to see that these different principles of market order—status and standard—are intimately related to the commodity traded in the market. Relational analysis stresses the mutual constitution of the commodity and the market (cf. Emirbayer 1997). Chapter 3 discussed the consumer market in detail and showed it is ordered according to the principle of status. This finding, however, gets its full meaning only when it is related to the other principle of order—standards—which I have focused on in this chapter. These two ideal-types are mutually exclusive, and comprise a basic distinction in the literature on markets (cf. Aspers 2009).

Manufacturing Garments in the Global Market

THE PURPOSE OF THIS CHAPTER is to analyze the market for garment production from the perspective of the sellers—that is, the manufacturers. In this way, we can get an even better understanding of this market in which BGRs face garment manufacturers. It also makes it possible to analyze the global dimension of this industry, and the extent to which this is a global market. Manufacturers' market identities derive from their commitments as producers and their interactions with retailers. I have already argued that this market is ordered according to the principle of standards, relating to the price/quality/delivery scale. In this chapter, I shall look at how manufacturers orient themselves to standards, and how evaluation according to standards generates their identities.

The globalization of the garment industry has given rise to enormous business opportunities for manufacturers, many of which did not even exist in the 1970s. However, it is wrong to say they have merely benefited from globalization; to a large extent they have made it happen. Some tend to see globalization as a threat. This fear is in some respects justified, and many people have been more or less forced to change their lives, not only in the developed world, where garment factories have been closed, but also in developing countries where it has forced people to adapt and to turn from farming to industrial production.

Many actors in the garment industry in developing countries have also benefited from globalization. One person with experience in the Indian economy told me about the opportunities of factory owners: "Yes, they make money. The garment business is a good industry. If you have a good run for two years, you can probably make five times your investment." He went on to describe the dangers of this trade: "When things start going wrong, or your fabrics get spoiled in dying or printing, you can be wiped out. It is that kind of high-risk business." The volatility does not just come from changing demand, where entire regions that specialize in a certain type of product can get into trouble. Such volatility is sometimes amplified by manufacturers' behavior, which means that those who get "good business from a buyer" tend to overbook and risk getting caught up in a negative spiral. The following remark by an industry insider summarizes a common view: "Making garments is a very, very detailed process; a garment goes through thirty-two or forty different stages. It's 75 percent planning, and 25 percent firefighting. This is how the business is run."

I will not discuss here the many markets in which manufacturers take part upstream in the production chain. I have not studied the market in which garment manufacturers working for global buyers hire workers, which would include the perspective of the workers. This would be yet another step of the analysis (see also Appendix III). Neither will I be able to talk about the ownership structure and the financial market of the manufacturers.

The chapter begins with a discussion of the industry from the perspective of the manufacturers. This discussion focuses on the production process, but also includes the steps prior to the production of fashion garments. The organization of production is discussed, too. This is followed by a discussion of the manufacturers' fashion input in the production process. Then, I bring up the different aspects that are relevant for manufacturers in their relations and negotiations with the buying side, namely the BGRs. A corollary of this is the identity formation process for the manufacturers, which we look at next. Before summarizing, I discuss the role of competition, standards, and culture in this market. This leads to the conclusion that though retailers and manufacturers take part in the same global market—despite being on different sides—their conditions and opportunities are radically different.

The Industry from the Perspective of the Manufacturers

Garment producers come in many varieties. They differ in terms of size, skills, what they manufacture, and the kinds of customers they have. Manufacturers are located in different production countries with lower labor costs than the countries in which the important decisions are made regarding design and marketing. One can say that design involves the top actors in the industry, whereas production or "simple sewing on the cheapest garments," which sometimes is carried out by home workers (Peters, Durán, and Piore 2002: 229), involves those at the bottom. The general trend, however, seems to be that many global production chains are becoming more symmetrically balanced in terms of power between producers, buyers, and brokers (Gereffi, Humphrey, and Sturgeon 2005; Tokatli 2007).

The Situation of Manufacturers

Each manufacturer is embedded in a flow of interactions, some of which exist only for a short time and at arm's length, while others are characterized by close collaboration that continues for years (cf. White 2002; Fligstein 2001; Gadde and Håkansson 2001; Uzzi 1997). Garment stores are concentrated in the city centers, and shopping malls in the cities of developed countries. Factories, in contrast, are often concentrated in industrial districts (Cawthorne 1995; Bair and Gereffi 2001). Moreover, smaller garment manufacturers are more likely to cater to the local market (cf. Cawthorne 1995: 47, 50), although not necessarily from choice, as the following anecdote shows. An Indian entrepreneur mentioned she had considered catering to the domestic market "many times." She explained the reason for this: "You know, when we have finished a shipment, we always have some leftovers. We always make some extra, so that last-minute rejections [will not stop the shipment] … So we always make five percent extra." After a short phone call (in this business there are many), she continued: "Many exporters have their own retail outlet. A lot of stock is left, and it is easier to sell it." The phone rang again and she switched to Hindi. There are, however, some problems with selling to the home market. One is quite simple: the upper classes want to distinguish themselves from other groups, as Simmel already suggested, and might shun everything that is domestic, which essentially means that those who have money spend it on imported garments. In India, for example, the upper class seems to wear either expensive Western clothes or tailor-made traditional garments. This leaves little room for factory-produced items that can be sold with high margins. The consequence is that it is mostly the local markets, located at street corners, that are flooded with garments of lower quality.

The workers of the garment supplying firms live in areas nearby or in some cases also in the middle of these industrial districts. I have, for example, observed people living between an industrial district and a dump area that was also used for pasturing their pigs. Some manufacturers also start out on a small scale in non-industrial areas. One manufacturer I interviewed who had a factory in an industrial area in New Delhi, explained how he started up his business: "When I started, I did it in a small place, which wasn't an industrial area. It was just a basement, and [I took it] from there. I took one order, supplied to one buyer. Finally when we were more established, and things were up and running, we came here." This is a common way of starting a business. The following example supports this kind of industrial trajectory. During my fieldwork, I went to one small factory, which at the time of my visit had about 20 employees. It was a two-story building, and three people were working in the storage room. It was very dusty, and it was piled high with swatches of cloth. People were climbing this cloth-mountain to sort them. Fabrics were cut and put together in other rooms. A staircase without a rail led up to the second floor, and the office was a small room that had windows to the other rooms so the workers could be observed. This "factory" was located in a residential area, which is illegal, and the alley that led to the entrance was a muddy path between houses from which the wash dried between numerous telephone and electrical cables that criss-crossed the buildings. Production in residential areas does exist, but the larger production units are located in industrial districts.

Researchers, beginning with Alfred Marshall, have argued that there are many advantages to industrial districts. These districts are more or less self-supporting. There may, for example, be small stalls or tents from which a cheap meal can be purchased. Fruit and food sellers, who know when the workers take their breaks, also circulate in these areas. It is not only the physical proximity and the advantages of their logistic network that matter; personal networks and access to labor are also advantages for firms that are located in industrial districts. Access to labor means primarily access to skilled labor with experience of different kinds of demanding production. However, it also means having access to less experienced workers, who essentially are recruited from the reserve army based in rural areas. These people contribute to urbanization. The following biographical excerpt is typical: a woman who "moved here [to the factory] from her village four years ago, finding work as a helper in a small factory making short pants for men and boys. She used to clip stray threads after a more skilled worker sewed the pants." One should remember, however, that though many low-wage and low-skill jobs are created in developing countries by companies producing garments as a result of globalization, some high-skill jobs are also created (Bair and Gereffi 2002: 45).

A number of other aspects are important to manufacturers in this industry. Especially with an industry like fashion, which deals with "perishable" goods, transportation and road quality are of great importance. Economic actors in developing countries face other kinds of difficulties than their peers in developed countries; a reliable electricity grid is an important issue in the former, but almost taken for granted in the latter. In some developing countries, power cuts are quite frequent, especially during the summer when all the air conditioners are running.

Numerous manufacturers are located in industrial districts, but it is hard from the outside to tell those factories that produce garments from those that make, for example, furniture. One conclusion is that no visual differentiation is made among garment producers when it comes to their sites, which contrasts with what BGRs are trying to do with their stores in places like London's high street.

The factories look similar from the outside: observation in industrial districts indicates similarity, not only between the factories and how the work is organized, but also in terms of physical appearance. When one enters the buildings, however, they also look the same from the inside. Many firms divide production into different working areas. There is usually an office area, and then a reception area for the fabrics and other goods, a place for cutting the fabrics into patterns, followed by one for sewing and other forms of treatment. The products are then perhaps moved to a spot for washing, which is followed by packing and delivery. The washing machines are often the largest machines in a factory. These machines, the number of workers, the constant stream of commodities into and from the site, as well as the noise of the sewing machines, make it clear this is industrial production.

My point is that production of garments should be understood in relation to the standard market for which the production is organized—it is not enough merely to look at the product itself. How then is production organized? An observer from the 1950s would probably recognize most of the production units in use today. Some firms of course have computers to get patterns directly from the buyers, but that is not always the case. The people glued to sewing machines operate them manually, which requires no computer skills whatsoever. That production technology has not changed much in this industry during the last fifty years or so (cf. Johnson 1985: 57) is also clear from the public relations material that manufacturers issue. It is quite common that they show pictures from the factory, in many cases depicting workers operating sewing machines.

These observations on work organization suggest that the principles characteristic of the peak of the modern industrial period—namely Taylorism—still apply. The orientation is towards function and efficiency, not creativity and aesthetics. Tayloristic principles are common also in other labor-intensive industries, such as footwear (for example, Knorringa 1995: 127). At a more general level, this industry (or more concretely the production side of this market) is fairly bureaucratic-Tayloristic.

Weber saw this form of organization—most likely in the organization of large German corporations (Swedberg 1998: 63)—as essential to rational modern industrial capitalism, with bureaucracy as its leading organizational form (cf. Parsons 1929: 37). Weber, without pursuing this in detail, argues that discipline in organizations applying scientific management ultimately comes from the military ([1920–21] 1978: 1156–57), and discipline is still a central concept in garment production. The idea of bureaucracy presented by Weber now belongs to the sociological mainstream, and needs only a brief summary here. Following Parsons's interpretation, the main characteristics of bureaucracy are "rationality, resting on a complex, hierarchically organized division of tasks, each with a sharply marked off sphere of 'competence'; specialization of functions, whereby a special premium is placed upon expert knowledge ... and impersonality" (1929: 37). This form of organization is appropriate for calculation, which Weber—and interpreters such as Parsons—argues is the core of modern capitalism. Taylorism lends itself well to rational industrial capitalism since it facilitates the calculation of costs and the planning of production (Weber [1920–21] 1978: 296).

Calculability merits particular attention in this context. The form of (economic) bureaucracy that Weber speaks about, summarized as a machine performing according to the general intention of its owners, is well adapted to an economy and markets characterized by relative stability. As Weber himself pointed out, stability is a condition of calculability (Parsons 1929: 37). Moreover, from what has been said so far concerning bureaucracy, rationality, and calculability, it is hard to disagree with Swedberg that "the main theme of rational capitalism is no doubt predictability and, in this sense, stability" (1999: 30). Moreover, Weber connects bureaucracy and in particular the calculability of the Taylorist system—which is also called "Scientific Management"—and its principles of organizing labor and work (cf. Weber [1921–22] 1978: 101–3, 150, 974–75, 1156–57; cf. Kocka 1980: 97). One should, at the same time, remember that his discussion of bureaucracy refers largely to the upper segment of administration.

Whether one calls it Taylorism, Scientific Management, or Fordism is of less importance; the main thing is the rational organization of work in many small steps, according to a piece-rate method of production and pay, and producing standardized products. Hierarchy, calculability, subordination ("tell the workers what to do and supervise them"), and the assumption that actors are rational and self-interested is a key component of this approach. Though this form of organization is often a mixture of hierarchy and markets, the firm, given that the workers have sold their labor, is in control and can give orders.

This way of organizing work does not allow workers any scope for initiative, and the analogy made by Marx, that the worker becomes an appendage of the machine, is largely still true in the garment production sector. The point is that much of what is true of bureaucracy is also true of Taylorism, and both organizational forms, I claim, correspond well to the form of industrial capitalism that one sees clear evidence of when observing and talking to people on the production side of the global garment industry. Taylorism and its economic logic, so it seems, also informs us about contemporary working conditions in this industry.

A garment factory needs a large work force to produce the garments it has promised to its buyers. Though many buyers demand that their manufacturers do not subcontract, some admit that they do so, predominantly during periods when the capacity of the factory is insufficient. But as one manufacturer said, "there can be a lot of problems with the suppliers" he uses to help him out, and quality and consistency may suffer.

One form of subcontracting is to hire jobbers. This is more common among smaller suppliers and was not an issue central to my study, but many of those I interviewed brought this topic up, sometimes even as their first issue, as if they expected me to ask about this. This suggests that people in the garment industry are aware of how sensitive this question is among final consumers in the West. One head and owner of a smaller manufacturing firm in India explained why he used a "contractor" (jobber): "You know, in India there are many labor laws, and a lot of labor problems. I don't want too many headaches, so it is easier for me to give it [the job] to ... a contractor; they do the work, and they look after the labor." Given this relationship the subcontractor, who in this case worked only for the person I interviewed, is paid per garment, which also means it is, as he says, "up to him how he pays his people ... so less of a headache for me." However, manufacturers do not always inform the buyer that they are using subcontractors.

The Production Process

The organization of this industry essentially reflects the bureaucratic principle of Taylorism, representing the production process in which the manufacturers have a central role. Their role is even more central if the production is oriented towards full-package solutions, which means the garments the manufacturers deliver are ready for the racks in the stores.

The production of garments is a technological process. Before one can talk of garments, a number of steps must be discussed (Gereffi, Spener, and Bair [2002] have much of value to say on this, in addition to the practice-oriented literature). In the following, I briefly summarize the garment production process. Here, I follow a cotton production chain. The production process depends on the material and so do the dying techniques.

Cotton is harvested and is spun into yarn, which is woven. In most cases, spinning and weaving are integrated within the same mill. These processes generate unfinished cloth ("greige"). Afterward, the cloth is usually dyed, bleached, or otherwise prepared before it is sold to an apparel producer. Cotton can be manufactured in different qualities—for example, thin or thick. They are later trimmed and cut, and they then go through a number of steps. Garment production includes assembly, sewing, laundry and finishing, packing, and distribution. All these steps include control.

The production of fabrics is not done independently by the manufacturers. Many producers of fabrics have close links to designers and they get feedback about trends from their customers, namely the garment manufacturers. Fairs also occur, specializing in both the cultural aspects—what the latest fabrics/trends are or will be—and the latest technological systems and innovations. The business-to-business market between manufacturers of fabrics and the buyers (garment manufacturers) is price-driven. Spinning and weaving are capital-intensive, whereas production of garments is labor-intensive (Weil et al. 1995: 181).

Fabrics are input materials for the manufacturers, and lie upstream in the production chain. It seems, however, that they have traditionally been standard markets, though the role of fashion has increased over time (Marshall 1920b: 802). The fact that it has long been possible to trade in the futures of some input materials suggests that these are standard markets. Alfred Marshall (1920b: 802) refers to the futures market for cotton. That production of textiles is standardized is explained by Marshall (1920b: 56–57) in terms of "natural standards" of cotton and wool. Over time, however, fabrics have benefited from more advanced science and greater variety, and the more buyer-driven the tendencies in the design of fabrics, the less standardized it gets.

An important aspect of production is consistency. A manufacturer used the following control system with a British customer. Production begins with checking the material, then the handmade parts are produced, which are checked; then comes stitching, and further checking, and one has to make sure that the size is right, as well as the buttons, the embroidery, and the appearance of the garment. Then, the garment is washed and checked again. Afterward, the labels are normally put on. The packaging, the folding, everything is checked. Only if it passes the last step will the manufacturer ship the garments. If they do not meet the standard, the garments are discarded or sold in local markets. Quality control, which in the broadest sense also includes the code of conduct, implies, as one manufacturer puts it, "[that] there are thousands of things that need to be approved in garments in accordance with the buyers' wishes." This is further evidence of what was shown in the last chapter, namely that the buyers have the upper hand in this relationship.

Fashion Input

Earlier, I argued that the production process is fairly standardized, and this supports the idea presented in chapter 4 that one should treat the market in which manufacturers face BGRs as a standard market. It is evident from my research that the meaning of the garments as fashion commodities is constructed in the final consumer market. The garments that BGRs and other sellers have on display become fashion when worn by consumers. This does not mean the BGRs' designers create everything that they sell. However, that the fashion input from manufacturers is sometimes very limited receives support—for example, from one designer working for a manufacturer in Turkey. He said he meets the buyers "once or twice a year," which of course is not often, though people can stay in contact using other means, like the Internet. The buyers, another representative of a manufacturer told me, "are mainly involved until the orders are in place, after that the work is handed over to the local office, the buying office, then they [the people at the buying office] follow up on the production, the quality, the delivery." This means that manufacturers meet buyers only "at the beginning of the season." The buying office does not deal with fashion. This is indicated by a person working at a buying office: "we are not in the design process; we just have the information [about fashion]."

The manufacturers—to underline that this market is oriented to standards and production and not to fashion and design—have much more contact with the people at the buying office, as one manufacturer told me: "The [representatives from] buying houses come very often; they come to see the fabric, the printing, the process; they check the sizes, we send them samples; they check the measurements to see that they are according to the requirements."

Design input from manufacturers comes largely from designers who know about the market the manufacturers' buyers come from. I covered this issue in interviews, and asked whether the designers the manufacturers were using were employed or were "independent designers." In one interview, I got the following typical reply: "They are mostly freelance designers." By way of further explanation, I was told: "We hire the designers on a freelance basis, but we also have in-house designers, but not at a very senior level." Their own staff, thus, carries out only less advanced tasks. Sometimes the designers specialize in different markets. Another interviewee told me: "We have different designers, and the buyers also have their designers, and some ask [us to design and develop a fashion line that is only for] their collection, so we develop collections specially for those customers, country-wise, [since] colors change, bodies change [according to the country]." This means that the manufacturers can make a collection and selection, "keeping their buyers in mind." The consequence is that "if a company is working with French buyers, then it hires French designers."

The dependence on foreign freelance designers, who are expensive, also means that fewer local designers get a chance. Nevertheless, manufacturers "all hire European designers, either they work there and keep sending them the concepts, or they build it up, and [the designer] comes here for two weeks or three weeks and builds up the whole line for them." It is difficult to estimate the number of freelance designers, but from an informant with twenty years in the industry, I was told that 30–40 percent of manufacturers who cater to the BGRs use this strategy.

Manufacturers must adapt to the characteristics of different buyers; even buyers from the same country can have different markets. Products are tailored to particular consumer markets. This also means that manufacturers "have to make a different collection for each buyer, [because] pricing [policies] differ. Some ... will sell the same piece at a higher price than manufacturers in the lower segment of the market." However, the different prices in the consumer market—which consumers of, say, white shirts can observe—are not reflected in the producer market.

Design input on the part of manufacturers is different from design conducted by the BGRs; in practice it means that designers working for a manufacturer must listen and adapt to the demands of the different buyers, as research (e.g., Tokatli, Wrigley, and Kizilgün 2008) and the following conversation shows. I talked to a designer at a manufacturer about the collection they made for a BGR and asked whether there could be a problem if they showed the same thing to everyone, and all the buyers wanted to have the same pieces from the collection. The designer replied:

> Everyone's taste is different. Someone in the United States has different taste [than] someone in London, and someone in Canada is likely to be different again. So I have to adapt to their [differences]. I show [them] my ... collection. The person in the United States tells me to make this change; the Canadian tells me to make another. I have to take their views into account.

In a conversation I had with the head of a firm that concentrated on designs with a very ethnic Indian look, which was in vogue when I did my study, I asked whether this specialization might be a problem when fashion changed. This informant replied: "You see, we are working for an ethnic look [in our] garments. Ethnic-look garments only." I suggested it could be both an advantage and a disadvantage to have an ethnic look. My informant pointed out that fashion changes all the time, and that only those able to keep up will survive. In other words, while his firm was currently geared up to satisfy the demand for ethnic styles, he had to be constantly alert to general fashion trends and be ready to switch direction.

> To stay in tune with developments, manufacturers also have to travel, to know what the trends are, and what they are going to be for the next year, for we work one year in advance. So ... we have to attend the fabric fairs, to go and see what we have to design, what we have to offer the buyers, and they also have to bring their own instructions, and we work together very closely to make a collection for them.

This again underlines the importance of manufacturers tuning their fashion input to their buyers' needs. This process, of course, shows many similarities to the working process of the BGRs described in chapter 4. According to one manufacturer:

> First of all, we start with the colors that are going to be in fashion next year, then the fabrics. We go into what kind of fabrics they [the buyers] might be interested in, then we start [to design] the collection, and [then] the embroi-

dery, the fabrics. It's a lot of work because what one buyer likes, another buyer may not be able to sell.... So there is a lot of work involved in each and every one of them, and it should not look cheap. So it is the buyers who decide ... because they are the ones who are selling to the markets, and it is their decision.

Because this process takes place up to one year before the season, manufacturers cannot accommodate changes in fashion that happen after they have made their collections. Information and inspiration come not only from the international scene; manufacturers' designers are also inspired by their local market.

Keeping up to date with fashion trends is an important issue for the manufacturers, and it is of course crucial if they want to provide fashion input for their buyers. One designer who has worked for global brands as well as BGRs told me how he obtained information about trends: "Their [BGRs'] design departments select the trends. And they also inform us [about] their company's trends." This means, I was told by one representative of a manufacturer, that the BGRs "inform us what color is to be used for the coming season, as well as what fabrics will be used, so we have all this knowledge and we design accordingly so [that] they buy it."

Some manufacturers are open about the support they get from BGRs: "they [the BGRs] help us [by informing us] what kind of product they are looking for. We can make very nice designs and everything, but if it doesn't sell, what's the point? They are in the market ... all the time, and decide what is going to sell and what [is] not." This contains an important insight, namely that it is very hard for everyone, but especially for manufacturers, to have detailed knowledge of what will make it into Western consumer markets twelve, three, or even one month from the conception of the design. This observation, amongst others, supports the argument of the centrality of the consumer market.

One manufacturer described how the staff of her firm and the BGRs' staff "work as a team." "The buyers have their own designers, [who] work in their established style." In the next step, she continued, they "bring us their sketches and they [then] see what we can offer them, the fabrics, and—each exporter has its own plus points, we may be good in some embroideries, and another may be good in denims—the buyers decide [according to their preferences]."

Though it can be described as teamwork, manufacturers' fashion input may be indirect, and in some cases only a point of departure for the discussion. One head of a manufacturing firm said: "They [the BGRs] give us their design; they tell us all the things they want." This means that, in the end, their designers "will take ideas from our showroom, from our collection, [and] make changes according to their collection, depending on what can sell."

The teamwork referred to earlier can take place only in cases where the manufacturers—or, more concretely, the people working for a specific manufacturer—get a feeling for what its buyers want. The BGRs "have their own designers, and we have our designers, and they have to merge together to make a product that will finally sell in the market, to the masses."

The degree of design input may consequently differ. Some manufacturers have no fashion input whatsoever. Among smaller manufacturers that only cater to smaller firms, not to BGRs, the process starts with the firm getting a garment, an "actual" piece, that the firm is asked to copy. It must also come up with a price. This ties into the major debate on counterfeit products, often associated with producers in China (Crane and Bovone 2006: 328), which is a substantial problem for many brands.

To sum up, although we should understand this as a standard market centered on production, manufacturers too may provide design input. But such input can be useful only if the two parties know each other's strengths and preferences. This means that the ongoing dialogue is often part of a relationship that may have existed for years, which is typical of industrial business relations (cf. Darr 2006).

Identity Differentiation and Strategies

Manufacturers operate in a buyer-driven market, which means they must appear attractive to the buyers. Differentiation, as already mentioned, is an important aspect in a status market and it is a condition of carving out a market niche. In "standard" markets, by contrast, actors try to outperform their rivals by scoring higher on the standard measurement (that is, producing the right quality and delivering on time). Thus, even though the status of firms in the final consumer market to some extent rubs off on the manufacturers, neither the technological and organizational differences, nor any other aspect are enough to enable buyers to orient themselves towards the status of the manufacturers. The principle of standard is, consequently, a better explanation of order than status, because it is a more entrenched social construction.

Even though manufacturers are able to differentiate amongst themselves, this takes place within a broader frame of similarities, including self-presentation, how work is organized, and pricing. There are also many similarities in the ways manufacturers market themselves. The information material that manufacturers send to potential buyers puts the spotlight on production capacity; how short the lead-time is; what kind and quantity of machines they have; how well they check quality; and their relations to purchasers. This is information that one can easily find on the Internet in manufacturers' marketing materials.[1] This kind of "marketing" would be unthinkable on London's high street. Moreover, production technology is not secret in this industry. The secret is the design of fashion garments, which, however, gain "value" in the consumer market when presented in the context of the brand. Knowing about the garments that are in production, unless they are identified with a particular brand or firm, is of little value. It is only once one knows which firm is producing what that the information becomes useful for competitors.

What strategies do manufacturers use to survive and make a profit in the market? One strategy is to work with a limited, but not too small, number of buyers: "it is better to work for a few buyers, at least five or six. If anything goes wrong with a buyer, there are more to work with. At least you can survive in the market. If you supply only one buyer, the stakes are much higher—if that buyer goes bankrupt, you are finished." A manufacturer does not want too many buyers either, because this makes it difficult to organize production. It is therefore enough to have a handful of buyers. Costs arise in reorganizing production lines and maintaining business relations. Thus, a large manufacturer prefers to work with long runs with a few large buyers, which means there is a mutual interest in establishing relations. One dimension of the relationship is that manufacturers get some fashion input from their buyers. This is especially important if a manufacturer sticks to only one buyer, as, in the words of one manufacturer, "he is [then] not seeing the outside world." This means that a manufacturer must be part of a network of many actors to acquire information (cf. Granovetter 1974).

One strategic question concerns taking on orders when a firm's production capacity is already full. In order to comply with the demands of buyers who want quick delivery, a manufacturer may sometimes have to outsource some of the production. Manufacturers operate in a business environment in which it is hard to turn down an order from a long-term buyer. In addition, strikes and logistical problems may cause difficulties for manufacturers. This can more or less force them to subcontract. This, I was told by one manufacturer, "happens rarely, perhaps once a year or so. 'If I need 1,200 and have the capacity to produce 700, I may ask someone else to do the extra 500.'" On being asked whether they pass this information on to the buyer I was told that "the buyer doesn't have to know." "Overbooking" —that is, taking on more orders than one has capacity for—is a risk that manufacturers sometimes decide to take. Other risks can be more difficult to deal with, such as events in some of the markets that the manufacturers are involved in "upstream" in the production cycle, such as labor markets and other input markets.

Manufacturers' strategies differ. Some discriminate, and try to work with, for example, medium-sized BGRs from the UK, whereas others take a broader approach. I asked owners of garment factories about this, and the following was a typical response. On being asked whether he had different buyers, some larger than others or of the same size, one respondent replied: "I work with bigger buyers, but with small buyers too, and so I'm working with every type ... I'm in the market. I have to sell my product." This strategy, to cater to virtually all consumers would not be successful in the final consumer market, however, since this market demands that firms have an identity. It may not even be successful in the production market, but here manufacturers can at least orient themselves to the standard.

As I showed in the chapter on garment buyers, there is an advantage in developing long-term relations for both manufacturers and BGRs. Many of the manufacturers I talked to expressed an interest in developing this kind of relationship. One manufacturer had been in a relationship for eight years, and stated that the greatest advantage of a long-term relationship is "understanding." This means that one side understands the situation of the other, and both can talk about the production problems that occur, whether related to delivery or changes of design. Communication of this kind tends to be rather straightforward and he says that they do not hide anything from each other. Instead, trust and reciprocity become important in this network-oriented relationship. The concrete effect, as well as the means of maintaining the relationship, is that the manufacturers visit their buyers in their home countries, and vice versa. We shall now look more closely at an issue that may seem to be at the core of the relationship, namely price.

Price and Global Competition

To branded garment retailers, prices are just one out of several crucial dimensions that they use to sort out manufacturers. How manufacturers perceive price reflects this. The following quotation from one head of a manufacturing firm summarizes manufacturers' view of prices well: "So finally, when the [test sample of the] product is made, to the satisfaction [of the customer], then we go into [the issue of] prices, and whether it will be sellable or not sellable." What does sellable mean here? It refers not to the producer market in which the manufacturers face the buyers, but to the prices that the BGRs can set in the final consumer market, in which the BGRs face final consumers and are under pressure from competitors. Does this mean, to refer to the discussion of the previous chapter, that pricing so to speak travels "backwards"? I was told: "Yes, it goes backwards, they [the BGRs] have their target prices, and we see if we can do it or not.... So it is up to us."

In this sense, pricing is not so much a delicate issue as a matter of "take it or leave it." Still, the global dimension of this market, in contrast to the consumer market, means that manufacturers are under great pressure from buyers, who are able to make competitors from several countries compete for the same order. Does this mean, I asked, "that it may be difficult to negotiate about the price?" As might be imagined, the answer was, "Yes," and the explanation, in the words of a manufacturer is that "there are goods made in India in the stores [of the BGRs], and goods made in China. So ... people will always compare prices." This, she said, makes them think, "Why is this product, which looks almost the same, [sold at only] half the price." In her opinion, the buyers "want lower and lower prices, and they are not wrong to do so because they are getting [lower] prices [in their stores].... But it is becoming more difficult [for us]."

The assertion that there is a price/production/delivery standard in this industry receives support from the publicly announced prices for garment production. One can sometimes see such prices even in the company profiles that manufacturers use for promotion. The following comes from an Indian company profile: "Men's half sleeve shirt, one pocket flat pack, 100 percent cotton polin (92 × 98) [a cotton quality], dyed $2.80; printed $3.10." What is important here is neither the fashion nor the "look" of the shirt, but the production method and the quality of the fabric. The fashion input can, and apparently is expected to, come from the buyer.

In the following interview extract, a designer working for a manufacturer recalls a meeting with a British buyer. It further explains the role of price. The interviewee told me that he and other team members had prepared by finding out more about the buyer's design preferences. The buyer had also given some basic instructions on what kind of design they were looking for. He continued...

> They [the British design team] come to our office, we discuss various matters and many merchandisers, and the buyers are there of course. The buyer says "I like this T-shirt, I want to buy it, I want to have it in our collection." The buyer then says, "OK, what's the price?" That question goes to our company's merchandiser. And our merchandiser says "It's two pounds" and the buyer says "It can't happen; we cannot buy this." At this stage, we come together with their designers and design new stuff, which they like and can buy. So we can reduce the template of the prints. For example, if the print used in the T-shirt has four templates, we can reduce it to two. And if the buyer likes it, they buy it. That's what we discuss.

Price is connected to the design input, but (as this case illustrates) is more tied into the cost of production.

Thus, producers in this "standard" market do not compete as retailers in a status market do, by aesthetic differentiation, but by having a better price/quality/delivery combination. Alternatively, in the words of one agent representing a manufacturer: "We try our best to negotiate with buyers and give the best price, and make sure that the supplier is of the right quality, and delivers on time." This is to say that one cannot separate price and quality (Chamberlin 1953). Competing manufacturers hold largely structurally equivalent positions, not only in terms of the market, but also in terms of information flow (Burt 1992).

In order to position themselves, manufacturers use references from purchasers and samples of products to prove their ability to meet certain standards of price and quality. Consequently, they do not compete merely on price, assuming that the other requirements have been met. Instead, they compete on quality, assuming they are equal in other terms, including price. The preoccupation with price, however, is easy to understand since prices are relatively easy to calculate and can be seen as reflections of quality and the ability to deliver on time. This discussion not only shows that one can talk about an underlying value (in this case, a production/quality/delivery standard) in this market. It is also possible to talk about a culture that prescribes how negotiations and interaction take place between manufacturers and BGRs, a topic to which I shall return.

Given the global dimension, is it then fair to talk about increased competition in this industry? It probably depends on whom you ask, but my finding is that competition has increased. One Indian manufacturer told me that he faced tougher competition than in the past, and mentioned that the competition comes not only from other Indian manufacturers, but in the first place from China, Bangladesh, and other countries. This he notices in negotiations with the customers who say that "'We can get this in China for $2.50', [so] what can you do?" Another Indian manufacturer with many years in the industry sees increased competition, and feels squeezed between the buyers who demand lower prices and higher quality, and her contractors whom she cannot pay less. More specifically, she feels the threat from China: "They [the buyers] ... always compare [your prices] with the prices in China. 'We are getting two dollars in China, but three here; unless [you cut your prices] ... we will place the order in China.' So there is a lot of competition with prices, and many people have to run their factories almost on a non-profit basis."

The competition, thus, is not only with manufacturers located in the same industrial district. It is, in fact, likely that a manufacturer in Turkey will have to compete with a manufacturer in India or China. Firms can have different cost structures, but the ability to produce the same things. How, then, can a firm in Turkey, with higher production costs, compete with a Chinese firm? This clearly global dimension of competition must be understood in relation to shifting fashion trends. If firms could plan and wait for ships to take the goods from Bangladesh or China, which are typical low-production-cost countries, there would be few reasons to buy from other countries. However, with lead-times of three weeks, surface transport from China or Bangladesh, with much longer lead-times than three weeks, is not an option. These garments would have to go by air, substantially increasing costs. Thus, manufacturers closer to the consumer markets have an advantage when it comes to cutting-edge garments, items that need short lead-times. More basic commodities, such as socks, underwear, and regular T-shirts, are less affected by the vagaries of fashion, and one allows longer lead-times for them, and thereby lower relative production costs.

Manufacturers face their competitors not only indirectly, in negotiations with the buyers, but they can also observe their competitors when they visit the buyers' home markets. One manufacturer told me that when he visits Europe his buyer "shows me all the products; I can also see in the stores what is made in Bangladesh [and] what is made in China."

It is clear that the decreasing cost, which one can measure in real terms but sometimes also in nominal terms, of fashion garments enjoyed by European and American consumers is partly due to the abolition of trade tariffs, but to a large extent also to increased competition. This means that a country like Turkey, which used to be a cheap country, has increasingly come under threat—in common with most producer countries—from China, which has increased its exports substantially over the last ten to fifteen years (see Appendix II). The important point here is not the circumstances of particular countries, however, but the structural character of the global conditions characteristic of a standard market.

This market, to sum up this discussion on price and competition, is ordered around a standard. The crucial task of the manufacturer is to respond to the buyer with a price, based on the requisite quantity, quality, fabrics, shipping, and lead-time. Competition is fierce, but it is impossible to judge how many producers—for example, out of the 30,000 or so garment producers in India—are competing directly. It is, however, obvious that they do not know about each other in the same way retailers do. To the manufacturers, it matters less at the end of the day who the buyer is, as long as it fulfills its part of the standard transaction—that is, pays upon delivery of the goods.

Fligstein (2001) has suggested that hardly any markets are global. I think he is wrong, but it is easy to see how he can come to this conclusion. Fligstein's market model draws on Harrison White's work on markets. White's theory, as White is well aware, is only a theory of one kind of market, so-called producer markets. A central idea of this theory, which can be traced to Alfred Marshall and Edward Chamberlin, is that producers differentiate their products and occupy niches in the market that they essentially stick to (White 1981, 2002). A Whitean producer market is made up of a "handful" of producers. Fligstein assumes this to be the case for all markets. Many markets, however—not only those that neoclassical economics describes, but also the market this chapter is about—have more or less standardized commodities. A standard-oriented market can harbor an indefinite number of buyers and sellers, but what I call a status market cannot.

The Market Culture

This market has a culture (cf. Fligstein 2001: 18), which is central to the solution of the second prerequisite of market order, namely what behavior is approved in a given market. Consequently, when representatives from the BGRs and the manufacturers meet, they follow the informal rules of "this is how we do it here." This culture makes it easier to know how to behave, and in this way it contributes to the order of the market. This culture is colored by the different national and local cultures of the manufacturing and buying countries, but there is also a business culture that reaches across markets. What I shall focus on here is what sets this market apart from other markets in terms of its partial market culture, not the lifeworld-base and cultural characteristics that it shares with other markets.

If one analyzes the situation between a larger manufacturer and a larger retailer, it is clearly the latter (the buyer) who is the strongest (cf. Giuliani, Pietrobelli, and Rabellotti 2005). One should also remember that most of the product-value is added in the final stage, where retailers face consumers. This is fundamental to understanding how retailers have power in negotiations with vendors, and thus determine not only the conditions of business, but also the business culture. The power that larger buyers have over manufacturers is partly due to economic resources, but it is also due to their structural position (Burt 1992). Buyers can, for example, force manufacturers to keep production running even on holidays to meet deadlines.

The contracts between buyers and manufacturers set the terms of interaction. The buyers, then, make sure that the products are delivered and shipped on the right day, and that the manufacturer ships the right quantity at the quality demanded, produced according to the specifications, and under the ethical and environmental conditions that the contracts specify.

This does not contradict the fact that not all deals are made with a signed contract, another aspect of the culture of this industry. A manufacturer informed me that in the long-term relations they have with buyers, everything is "open." Moreover, some buyers know that the producers need a margin in order to stay in business. This means that they accept a markup of 10–15 percent. The power relations between the two sides are thus reflected in the culture, or more specifically, in "the way of doing business."

That this market is different from the consumer market is noticeable, for example, in the way people in the industry dress. They are business people and do not aspire to be particularly fashionable, especially not the men. The way people dress, and the kind of actors that are drawn to this market must be contrasted with the culture in the consumer market, which is ordered by the principle of status. In the consumer market, for example, it is very important how store personnel look (cf. Kawamura 2006). The interaction between the BGRs and their customers is embedded in a culture of fashion, not only of clothes but also of music, lighting, and much more, as I have discussed. At industrial fashion fairs where business people meet, styles barely differ from those characteristic of other industries—most of those who attend international B2B fairs are men dressed in suits.

One may talk of a global interface in this market, but one could also talk of a gender interface. Women dominate the industry on the buying side (not just as consumers) and men dominate the production side. Older men, whose understanding of the fashion sold to young women must be questionable, can have such sway in the producer market because the name of the game there is not fashion, but a standard governing the *production* of fashion. The perhaps obvious advantage of having women as both buyers and designers has not always been obvious, but positions within this industry can to some extent be seen as breaking the typical gender division of labor (England and Folbre 2005).

Another gender dimension of the culture is that women working as buyers may be unwilling to travel on their own, or they may not be treated with respect. One buyer told me what she has experienced: "It has happened when we [as women] visit a firm where I have felt, 'no, this isn't working out, they don't respect us.' If they do not look at us when we are speaking ... then this supplier won't work; one simply turns them down; they don't exist."

I then asked a provocative question: "This may sound like a question from the nineteenth century, but haven't you considered sending a man instead?" She replied:

> No, rather the other way around. If it doesn't work with women in this country, then we can't do it, just because our buying organization is almost all female. They must be able to accept that a young female assistant, who may be 22, comes into their office and tells them what to do. This is a business relationship between a buyer and seller; that takes precedence over the other issues.

This indicates the cultural dimension and the fact that the buyers have a major impact on how business is done in this market. This power may also be a source of change. The scenario of a 22-year-old woman giving orders, for example, to an older Muslim man is unlikely outside the global economic sphere in many Muslim countries.[2]

This market is about providing services for producing garments, and making a deal is not a particularly mysterious act. The general business culture is the common denominator and serves as a foundation for making deals in this market. The following episode referring to a fashion industry fair, reported by Skov, shows what I mean:

> I have observed, for example, an Eastern European buyer place orders with a Korean leather supplier with perfunctory English as the only common language. Each with his heavy accent, their talk included little apart from numbers; sample numbers, lot sizes, shipment dates, prices and letters of credit formed the mainstay of a lingua franca which was sufficient to close a deal. (2006: 780)

It is, in contrast, unlikely that these two actors could have talked about the design and development of a fashion line for a specific market. This market, to conclude the discussion of culture, has created a unique culture only to a limited degree. There appear instead to be many similarities with other industries, and one may then talk of a more general business culture. Nonetheless, the culture not only helps to set it apart from other markets, but is also a prerequisite for market order.

Order Out of Standard

Order in real life is often a combination of the two principles I have described: status and standard. I have argued in this chapter that standard matters most in this market. Buyers and sellers orient themselves to each other, and their relations and identities play a role. Status, however, can be a proxy or a signal effect of "quality." Both sides can learn from their counterparts, for example, by working with high-status firms. This, however, should not conceal the important fact that the standard of the market is a much more entrenched social construction than any status order of actors, or of buyers or sellers. This is to say that standard is the ordering principle in this partial order, which is the global market for the production of fashion. Everyone in the business knows the standard, and how well a manufacturer performs in relation to it determines its identity. Thus, though the literature on technology and its role in "path dependency" and order in a market relies on materially entrenched standards, they may not be more "entrenched" than ideal standards. Though firms on both sides of the market are judged according to how well they meet its standard, only the manufacturers gain their unique identity in this market, because they are evaluated on the basis of what they do by the buyers who make up the economic audience (Zuckerman 1999: 1403–1404; Phillips and Zuckerman 2001). The BGRs represent the economic audience that also determines what counts in this market.

The increased design input that some manufacturers are capable of is a competitive advantage because it means they can do at least some of the work that the BGRs would otherwise do, and at lower cost. Seen from the perspective of order, this is likely to affect their identities, and one may predict that in these circumstances status becomes more important. This does not mean the market becomes a status market, however. Another possibility is an increased segmentation of producers due to their different design input. This form of differentiation, of course, is to some extent already the case. The large number of Asian students at, for example, British design schools is likely to facilitate this in the future.

Evaluations in both markets and non-markets ordered by status (as described in chapters 1 through 3) are characterized by spatial proximity— that is, the construction of values, the discrete identities, and ultimately the order of status markets emerge in close interaction between actors. The standard-oriented market described in the present chapter and in chapter 4, by contrast, extends over quite large distances, though buying offices mitigate physical distance, and to some extent socio-cultural distance (Aspers forthcoming).

The existence of standards facilitates interaction and the evaluation process in this market. Moreover, industrial standards usually contribute to transparency since firms may have to document their adherence to a standard, such as the ethical codes of conduct that are important in this industry. Nonetheless, once standards have been set, both sides relate to them. Standards are often easier to understand than the logic of order through the principle of status.

Summary

Garment manufacturers acquire their identities as sellers in this market. Only those that buyers accept as garment producers are market participants. In contrast to the consumer market, order in the production market relates to the contract, though, as we have seen, informal transactions are also possible. The commodity in this market functions as a standard consisting of a price–quality function. Manufacturers acquire their identities in relation to how well they meet the standard. Purchasers control the standards of this market, which I have shown can be analyzed according to the principles of Taylorism. This was indicated in chapter 4, but it is confirmed in this chapter by the analysis of the suppliers' side of the market.

Order in production markets for garments is a function of relatively stable standards: The standard in the market is more entrenched than the social structure of named actors' identities. Thus, order in "standard" markets is constructed in the opposite way from how it is constructed in status markets. In addition, one should consider the culture, which undoubtedly is an important aspect of the construction and maintenance of order. Order in this market, I have argued, is a reflection of the power relations of the two sides. This means, in practice, that the interests of the buyers become institutionalized.

This chapter has shown that the producer market for fashion garments is truly a global market, which means that firms in Bangladesh may compete with firms in Bulgaria for the same order. The fact that it is a standard market means that thousands of firms all over the world in principle compete with each other. I have argued that the global dimension makes it easier for large buyers in particular to make sure they get good deals; a finding that is reflected in other industries as well (for example, Whitford 2005). Manufacturers are less flexible and operate under the restrictions of the country, the region, and the industrial district in which they are located. They cannot move production or affect production costs; essentially they must accept that orders may go to other countries, take losses, develop their business in a new direction, or move their factories to other countries.

Manufacturers have common interests, but they are also in competition. Each manufacturer in principle has access to the same information as the designers in European countries. A designer working for a BGR, however, has the advantage that she knows the identity of her firm and what their take on the trends will be. Though manufacturers get some information from buyers, they do not get the whole picture, just piecemeal. Upgrading under these conditions is not easy (cf. Aspers forthcoming). In this chapter, we have established that different kinds of markets exist. In the last three chapters, I used the notions of status and standard to distinguish different kinds of markets. The three prerequisites are met in different ways, depending on the kind of market we are talking about. In this standard market, the service contract is "what is traded," and the culture is essentially determined by the more powerful buyers. Prices are set in competition. It is clear, however, that the buyers have the upper hand and benefit more than the sellers from the competitive logic of this global market.

Chapter 6 _

Branded Garment Retailers in the Investment Market

THE PURPOSE OF THIS CHAPTER is to analyze order in the market in which investors evaluate branded garment retailers. This involves a switch in perspectives: the BGRs are still at the center of the analysis, but I do not view them from the perspective of consumers or of their suppliers, but from that of their investors. Seen in terms of the final consumer market, investor markets are clearly "behind the scenes." Most consumers, unless they also own stocks, are probably little interested in relations between the BGRs and the investors who control them. Consequently, the average consumer does not know that the firm that owns Zara is Inditex or that Topshop, together with Topman, Miss Selfridge, and other branded stores, is part of the Arcadia group. To investors, however, not only the consumer market, but even more so the production market of fashion garments is not their focus. The analysis in this chapter focuses not on the fashion output of the BGRs, but on how BGRs try to manage their identities in the investor market and how this is seen by investors.

This examination of the financial side of the fashion business will make it clear that BGRs' identities in the final consumer market and in the financial market are related. In this way, we pursue further the book's general aim, which is to see how different partial orders, with a clear focus on markets, are embedded in each other. We will see, nonetheless, that the financial market has a special status in relation to markets in the real economy, as the arena in which other markets and their activities eventually must come together to be "compared" with each other. To accomplish this comparison, money is central. This is not a fundamentally new insight; financial markets are to be compared to yesterday's clearing houses (cf. Braudel [1975] 1992). The chapter will also go into detail about the stock market. This will make it possible to clarify the central market distinctions.

I have discussed some of the evaluations in which BGRs participate, and I will continue in this chapter, this time focusing on the financial side and the market for investors. As this is a huge topic, I will restrict the analysis to the stock market. Despite the switch of perspectives, the analytical approach is the same; the idea is still to look at how order is maintained in the different markets in which BGRs operate. This requires answers to a number of questions: What role do other evaluations of BGRs, some of which have been the focus of previous chapters, play in this market? In what way, if any, do BGRs control and communicate their identities in this market to attract potential and existing investors? Do they try to control it in the same way, and are the same things seen as valuable as in the consumer market? Can we analyze the stock market with the same tools as those we have used to study the producer and consumer markets in the garment industry?

The focus of my empirical research is not the financial side, and I make no big issue of the fact that the firms I analyze are listed on different stock exchanges. My main ambition in this chapter is to show the interconnectedness of the different markets, not to provide a detailed account of stock markets. This idea of embedded markets is not reflected in the sociological research on financial markets and producer markets, two fields that have not communicated sufficiently. Here my aim is merely to bring these fields a little closer to each other. This discussion, however, leads to the idea that there are different kinds of markets—thus, we need different models to understand them. The analysis relies on the written documents that the firms issue, such as annual reports and websites, as well as published interviews.

We begin by looking at the evaluations already analyzed to see how BGRs represent and discuss them, followed by a discussion of their role in stock markets. The focus on the stock market will enable me to draw a general distinction between kinds of markets. The chapter discusses the specific value in stock markets. Next, I study the aspects discussed by BGRs in their annual reports and elsewhere, such as the materials they direct towards potential employees. I start by analyzing the stock market. Then I will discuss how BGRs gain identities in investor markets. I will thus analyze the four evaluations in chapter 3, but this time from the perspective of investors. This means I will look at how the store, the advertisements that firms emit, editorial fashion, and ethical production are represented in the material BGRs issue for investors in this market. I will also say something about the other ways in which BGRs present themselves to investors.

Approaching Financial Markets

It is by generating profit, or at least by not losing capital, that a firm can sustain itself in a competitive economic environment. Firms need money to do business, which they may obtain from a bank, an owner, a group of owners, or a combination thereof. Each investor demands a dividend, either in cash or in the form of the increased value of the assets. The stock exchange is the most explicit representation of capitalism, and it is seen by many as the essence of the economy and financial markets. There is, in addition, a methodological advantage to focusing on the stock market because firms' market activities are highly regulated. One would ideally carry out a detailed analysis of the different aspects, or evaluations, that investors make. Stock exchange analyses, industry evaluations, articles in business journals, and their historical evolution (for example, Smith 1981; Clark, Thrift and Tickell 2005; Preda 2005) are an object of study in their own right.

Though there are other ways to finance the business, and though capital structure differs between countries and between firms, the stock exchange is the nexus of most forms of capital, and it is in many ways the benchmark for other markets. Family enterprises are still common, and issuing bonds is yet another way. Different kinds of investors also exist, such as industrialists, risk capitalists, institutional investors, and venture capitalists. All of them may own garment firms or finance them in other ways.

Focusing on the stock market will leave out many firms, but stock exchanges prefer listing large firms, which generate more income for the exchange and which are better monitored, over smaller ones. The stock exchange is also a dominant force in the economy and firms outside it are likely to adapt to its demands, trends, and logic. Strict rules govern the kind of information that listed firms must provide and the form it must take. The general rule is that all actors in the market, existing and potential shareholders, must have access to the same information. When sales figures are presented, to take one example, they are relayed in a more or less global information flow within seconds. The annual report, or a news flash mentioning it, is shown on market actors' screens simultaneously. This reflects the ambition of transparency in markets. There are also strict regulations for insiders (actors) who, due to their position in a firm and the information they have access to, have the opportunity to profit by taking a position "ahead" of the market. Formal openness suggests it is possible to analyze the stock market by drawing mainly on official documents.[1]

Retailers' Identities in Investor Markets

The aim of BGRs is to make money for their owners in the fashion business. The current board may have had no say in the choice of business. Switching industries—for instance, starting a bank or selling tanks—is thus not a realistic option. This means that the reflexive identity of BGRs, which may be best represented by the will of the board, the CEO, and other directors of the firm (who do not have to agree), is seldom concerned with this issue; they take the collective identity that the company shares with its competitors more or less for granted. An investor, by contrast, can move his capital in a moment from one collective identity to another without having to bother about changing his own identity.

The financial markets evaluate firms according to their expected profit, but in order to be evaluated firms must be recognized by the evaluators (Zuckerman 1999). Profit is what matters to both BGRs and their investors, though some operate in the short term and others on a long-term investment basis. In this sense, all BGRs listed on stock exchanges compete for the money of investors.

Investors who own a firm can at least in theory set the goals of the firm, though the principal–agent problem is a well-known managerial dilemma (Miller 1992). The statements of BGRs make clear that they aim for shareholder value. One British retailer says: "Our primary aim is to generate steady growth in earnings for our shareholders and while we work on our broad range of expansion opportunities, our success is rooted in producing cool, fashionable, well-made products. Our business is fashion." A Swedish retailer puts it slightly different, but with the same goal: "[Our] aim is to grow with sustained profitability and thereby create shareholder value. Our ambition is to provide investors and other interested parties with adequate information for the assessment of [the firm]. We consider it important to maintain an open and continuous dialogue with the financial market." Seen from the perspective of the investors, a fashion company is similar to other companies, which also have the goal of increasing value for their shareholders. The aim of one steel company, for example, is stated as follows: "The group always endeavors to create value for its shareholders." The question is how to do it. How can the firm make itself attractive to investors? The stock exchange, as I will show, is an arena in which a BGR acquires an identity as an "investment object" in relation to other firms.

The Stock Market and Its Value

Stock markets, like those in Frankfurt, Shanghai, New York, London, or Stockholm, are market places in which different stocks are traded. The general definition of markets provided in a previous chapter—"a social structure for the exchange of rights, which enables people, firms, and products to be evaluated and priced"—also covers stock markets and their products. But stock markets constitute a particular kind of market, to be distinguished from, say, the producer market in focus in chapter 5.

The stock market was originally a physical place, and the first modern stock exchange is said to have existed in Amsterdam (Braudel [1975] 1992; Weber [1894] 1999). Today, some stock markets do not have physical locations. They are better described as a set of connected computers, and one cannot separate the evolution of such markets from "technological" developments (cf. MacKenzie 2006). Moreover, the stock exchange is often seen as the market *par excellence* (Smith 1989: 169). The main reason for this is its centrality for the neoclassical economic market model.

Neoclassical theory is a broadly correct description of the price formation of individual stocks (cf. White in Swedberg 1990; Kirzner 1973). Both Marshall and Walras studied the price mechanisms of markets. Their theories are good accounts of how a stock—for example, Siemens—acquires its price in the stock market (Aspers 2007). Walras used the Paris Bourse as a model for his theory (Kregel 1998; van Daal and Jolink 1993). Weber's definition of the market, I argue, is also mapped on the stock exchange, which he studied in detail (Weber [1894] 1999, [1896] 1999). Weber ([1894] 1999: 139–40). It stresses depersonalized exchange that is oriented to the items traded, but does not see a significant difference between the stock exchange and other forms of markets.

The neoclassical model is used as a blueprint for the creation of markets. A further conclusion is that the neoclassical model is a model of the prices of standardized traded items.[2] However, the link between theory and real markets is much more complex than the discussion of performativity suggests. Marshall made the point that "stock exchanges . . . are the pattern on which markets have been and are being formed for dealing with many kinds of produce which can be easily and exactly described, are portable and in general demand" (Marshall [1920a] 1961: 328). It was only later, in a second stage, that markets were made on the basis of existing market theories.

What are the typical features of a stock market? Price and evaluation are central components of stock exchanges. The stock market is characterized by standardized products, which does not necessarily mean it is a standard market. To know whether this is the case, one must look at the social structure, and more specifically find out which of the two components of the market—social structure and standard—is the most entrenched social construction. I see the price mechanism in these markets as a form of evaluation in a social structure made up of actors who switch roles. This means that brokers do not permanently play roles as buyers or sellers, and the identity of an actor in such a market is not connected to one of the two sides of the market; they share the general role of broker (trader). Traders can, from a theoretical point of view, be replaced by stockowners or investors. The fact that actors can switch roles between buyer and seller several times a day, and that there is a

TABLE 6.1.
A typology of markets. Kinds of markets, given fixed and switch roles and standard and status.

Typology of Markets	Fixed roles	Switch roles
Standard	Garment production markets	Stock exchange
Status	Consumer market for garments	(The bazaar)

more general role and collective identity, should be seen in contrast to the markets analyzed so far, in which actors are identified with the role of either buyer or seller. Also, firms may sell and buy their own stocks in the market, which means that a firm can operate as both buyer and seller.

Given this distinction between switch-role and fixed-role markets, and the previously introduced distinction between status and standard markets, we can summarize the different types of market in a two-by-two table (table 6.1). This distinction is of general value, because it does not apply only to the field of garments.

In this book, we have discussed three of the four types of markets presented in table 6.1. Actors in both producer and consumer markets have stable roles as either buyers or sellers. We saw that the consumer market for fashion garments is ordered according to the principle of status, whereas the production market is a standard market. The stock exchange is also a standard market, a notion that covers the more narrow economic idea of homogenous products (cf. Aspers 2007), but it is also presented as a market in which actors switch roles. We will discuss this in more detail later. The fourth possibility is not represented in this industry, but has been identified by Geertz.[3] So, we may then ask what the value of the stock market is that makes it an example of a standard market?

Capitalism and Value in Stock Markets

I have argued that all markets have a value. What is the value that prevails in contemporary stock markets and, one could add, investment markets? The answer to this question provides the key to understanding order in this standard market. Obviously, people may endow stock exchange trading with different meanings, but it is clear from the literature (for example, Abolafia 1996: 30; Norberg 2001; Hasselström 2003) that financial growth is the central value for brokers, as well as for their clients. Though there are different kinds of investors, such as industrialists, risk capitalists, institutional investors, and venture capitalists (Freeman 2005), all of whom are more or less risk-averse (De Bondt 2005), they all share a commitment to the value of the market. To excel in this market, to become successful, is to make as much money as possible. Actors use the fundamental value of capitalism to evaluate each other's performance in this market. It is in relation to how well they perform against the value of the role of being a trader that actors' discrete identities are evaluated (cf. Geertz 1963: 33). That is, the different roles in the market—buyer and seller—are less important for the actors, though they are crucial for playing the market game that distributes identities in the market. What, then, is the "value" of capitalism?

Capitalism is defined as the "accumulation of wealth." This definition implies profit making. But as Weber ([1921–22] 1978: 164–66) noted, there are many kinds of capitalism, such as political, authoritarian, predatory, and rational, each with its own forms of profit opportunities (cf. Swedberg 1998). Weber defines a (rational) capitalistic action "as one which rests on the expectation of profit by utilization of opportunities for exchange, that is on (formally) peaceful chances of profit" ([1904–5] 1968: 17; cf. [1921–22] 1978: 637). The activities on contemporary stock markets fit this definition because they are "peaceful," due to formal and informal regulation. The stock exchange is in some sense the quintessence of capitalism, where money is the end of all ends (Simmel [1907] 1978), the value around which the market is structured. It is, put another way, the market in which what is valued in other markets are valued in terms of the value of the stock exchange market: money.

Discussion of the stock market leads to two questions, though they represent two sides of the same coin: (i) Why does each stock not constitute its own market? and (2) Why do not all markets simply merge into one? The first point might be valid if the price mechanism operated on the level of individual stocks, and if the culture and social structure were also specific of each stock. Is the price mechanism used to generate prices of a single commodity enough to constitute a market? If there were only one stock traded in a stock exchange, the answer would be "yes." Then, the price mechanism of that stock and the market would be identical. Nevertheless, the value underlying trading in the stocks of BMW or H&M is the same, namely to obtain money. Traders (investors) do not stick to one stock, however, but trade with many different stocks more or less simultaneously, depending on which are "cheap" and which are "dear." This means that actors (investors) do not identify one another with "the market" for a single stock; investors are identified with the stock market, with its culture, underlying value, and members. This suggests that the different stocks are traded within the same market. This makes it more like a bazaar, with many different stocks traded in one market "place," with a partial culture rather than the fixed-role markets we have seen in the final consumer market for fashion clothes.

The price mechanism constitutes the market in the view of economists, but sociological and anthropological market approaches often
include much more, such as preconditions of trade and social connections between market actors (cf. Beckert 2009). Though not everyone
shares Geertz's approach to markets, the following indicates the breadth
of his approach. It refers to a particular market place in Modjokuto,
Indonesia:

> Thus by the *pasar* [the market] we mean not simply that particular square
> eighth of a mile or so of sheds and platforms, set apart in the center of the
> town, where (as someone has said of the classical emporium) men are per-
> mitted each day to deceive another, but the whole pattern of small-scale ped-
> dling and processing activity characteristic of the Modjukuto area generally.
> The market place is the climax of this pattern, its focus and center, but it is
> not the whole of it; for the *pasar* style of trading permeates the whole region,
> thinning out somewhat in the most rural of villages. (1963: 30)

Does not Geertz's comment indirectly suggest that all stock markets all
over the world are simply one? One could make this claim as all market
actors orient themselves to the same value, and one can at least partly
trade the same stock in several different stock exchanges. The reason why
this is not the case, given the discussion of markets in this book, is that a
stock market is not only centered on the "accumulation of wealth," but is
also "kept together" by its culture through means of regulations (which
are still chiefly national), norms and sanctions, recognition of members
and the social structure, local knowledge, the organization that operates
the stock exchange, as well as stories about it. Furthermore, the information in the country where a company's head office is located, which is
often the country in which the stock's prices are effectively set (though a
company may be listed on several stock exchanges) is usually better than
the information available in other countries. This is because more analysts and journalists report on the country concerned, and also because
more people have access to information that may leak. One can thus talk
of different exchanges because they do not have the same market culture,
including different formal and informal institutions and narratives (cf.
Mützel 2007). The market cultures, though similar, represent the second
prerequisite of market order.

Consequently, place still matters (Sassen 2005) and the available stocks
also differ; these differences are pegged on the fact that they have different names (such as the London stock exchange or the New York stock exchange). However, the approach to order that I propose cannot of course
fall back on realism when it comes to space. This means that spaces acquire meaning—or, in other words, become spaces—in relation to markets, as well as the other way around. Thus concrete market places—an

important theme in the anthropological literature—such as the flower market in Carpentras become what they are because of the market (Pradelle [1996] 2006). In short, though the social structure of buyers and sellers (traders), and the central value ("capitalism"), are the same in all stock exchanges, the culture (including institutions) is not. It thus follows that there is not one market, but many, though they may function in similar ways.

A stock market, then, is made up of those who share a collective identity as traders in one "place"—for example, the London stock exchange. Different stock markets are still national, though they are gradually becoming internationalized. Before looking explicitly at the BGRs, it is necessary to analyze the situation in the market, to understand its order. The situation for branded garment retailers on the stock exchange is the same as for most other firms on this market.

Trading Fashion Stocks

I have talked about values in stock markets, and I will now discuss trading of stocks in more detail to show the social structure of traders but also how BGRs' identities are presented in the stock market. This also means taking a step further and analyzing the market place in which the stocks are traded. Most BGRs and other firms are not big buyers and sellers of their own stocks, though this may also happen. The stock exchange is in many ways impersonal, and though interaction sometimes takes place face-to-face, it is normally a face-screen-face setup that represents "market interactions" (cf. Knorr Cetina and Bruegger 2002). The depersonalized business trade means it is enough to say "yes" or "no" to the offers on the screen. It does not matter who the sellers and buyers are once an agent has decided to trade a stock; one stock is identical to any other (Marshall [1920a] 1961: 326). This must be distinguished from the fact that it is often of great interest to know who—for example, an insider or a major shareholder—is selling and who is buying. Table 6.2 shows the number of buyers and sellers and what prices they are willing to trade at, while table 6.3 shows transactions.[4]

These figures illustrate how the market may appear from the perspective of a single actor, such as a broker. All market actors can observe the number of stocks that are "on the market" and the prices are shown in real time. Furthermore, all members of a stock exchange have access to virtually the same information, and a member may relay this information to his or her clients, so that they too can operate in real time. Thus, this "double auction" in which both sellers and buyers are making offers, to sell or buy, is made visible.

TABLE 6.2.
Orders for a single stock on the Stockholm Stock Exchange, H&M (Series B), August 9, 2007. The bars—depicting the number of stocks that sellers ask and bid for at a given price—illustrate the Marshallian graph, where an "indefinite" number of buyers and sellers "meet." Frequency refers to the number of stocks offered, and not the number of buyers or sellers.

Buyer				Seller	
Amount	Bid			Ask	Amount
4,075	389.00			389.50	11,900
5,250	388.50			390.00	15,375
10,175	388.00			390.50	25,075
7,579	387.50			391.00	15,100
12,150	387.00			391.50	10,725

Trading takes place on the basis of the price mechanism, in which price competition of course is crucial. The automatic mechanism, which may partly be driven by computer programs, means you can buy and sell stocks, but you do not influence these deals directly. Once an actor dispatches an order, it becomes one among many, and the prices sellers are asking and those that buyers are bidding, as well as the size of the order, will determine the trading partner or partners. Consequently, the system cannot handle preferences for signing contracts with specific actors. The technological system has been constructed to make the market operate in accordance with the theory (cf. MacKenzie and Millo 2003). This system manifests how the third prerequisite of market order is met, namely the generation of prices.

Evaluation of Stocks

I have very briefly described the stock market. I will now look more closely at how people evaluate stocks. This market is one in which firms are evaluated by potential and existing investors. Obviously, both sellers and buyers evaluate the stocks in question. In between, there may be many layers of, for example, analysts, who of course may pose demands and thereby shape firms according to their theories and modes of valuation (Zuckerman 2000). Furthermore, the principles of evaluation are by no means stable over time. Organizational analysts have shown that there are many stakeholders, such as credit rating institutes, both inside and outside firms, that affect how firms should be valued and of

TABLE 6.3.
Stock contracts (H&M), August 9, 2007. The figure also shows the price (in SEK / Swedish krona), the number of stocks traded, and at what time each contract was "signed." In this case, two firms, Credit Suisse and the now defunct Lehman Brothers, operated as both buyer and seller, as well as carrying out "internal trades." As can be seen, several contracts between different brokers were made at the same time, which of course would be impossible for a real auctioneer.

Buyer	Seller	Amount	Price (SEK)	Time
Lehman Brothers Intl.	Lehman Brothers Intl.	450	389.00	15:17
Credit Suisse Securities Europe Ltd	Bankaktiebolaget Avanza	100	389.00	15:17
Credit Suisse Securities Europe Ltd	Credit Suisse Securities Europe Ltd	3,275	389.00	15:17
Kaupthing Bank Sverige AB	Credit Suisse Securities Europe Ltd	3,000	389.00	15:17
NeoNet Securities AB	Credit Suisse Securities Europe Ltd	1,700	389.00	15:17
Bankaktiebolaget Avanza	Credit Suisse Securities Europe Ltd	1,000	389.00	15:17
Kaupthing Bank Sverige AB	Bankaktiebolaget Avanza	300	388.50	15:16

course how businesses are organized (for example, Power 2005; Zorn et al. 2005).

Here, I focus on stocks, and ask "Upon what value is a stock based?" Evaluation of stocks is forward-looking—that is, the orientation of the buyer and sellers is towards the development of the stock. There are, in principle, two kinds of analyses, the fundamental and the technical.[5] Fundamental analysis concerns the prospects of the firm, its markets, the industry, and the economy at large. This analysis is based on reported facts concerning the economy and the firm's accounts (which firms summarize in their reports), market trends, the written reports that are issued by firms, as well as what is produced in the media by analysts and others. Obviously, these "facts," such as credit ratings, are based on values that depend on other values and others' evaluations (cf. Keynes [1936] 1973). These evaluations are like a web; they refer to each other, but with no fixed points of reference. Technical analysis is all about analyzing the movements of stocks, and essentially disregards fundamental information. This is, then, a form of meta-analysis.[6] In reality, a number of different methods are available (Smith 1989: 11–66), which actors can combine.

Investors care mostly about future profit opportunities, and this is the form in which the evaluation in this market is cast, in general.[7] Profit is revenue over expenses in a particular accounting period. Firms have costs because of what they "are" (aim to be), which means they differ depending on the position they occupy in the final consumer market (Podolny 2005). Obviously, one can never conclude from the identity of a firm whether it is profitable or not. To know more about this, one must take into account not only the situation of the firm, but also the collective level of the market (cf. White 2002).

The notion of profit has two meanings. The first is simply what is represented in balance sheets, representing the results of the past financial year. Though this is interesting, there is another aspect of profit that is forward-looking. Economic investors hope to make a profit, in the sense that they will make more from their investment in the future than what they know they can secure by other means. This is one driving force behind investing money, and it is here that not only actors' different knowledge (Hayek 1945), but also their different sentiments matter, as Pareto made clear (Aspers 2001). Finally, hope is a key aspect that must be considered in the process of how actors bet on the markets and on individual stocks.

Economic Evaluation

In order to look more deeply into the investor market, I shall now study the materials that BGRs issue as information and how they present themselves to existing and potential investors, so that the latter can judge how profitable their investments may be. The idea is to capture how, for example, the markets and non-markets in which BGRs operate—described in chapters 1–5—are reflected in these materials. This is a way of studying how firms use identity management, by concealing or highlighting information (cf. Simmel 1964: 334). I also try to capture those dimensions that investors see as important. I did not take the further step of asking investors about their views and how they interpret this information.

I analyze four branded garment retailers, two British and two Swedish. The analysis concentrates on official documents, websites, and different kinds of reports (the annual report being the most important).[8] Given that legal systems and traditions in Sweden and the UK are different, one should not restrict the analysis to annual reports. Company sites are examples of other sources of information that I have included. One may then pose a more concrete question: How do BGRs try to manage their identities to affect how investors perceive them?

If it were possible to translate all information about fashion, strategies, and markets into numerical terms, there would be no need for extensive text in the annual reports, nor would we need pictures. However, the numbers are at the back, and the text and the pictures are at the front of the annual reports. This indicates that firms think it is important to communicate visually to investors. It should be noted, however, that what is most interesting is the profit, and the less extensive quarterly reports focus much more on the numbers in combination with predicted future development than the annual reports, which also present other kinds of information.

Presentation to Investors

The different evaluations discussed earlier affect the identities of the BGRs in the eyes of consumers, but they also matter to investors. However, the question is to what extent these identities are reflected in the information material directed towards investors. The information firms issue is limited. Though many of the figures in an annual report refer to the past, much space is also devoted to informing investors about plans for the future. One firm looked back on a year of falling profits, but the statement by the chair did not discuss the reason for these problems. The strategy instead was to look ahead: "We feel confident that we will use this experience to return to our growth track and build a stronger business for the future." The unique economic identity of a BGR, as seen by an investor, is essentially a function of its future economic value. This is an economic calculation, which translates other values into an economic value.

How are the stores of the BGRs presented in the material they issue? BGRs tend to mention the number of stores they have, and perhaps if they have opened, or plan to open, or close, stores in the coming year. Location strategies are also something that they discuss. The "store portfolio" of a firm refers to the range a firm represents. It may include different "concept stores" that offer its customers more specialized products (for example, underwear). Pictures from stores, however, are not frequent. Firms, moreover, may refer to its stores as sites of a "high degree of innovation."

Advertising is the second activity I studied. Advertising is often explicitly discussed, but usually under the more general heading of marketing, which is a more business-oriented concept. Some BGRs stress the usefulness of traditional marketing, such as advertisements in magazines and on billboards. Marketing has many functions and one is, as a BGR writes, "to maintain our brand profile." Several firms include examples of the advertisements they have run, and all documents include fashion pictures.

There is also talk of a "marketing strategy," but this is neither a central nor a well-developed issue in annual reports.

I found no traces whatsoever of editorial fashion in the annual reports. One possible explanation is that the BGRs cannot control their appearance in editorials, as discussed in chapter 3. One may say of course that the inclusion and exclusion of BGRs' clothes in the different fashion magazines, which are status distributors, matters for the BGRs' market identities; hence, information on this should also be included in their reports. I did not investigate whether this is discussed (which would indicate it is part of the reflexive identity at which they aim) within the BGRs, however. What I can conclude is that investors do not receive information on these activities, although it would be a means by which they and others could judge how fashion journalists perceive the different BGRs. One can thus see this as a way in which BGRs try to control their identities in relation to investors by restricting, or more generally controlling, the information they give out.

Ethical production is probably the only one of the activities analyzed here that attracts readers who are not investors to the annual reports. Journalists as well as ethical and environmental activists, organized and non-organized, read the reports to check how the firms are doing according to ethical standards, which one can see in the press that reports on firms, as well as in different reports on ethical trade put together by NGOs. The following is the policy of one firm made explicit in the annual report: "The business aims to comply with all locally applicable health and safety regulations in the countries in which we operate." I interpret the way ethics is presented in the official documents primarily as a way of providing information and trying to control identity in relation to investors. Thus, a strong ethical commitment may, or may not, be a profitable component of identity building in the final consumer market.

A firm that does not sell fashion, but which is "just" ethical, is not taking part in the same market as those selling fashion. If the firm is a fashion-oriented BGR, it shares, by definition, the underlying value of the market. This means it can be included in the same collective identity as other BGRs. Investors and firms that have significantly different interests—that is, value different things—will not be part of this market (cf. the discussion of differentiation and cohesion of markets in chapter 1). This, of course, does not hinder the making over time of a new and separate market that is centered on ethical values but also offers advanced fashion. It may, however, also be a good strategy to attract investors to turn to ethical production.

It is my finding that ethics is not a central dimension in annual reports, though many firms issue this information on their websites. The Swedish firms in this limited sample did discuss this matter in their annual reports, while the British firms did not. The general finding, however, is that this issue is discussed in reports and documents that are somewhat separated from both investors and final consumers. BGRs seem to direct this kind of information to certain stakeholders in the debate.

Moreover, it is possible to connect firms' economic activities to their non-economic activities (which they may be more or less in control of). A firm that is named and shamed—for example, because one of its manufacturers employs child labor—is not merely shamed. Shame comes with an economic cost, and negative publicity may, for example, lead some customers to boycott the firm and its products. In this way, non-economic activities, in which the BGRs do not directly take part, affect their identities and profit.

The material that BGRs issue also covers other aspects. What this part of the study shows is that many things that the BGRs do and inform investors about are of no particular interest to final consumers, such as cold and short springs that leave BGRs with unsold stocks of garments that must be put on sale, with lower revenues and hence decreased profit as a result. This will mean a lot to an investor, however. To consumers it does not matter if a BGR has a huge stock of unsold garments in its warehouses. To reduce the money tied up in production, firms try not to hold stocks of garments. This is due not only to lean production, but also to the fact that clothes are "perishable," and their value may decrease substantially when fashion changes. It is common to include a review of the supply chain and its management. Exchange rates and currency options are other issues, and, before their abolition, quotas were also discussed. In addition, firms comment on sales figures and sometimes employment policy.

BGRs provide less information on how different activities affect their position in the market. They tend to discuss the general market position of firms and the different markets in which they operate (which often correspond to countries). In addition, trends in markets as well as market shares are often mentioned, and prospects of the growth or decline of the different markets are discussed. The costs, such as production costs, that firms face are also covered. A firm's credit rating is another issue that is occasionally mentioned. Even disregarding the large amount of information included in the accounting section of the reports, a substantial amount of information is presented numerically. Finally, from an economic perspective, it matters little what relations a BGR has with its manufacturers as long as they are profitable; manufacturers are therefore not a priority in the information directed towards investors.

The information that firms issue in annual reports and other kinds of material are vital to investors and analysts. Information about how the firm is doing, regardless of whether the firm is doing well, is of interest to investors when they come to decide whether they should sell or increase the number of shares they hold in a certain company. Investors do not value garments as pieces of art, as a fashion editor or art historian may do. Garments are instead seen as purely economic items made to generate profit, if such items are considered at all. I have argued that it is possible to connect different evaluations that are obviously interdependent through these "renditions"—that is, interpretations through a mediator, instead of through direct communication. I have shown that the logic of the valuations governing the U.S. stock exchange, and the firms listed on this exchange, have repercussions also for firms in other countries (Davies and Marquis 2005). At a more general level, this is a sign of how the value of the financial markets has gradually penetrated not only other markets, but also non-economic partial orders. A final observation is that most investors are men, and most of the fashion produced is for women, which suggests a further socio-cultural distance between interconnected and interdependent markets.

Summary

In this chapter, I have analyzed the market in which the BGRs face investors. More specifically I have analyzed the logic of the stock market and showed how this market is connected through renditions to the other markets and non-markets I have studied. The underlying value in the financial market in which stocks are traded is wealth accumulation, to which profit is central, but mergers and acquisitions are additional ways of accumulating wealth. Not only investors, but also BGRs value profit, or as one BGR states: "Our aim is to generate steady growth in earnings for our shareholders." This value, to recall, is not the same as what is valued in the final consumer market as expressed by the same BGR: "Our aim is to retail and wholesale high-fashion quality products at affordable prices." One can assume that wealth accumulation is a goal shared by all firms listed on a stock exchange, but in the case of BGRs this accumulation takes place in fashion markets. The stable value of wealth accumulation (cf. Simmel [1907] 1978) is the ordering principle of this market. This is to say that firms—for example, BGRs—gain identities as a function of how profitable they are, or are deemed likely to become. The value of this market is assumed; in other words, it is an entrenched social construction. This market is thus an example of a standard market, and this is how the first of the three market-order prerequisites is met. Each stock exchange has a partial and unique culture, though stock exchanges grow more similar. This is how the second prerequisite is met. Finally, the price mechanism means that prices are set, meaning the third prerequisite is also met.

I have shown how firms' activities directed towards making a profit are presented to investors. A substantial part of the chapter was devoted to an analysis of the stock exchange. In this sense, it is only indirectly an analysis of BGRs. I have indicated that a more detailed study could identify different kinds of investors. The stock exchange has been researched by sociologists (for example, Abolafia 1996; Smith 1981; MacKenzie 2006), but more must be done before we know how it operates, and especially how it is interdependent with other evaluations and the social structure that is connected with these economic and non-economic evaluations. In particular, we need more research of the kind that would help us understand how key actors think and how they assess situations, and thereby how markets are interconnected.

I have shown that the stock exchange is not like the final consumer market or the production market for garments, but a market of a different species, as Harrison White (1992) says. In contrast to the fixed-role markets discussed in previous chapters, which are characterized by the fact that identities are tied to one side of the market, switch-role markets are characterized by the fact that actors' identities are not so tied. Instead, actors may share more general roles, like "investor" or "trader." This is an important, but neglected distinction within economic sociology. The neoclassical model is, in the language of this book, a standard and switch-role market. I have shown that many markets are status markets, but also that in many markets actors do not switch roles. A grasp of these two distinctions improves how we conceptualize markets.

The chapter has also addressed another important issue already discussed in this book, namely that markets are interconnected. I have discussed how production and consumption markets are interconnected and embedded in each other, which is to say that decisions made in one take into account what goes on in the other, and may have consequences for the other market. These markets are reflected in the financial markets, though in that case they are "reduced" to numbers. Financial markets are the apex of different activities that come together and are measured in monetary terms. Though Simmel neglected the role of the market in his study of money, he made an important observation: "[O]ne of the major tendencies of life – the reduction of quality to quantity – achieves its highest and uniquely perfect representation in money" ([1907] 1978: 280). The literature clearly shows that the importance of financial markets has increased over the last thirty years (Zorn et al. 2005: 272), and one can also say that economic logic has acquired more influence in public debate as actions increasingly are justified according to economically rational principles (cf. Boltanski and Thèvenot [1991] 2006). This puts information and knowledge at the fore.

It is, however, not obvious that actors at one end of interconnected markets know what is going on at the other. It is this phenomenological perception of, for example, other markets, seen from the vantage point of one market, that constitutes the reality to which actors orient themselves. The vantage point is primed by the value of the evaluation. From the perspective of investors, BGRs are seen as economic identities resulting from a large number of activities. I will address this issue in the final chapter of the book.

Chapter 7

Markets as Partial Orders

THIS FINAL CHAPTER HAS TWO PURPOSES. The first is to discuss the findings of the book and thereby put the study in the context of, and in relation to, the existing literature. The second is to discuss the idea of order and most of all partial orders. This means, more concretely, asking in what way markets and non-markets are embedded in each other. This chapter discusses more generally how partial orders are interrelated. I begin by summarizing the findings of the study, and then I turn to the question of partial orders.

Discussion of the Study

The central question of this book is order, which is contrasted with ideal-typical chaos. Social life, however, is not in chaos. I have focused on order in the global fashion industry, or to be precise, certain parts of it: the markets and non-economic evaluations in terms of which BGRs operate. These partial but interconnected orders are of course socially constructed. I have, however, left out many more basic social constructions, which are taken for granted in this industry as well as in other parts of social life.

The empirical analysis started with a set of competing markets, one of which is the market for "affordable fashion." Within this market, each BGR acquires a discrete identity, which we can identify analytically as due to differentiation on the basis of BGRs' shared collective identity. It is in the consumer market that BGRs are evaluated and paid for what they do, and hence acquire their unique identities. I showed that BGRs' identities result from undertakings that are evaluated, and the BGRs have control of these only to some extent. I then turned to the market in which the BGRs operate as buyers of garments, or, as I argued, of the service of producing the clothes they then sell to the consumers. This market was also discussed from the manufacturers' perspective. Finally, I analyzed BGRs in relation to their investors.

The first contribution of the book is the discussion of order. I argued that in sociology the question of order has essentially assumed realism or has reduced the question to an epistemic issue. My idea is to use a social constructivist perspective, in which order is understood in relation to the special role of man. People have this peculiar characteristic of, on the one hand, being part of the same world as other identities—for example, things and events—and on the other, the ability to reflect on their being in the world (Heidegger [1927] 2001), which I catch using the notion of "reflexive identity." The idea of a socially constructed world made up of meanings is central to the question of order. The partial orders we have discussed are social constructions, and I have argued that though a given order tends to last, all social constructions are susceptible to change— indeed, social constructions are stable only in relation to other social constructions. This means that a social construction may be entrenched in relation to, and serve as the basis for, another construction that is less entrenched. This we may call the ontic structure (following Heidegger), which makes up the socially constructed order. The explicit discussion of entrenchment is a way of speaking of social constructions without falling into the trap of seeing social constructions as merely a matter of "text" or "discourse" that can easily be changed. Although I hope that the reader will see that, by addressing the question of order from a social constructivist perspective, this book makes a contribution to the question of order, it should also be said that it does not address the question of ontological order, which is the question of Heidegger ([1927] 2001). Thus, this question remains to be researched.

The second contribution is to the sociology of fashion. I have studied the largest segment of the fashion industry and argue that fashion should be tied to a discussion of the economy. Moreover, the social structural approach to fashion has provided us with an enhanced perspective: only when the social structure of identities is relatively more entrenched than the object, and when a change of garment styles takes place, can one talk of fashion. I hope that the theoretical contribution concerning fashion, change, and innovation presented here will prove useful far beyond fashion in clothes.

The third field to which the book contributes is economic sociology. My strategy was to look at markets. I analyzed the conditions of markets, and stressed the role of order. In presenting this perspective, I drew analytic distinctions and took markets apart. Other approaches to markets, such as ANT and cultural approaches, have been criticized for lacking theoretical clarity when it comes to understanding markets, their preconditions, and different incarnations. I shall now turn to a more detailed discussion of markets, drawing on the findings of the book.

I have discussed the three prerequisites of market order. When these are met, one can talk of order in the market. The first prerequisite has to do with what the market is "about." I have shown how the market for "affordable fashion" is different from, say, the market for airplanes, but more importantly how it also differs from the haute couture and mail-order markets, though these markets too are concerned with fashion. One can talk of the differentiation of markets, so that "things" that in one sense are similar are traded in one and the "same" market. They can be ordered according to either status or standard.

The second prerequisite refers to the culture of the market—that is, the "rules of engagement"—defined in terms of informal and formal institutions. The concrete problem that is solved concerns "how to operate in the market." I argued that much of this is met in a similar way in different markets (such as when the same law is used in markets across a nation, Fligstein 2001: 19), so that one can talk of a general market culture. Thus, markets are rooted in the lifeworld, and in this way each market rests on a bed of assumed meanings often expressed in terms of "culture." These are taken for granted both inside and outside markets. Today, one may even talk of a well-established market culture that is part of the lifeworld. I also showed how a specific market is often characterized by its own unique cultural elements.

The third prerequisite, finally, has to do with how much something is worth, or in other words, the problem of how to evaluate and price what is traded in the market. I argued that prices emerge in different ways depending on the kind of market: status or standard, switch-role or fixed-role.

The literature has identified three ways of bringing activities and things together so order is created: market, hierarchy, and network (Thompson et al. 1991). I have dealt with all these forms of coordination, but with the focus on the market. The garment industry was an important part of the Industrial Revolution, and production was for a long time concentrated in organized firms (hierarchies) that traded with each other in markets. Much later, subcontracting in the industry and specialization of firms meant that the production chain of garments was extended and divided. Since the 1970s, this has gradually become globalized. In the garment industry, however, one can observe that coordination between suppliers and especially European BGRs takes the form of networks.

Of these three forms of coordination in the economy, the market stands out as the most central. It is only in relation to the market that the other two basic forms of economic coordination—hierarchies (firms) and networks—can be evaluated. Thus, the competition in markets makes it possible to relate what is done within a firm (hierarchy) (cf. Coase [1937] 1988; Williamson 1981), as well as in the network (cf. Burt 1992), to the alternative of the market, an issue that Brian Uzzi (1997) has studied. This is possible because what is offered in a market is signaled by the market price. The market is also the benchmark for evaluating the network relationship for both the leading firm and its suppliers, based on calculable offers and costs. Because this benchmarking is conditioned on the calculability of prices, it applies predominantly to standard markets. Calculation in status markets is a more complicated issue since more aspects must be processed simultaneously, such as price, status, and "quality" (cf. Uzzi 1997). This short discussion of these three basic forms of economic coordination suggests that the market has a special role. It suggests, furthermore, that many problems of organizations and networks can be addressed only in relation to their embeddedness in markets.

This study has shown not only the interdependence of markets, but also how markets and non-markets are embedded in each other. Though the idea that markets are embedded in each other is mentioned by White (2002), no prior study has tried empirically to investigate this matter in depth. I have shown how order in one market, or non-economic evaluation such as editorial fashion, affects and depends on other markets but also non-markets. The finding that markets are embedded in other markets suggests that the traditional notion of industry should be understood as a set of interconnected markets and non-markets, centered around one core market. In this industry, it is the final consumer market for fashion garments. For example, the construction of order in the final consumer market penetrates the producer market much more than the other way around. This stresses how the different activities and evaluations in an industry are interconnected, but also that there is no overarching plan, control position, or even viewpoint; there is a set of interrelated partial orders, each of which is constituted in relation to other partial orders. In each evaluation process that is stable over time, such as the markets studied in this book, at least some form of rudimentary order emerges. I have shown that the principle of order in the consumer market is status, while in the producer market the service contract for garments is more entrenched than the order of actors on the two sides of the market, which means that one can talk of a standard.

This study has consistently used identity as its core concept, alongside order. Identity has been my entry point, and at four levels. I started with the collective identity shared by all BGRs, which sets them apart from, for example, independent designers, but also, of course, from garment manufacturers and other identities. If we look at the consumer market, each BGR acquires a unique identity in relation to other BGRs. Their unique identities, however, are the result of consumers' perceptions of several different evaluations, each of which constitutes a discrete identity. The fourth and final level is the reflexive identity, which constitutes the "existential" level—in other words, what the BGRs want to be perceived as in the market. Among the four types of identities discussed in the book that acquire their meaning in relation to each other, only the reflexive identity has the capacity to pose the question: "Who am I?" Though I have studied the reflexive identity of both organizations and persons, it

Manufacturers and
investors

BGRs' unique identities in the
fashion consumer market

BGRs (examples of four
discrete identities)

Final consumers

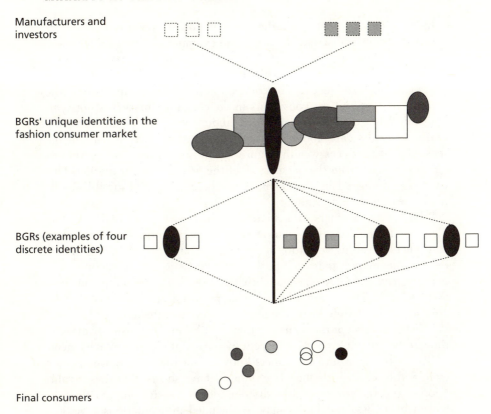

Figure 7.1. Formation of the unique identity of one BGR from its discrete identities in the eyes of the final consumers (schematic figure). It is their role as consumers that constitutes their viewpoint, which makes up the unique identity of BGRs from a number of discrete identities. Here, only the four schematically represented discrete identities—in this case, fashion stores, advertising, editorial fashion, and ethical production of garments—are included in the formation of the unique identity of a BGR (represented by the thick line). The dotted actors, representing manufacturers and investors, do not become part of the formation of the BGRs' unique identities in the final consumer market for "affordable fashion" as seen by the consumers.

is clear that the organization is reflexive only in a "derivative" sense, drawing on the reflexive capacity of its members. The question "Who am I?" correlates with "Who do I want to be?" To analyze action from an identity perspective is to identify the possible discrepancy between "who I am" and "who I want to be." Even actors who are what they want to be wish to maintain it. This is to say that identity management applies to all actors.

In my analysis, I stressed the construction of the more research-oriented notion of discrete identity. As an example, one may look at how the investor market is connected with the consumer market, through "renditions," in the form of mediated information that flows from the firm or through the media. The connection between the investors in the investor market and the consumers in the consumer market is not symmetrical: While consumers rarely care about the investor market for the BGRs, investors care about the final consumer market, at least in the sense that it produces wealth. Figure 7.1 illustrates the construction of identity as seen from the perspective of the final consumer market. This issue was discussed in chapter 3, but is here illustrated graphically to make it easier to understand.

What final consumers value matters in the formation of BGRs' unique identities in the consumer market. The unique identities are central to consumers' meaning structure in the final consumer market. It is, moreover, in this market that each of the different BGRs—that is, companies that are *seen* as BGRs—has a niche corresponding to its unique identity (White 2002). The research, so to speak, performs an analysis of the discrete identities that make up the phenomenology of the unique identities.

BGRs must accept the identities they acquire in the consumer market, though they may try to control them by means of identity management. BGRs try to make sure consumers know about the positive things they emit, and to conceal the negative things. I have shown that these evaluations—and the corresponding discrete identities—are only partly controlled by BGRs, and BGRs may be included in evaluations that they have no interest in taking part in, or which they cannot control. Another dimension of identity management is control of information to the consumers and investors about what firms are doing. This is particularly important when evaluations are not public or transparent. The media can play an important role and relay information concerning different evaluations and activities so that, for example, consumers find out about firms that are not treating their workers well. However, as this relay process is never neutral, I prefer to speak of renditions. However, at the end of day, it is the consumers who say "yes" or "no" to what the BGRs are doing.

The phenomenological approach to identity taken here also makes it possible to analyze material objects, such as clothes and events and fashion fairs. It is nonetheless important to recall that these non-human identities acquire meaning only as a result of their "interaction" with persons. It is in direct or indirect contact with them—for example, physical contact or observation—that people attach meaning to them.

In addition to its empirical contributions to the discussion of order, markets, and fashion, the book makes a number of concrete points. The trend towards consumption, design, marketing, and branding started long ago, but it is only recently that sociologists of fashion and culture have begun to research it, realizing the potential this field offers for enhancing our understanding of society. Production has long been the central issue in economic sociology. One ambition of this book is to bridge the two literatures, especially by showing how consumption affects producer markets more than the other way around. Thus, the unique identities that BGRs acquire in the final consumer market cannot be separated from the production of fashion, just as this market too produces fashion; there is no "mirror" that "reflects" only fashion or any other phenomena. The branded garment retailers I have focused on are not trend leaders, nor is their status as high as that of haute couture fashion firms or the increasingly important ready-to-wear firms. BGRs must therefore consider what happens in other markets, in which garment firms with more status operate. It is nonetheless accurate to view the BGRs as co-producers of fashion. They represent the largest market for garments in the Western world, and some of them operate in several markets. The logistical advantages—including, for example, the shortening of lead-times—enjoyed by the large BGRs are just one thing that puts them ahead in the struggle to define fashion.

Partial Orders in the Economy

Order is the central question of this study, and it is now time to expand the discussion of connected evaluations to partial orders, which is the unit of analysis. This will lead us to a discussion of markets and interconnected markets. Our object is partial, not local orders because the latter notion is not appropriate, for example, for describing the global, but still partial order of the production market for fashion garments. Markets are examples of partial orders, and I have argued that the components that are central for the understanding of markets—identities, values, social structure, and culture—are co-constructed.

A central condition of the existence of partial order is that people perceive and act in such a way as to furnish evidence of such an order; in other words, it is characterized by some sort of predictability. Thus, actors in a partial order share not only a commitment to the value governing the market—for example, "affordable fashion"—and the market culture, they also perceive and act in similar ways. This means that perception and practice reinforce each other and social constructions become entrenched and part of the meaning structure (Berger and Luckmann [1966] 1991). The existence of order is conditional on people orienting themselves to the same social construction and having similar expectations (cf. Luhmann [1984] 1995). In other words, actors' expectations of other actors and the "environment" are largely realized.

Addressing the issue of partial orders is one way of contributing to the discussion of so-called "clearly demarcated units of study" (Emirbayer 1997: 303), instead of referring to "society." Both the idea of "fields," as Bourdieu calls his units, and "social molecules," which is the Whitean notion, point to smaller units of analysis. Though the discussion of social units that simultaneously address several components is inspired mainly by Bourdieu and White, Simmel ([1922] 1955) was probably the first social scientist to address simultaneously the issue of social structure and values at the level of actors.[1]

There have been other attempts to identify smaller units of analysis. Zelizer has suggested that we should study the economy using what she calls "circuits of commerce," which refer to "interchange, intercourse, and mutual shaping" of ties between actors who are linked together and shape each other in networks (2005: 293). I think her approach, which is clearly aimed at bridging the cultural and structural approaches in economic sociology (Zelizer 2005: 292–93), is a move in the right direction, but the idea needs to be made more concrete.

I have tried to study partial—though also interdependent—orders, mainly in the realm of "the economy." Of course, many have taken this approach before, and I shall briefly discuss some of them before returning to the idea I am proposing, partial orders. Here I shall concentrate on some alternatives to make my point clear. I begin by discussing Luhmann's (1982: 191–225, [1984] 1995: xli) systems theory approach to the economy. His approach does not address many of the core issues in economic sociology, such as how markets operate and how consumers make decisions. However, it is Luhmann's ambition to see how the different—and increasingly differentiated—social parts hang together, without being parts of a clearly identifiable "whole." The economic whole is for Luhmann an autopoetic (self-reproducing, as well as closed) system that communicates by means of money. His idea, if we "develop" it and talk of "subsystems," means that actors in, say, one market, cannot really comprehend what goes on in other markets. I have shown how actors in one market—for example, the consumer market—take on what happens in other partial orders, of which some are markets. It is cognitively impossible to take in "everything" and, as Hayek (1945) and others have argued, actors act on the basis of their cognitively limited knowledge.

Weber (1946: 323–31, 333–57) divides society into spheres, each of which displays a certain amount of "autonomy" (*Eigengesetzlichkeit*). Each sphere has a logic, a meaning, and an end (or value—cf. Zetterberg 1997: 94). This idea of the modern society, however, does not account for variation on a smaller scale—for example, variation within the economy.

In addition to these approaches there are discussions of, for example, knowledge society (Bell 1973), postmodern society (Kumar 1995), consumer society (Slater 1997), risk society (Beck 1999), and network society (Castells 1996). These labels are misleading because different kinds of societies, such as "peasant society" and "industrial society," can exist in parallel. Other kinds of economies exist, such as the aesthetic economy (Entwistle 2002; cf. Negus 2002), the cultural economy (du Gay and Pryke 2002), the knowledge economy (Powell and Snellman 2004), and the technological economy (Barry and Slater 2005). These notions refer to broad tendencies and often to the "substance" of the economy. Some approaches do not focus on the substance of the economy, but on its institutions, and these argue that the institutional setup, sometimes at the level of nations, explains the differences we observe. The "varieties of capitalism" literature, ultimately drawing on Weber (Swedberg 1998), operates with countries, or national regimes, as units with different institutional settings. The varieties of capitalism tradition focus on "variation among national political economies" (Hall and Soskice 2001: 4; Hall and Gingerich 2004; Deeg and Jackson 2007). This approach assumes that markets within a nation are more similar than, for example, markets in the same industry that encompass many nations. However, observation of stock markets, many financial markets, and the global market for production of fashion garment indicates that markets, in contrast to nations, may very well be the most relevant unit of analysis.[2] The varieties of capitalism approach, and the other attempts to capture the economy within the framework of a single notion, are in need of smaller, clearly demarcated units that can handle the observable variation in the economy.

I argue that the more sweeping notions, which we often use out of habit, such as "the economy" or "capitalism," may largely be replaced by more phenomenologically real, and scientifically more fruitful, social units: partial orders, often in the form of markets. My point reflects what anthropologists have argued, namely that one should see the economy as "multicentric" and made up of "different transactional spheres," which means there is no "one piece—homogenous sector or sphere" (Dalton and Bohannan [1962] 1971: 164), that can be called "the economy." I take the anthropological idea further, and make my observations, not as they do from the perspective of tribal and peasant economies, but from within contemporary Western society. I elaborate on this in the next section, arguing that the economy—and the same kind of question that, in particular, the varieties of capitalism that literature addresses, namely observed differences of various kinds (profit, labor contracts, and so on)—can, and should, be analyzed and understood at the level of markets rather than nations. The production market for garments is a good example of a market not bound by nations.

Markets and Other Partial Orders

I will now look more closely at markets as differentiated units within the economy. I have argued that identities emerge out of evaluations within the framework of market and non-market processes. This book focuses its analysis on identities, but they are co-constructed by means of value, culture, and social structure. One strategy I have used is to analyze (or take apart) markets and their components. A related strategy is to study these parts in relation to each other (a relational analysis). It is not possible to analyze each component—value, structure, identity, or culture—in itself; each must always be related to other social phenomena. The approach I suggest is to view social phenomena as gradually evolving in a reinforcing process of entrenchment of the meanings of their participants; in other words, the entrenchment of social constructions is social reality.

Which of these components that makes markets different is the most entrenched, and in this sense is the one that brings about order more than the others? It is important to note that though all components bring about order, one is usually the most entrenched. I have shown that in some markets (so-called status markets) the social structure—that is, the rank orders of identities (firms and consumers)—are more entrenched social constructions than the prevailing value. In standard markets, by contrast, the value (the "good") is the most entrenched. These two ideal-types, status and standard, are mutually exclusive, and there is a "tipping point" so that one of them is always the most entrenched social construction. This means that order is entrenched in different forms of social constructions, but it is not given a priori, which would be the most entrenched form. Culture (cf. Geertz 1963, 1973) is important in all markets, and I have argued that partial orders, such as markets, that have the same form of social structure can have different cultures. In other words, culture, including what we call a market, may be what separates markets from each other. However, the culture of a specific market is often made up of the general "market culture," which is shared by all markets and today has become common knowledge and an integral part of most peoples' lifeworld. Markets, generally, can be seen as partial orders that are included in the economy. This book has shown that markets need not only a cultural foundation, including institutions, but also other markets to be ordered. Not only do markets order each other, but non-economic partial orders are also essential for creating order. They may be ordered by markets. The analysis of order in the fashion industry or in any other industry cannot be restricted to a study of what happens in what is called the economy.

Appendix I -------------------------------

Empirical Material and Methods

THE APPROACH I EMPLOY in this study draws on previous works (Aspers 2004, 2006a), and may be termed "empirical phenomenological." The idea is to connect theoretical constructions, second order constructs, with the meanings of actors in the field under study, first order constructs. Second order constructions are built on first order constructions. A scientific explanation is obtained if the evidence based on first order constructs supports the theory that is expressed as second order constructs. This is not Grounded theory, because the role of theory is central from the start. The explanation presented by the researcher must generate understanding, but to do this it has to relate to the understanding of the actors in their field. The key notion is, thus, meaning. It is people who are involved in activities and who think about things, who "hold" meanings, and the empirical phenomenologist starts with the "subjective" side of the actors, which is to study how individuals constitute meaning. Social constructions are entrenched meanings—that is, the result of actors who through interaction have created a social world, with various degrees of entrenchment, and these meanings are supra-individual or, as it were, supra-actorial.

Though I have mentioned the focus of the study in the main text, I have not presented how I have worked. This is the main purpose of this Appendix. I begin by discussing the empirical methods and the materials, and then I discuss the analysis of the materials and the principles for presenting evidence.

The Work Process

This project was launched on the basis of an ethnographic approach and based on a traditional design. I draw on the large existing body of research that deals with consumption and on the less extensive literature of sociology of finance, to cover the financial markets. I have to a limited extent used the marketing literature, to the extent that it is oriented to practical marketing. Its research is often done using a kind of naïve behaviorist approach, drawing on experiments with a limited connection to real-life situations; there are many studies based on students' responses that look at a very narrowly defined question. This means it is difficult to generalize and understand what is actually going on in the field.

The Empirical Material

Due to the scope of the garment industry, it is not possible to generate empirical material that is both "thick" and still covers all the different types of actors. There is, however, a large literature on this field, including textbooks for students, that are useful for getting an overview and practical insights into the different dimensions of this industry (for example, Brannon 2005; Dickerson and Jarnow 2003; Frings 2004). A substantial body of research is available on the apparel industry, especially on U.S. firms. In addition, a large number of organizations, both international, such as the International Apparel Federation (IAF), and national, are both export- and import-oriented. These, as well as the individual firms, have good Internet sites, which I have also used as a source. In addition, I have gathered written materials from the garment industry field, as well as business magazines and Internet sites covering various organizations, firms, and marketplaces. I have studied this material closely in order to understand the industry.

The empirical material underlying the results of this study is also based on several hundred pictures I have taken, public relations material from garment sellers, annual reports, my own observations in the field, twenty-seven interviews, and participant observation conducted from 2002 to 2006. The database Lexis Nexis has also been used, especially for identification of background material. I have also used some interview material from an earlier study (Aspers 2006a). I have left a substantial amount of the empirical material I gathered out of the book. It merely provides the background for interpretation of the concrete empirical material in the text. I did fieldwork for two months in India (two trips) and for one month in Turkey (two trips), and much more time was spent in Sweden and in the UK, which are the two countries on which I have based my analysis of the consumer market. The UK is of course a larger and more advanced consumer country and most of the systematic observations have been made there.

The empirical work in Sweden and the UK, and to some extent in Germany, was carried out in order to understand the buying side of garment chains, as well as the consumer markets. I chose India and Turkey because many garment producers are located in these two countries, of which Turkey is the most developed. Moreover, the study of several countries provides a better understanding of the industry. Thus, the "sampling" is primarily oriented to firms, not to countries. The theoretical question of order and markets does not call for analyses of countries (an assumption confirmed by my research).

My own fieldwork into the production side of the industry was carried out at factories and buying offices, as well as stores, shopping malls, industry recruitment fairs, wholesale districts, and garment fairs. I have spent a substantial amount of time observing and photographing garment stores. The pictures reproduced in this book give the reader some idea of the field, but their main benefit is as empirical material for analyzing differences in the visual presentation and locations of stores.

I have interviewed people on the buying side (that is, purchasers at retailers, importers, and others), as well as CEOs (who often were also the owners of the firms) of garment manufacturers. My questions focused on the industry, and their experiences as incumbents of roles (for example, buyers). Most of the interviews I organized as informal talks (cf. Aspers 2004: 10). The average interview lasted for about an hour. Most of those I talked to had more senior positions and long experience (usually more than five years) in this industry. I used a turn-taking strategy. That is, I asked one side, buyers, a number of questions and then let the manufacturers address questions that were partly raised in my conversations with buyers. The theoretical framework gave focus to the empirical work, which means I made sure I covered the research issues in interviews and observations.

I employed several strategies for selecting interviewees and study locations. I mostly talked to representatives of buyers who work in production countries and representatives of manufacturers. Most of the people working for garment producers in Turkey and India with whom I talked are oriented towards Europe, but a few of them also have customers in North America. Some respondents were network-sampled. This means I traced the chain from a retailer, through a buying office, to its manufacturers. I also chose producers because they were small, large, or because they engage in certain activities, such as garment fairs, and in some cases because they were suppliers to a BGR that I was studying. This strategy allows actors to define who is taking part in the market and who is not, thereby safeguarding actors' perspectives (Aspers 2004).

I occasionally used the following strategy to find firms in India. I asked my rickshaw driver to knock on factory doors to see if we were outside a garment factory or not. This was also useful because the front men seldom spoke English. Neither he nor I could have known merely from outside observation whether a particular factory was producing garments or not. In the factories I visited, only the heads and merchandisers could speak English, and they did not always talk English with each other. This made it less meaningful to spend a long time in the factories. I did not talk, for example, to suppliers of fabrics or to subcontractors—meaning, those located upstream of the garment manufacturers (cf. Jacobson and Smith 2001) in figure I.1.

The Analysis

The ethnographic empirical material is composed of several levels. The most basic is the researcher's knowledge founded on participation in the lifeworld. The empirical field is at some levels also part of the lifeworld of the researcher. There is a danger in viewing one's own everyday experiences as evidence. These experiences, however, are an indispensable foundation, a starting point, as well as the last resource of analysis available to researchers if they want to generate explanations based upon understanding (Gadamer [1960] 1990). Added to this is theoretical knowledge, and finally the empirical material of the field studied. The "evidence" is then not just the answers obtained in a series of interviews, but the evidence validated by researchers' general knowledge grounded in their lifeworld, theory, and the field of research.

In my case, I have tried to get an overview of the field by conducting fieldwork and reading magazines; I let the first couple of interviews be broad in scope, and relatively shallow in depth. Gradually, and in light of a general knowledge of the field, I was able to deepen the questions during my fieldwork. The analysis also developed the theoretical questions. The empirical material was generated in a theory-guided process. However, the theory has also changed in light of the progress made by the fieldwork.

Theoretical codes were initially generated building on the much modified Whitean framework, but codes (and corresponding theoretical notions) were also generated by the empirical work (cf. Aspers 2004, 2006a). Throughout the study I used the N-Vivo computer program. I also employed this program to organize and help analyze the large quantity of material. Only in the coding process of my analysis did problems with the existing approach emerge in detail, especially in regards to how it handled issues of value in markets. Thus, coding and detailed analysis were not only for the purpose of controlling evidence. They were also used to generate theoretical ideas.

Presentation

The different forms of material I have used are reflected in the evidence included in the book. The value of the evidence is essentially to be determined by the depth and scope of the empirical research presented in this Appendix, naturally in combination with how it is presented in the text. I have decided to include pictures, quotations from interviews, and field notes, as well as documents. A substantial form of evidence is built into the text in narrative form. This essentially means I make claims without necessarily using quotations or other direct references to the empirical material. The descriptive sections, as well as direct quotations, are part of the evidence for the theoretical arguments; they also give a flavor of the field. I have tried to present the material by including people's voices, my observations, and excerpts from texts. In most cases, it is possible to see what kind of evidence I am drawing on, but in other cases I have left this out and instead have focused on the big picture to, among other reasons, make the text easier to read.

Appendix II

Garment Trade Statistics

THE TABLE AII.1 SHOWS the fifteen leading exporters and importers in 2007 (USD billion) and their market share (World Trade Organization, Table II.69). Trade statistics show an increased market share for China as a producer country from 1980 until 2007, but the rate of change has remained the same over the last five years (a period in which China has increased its share). Some countries have appeared as exporters over the last twenty years, such as Vietnam. Also within Europe (Romania, which is not included in Table AII.1) and the vicinity of Europe (Turkey), it is possible to observe dramatic increases in exports. These increased exports must be seen in light of the diminished production of garments within developed countries, such as in Northern Europe, and the corresponding need for imports. Also, many countries in Western Europe are major garment exporters, though this is often re-export, which is to say that the clothes may at most be labeled in Europe before they are shipped. The total volume of the garment trade has also increased over time.

TABLE AII.1.
Leading exporters and importers of clothing, 2007

Billion U.S. Dollars (and percentage) (World Trade Organization)	Value 2007	Share in world exports/imports				Annual percentage change			
		1980	1990	2000	2007	2000–07	2005	2006	2007
Exporters									
China[a]	11.0	4.0	8.9	18.2	33.4	18	20	29	21
European Union (27)	103.4	—	—	28.4	29.9	9	3	7	13
extra-EU (27) exports	24.8	—	—	6.5	7.2	10	5	10	19
Hong Kong, China	28.8	12.3	14.2	12.2	8.3	2	9	4	1
Domestic exports	5.0	11.5	8.6	5.0	1.4	-9	-11	-7	-26
re-exports	23.8	0.8	5.7	7.2	6.9	8	18	8	10
Turkey[b]	14.0	0.3	3.1	3.3	4.1	12	6	2	16
Bangladesh[b]	10.1	0.0	0.6	2.6	2.9	10	19	28	4
India	9.7	1.7	2.3	3.0	2.8	7	26	10	2
Vietnam[b]	7.2	...	...	0.9	2.1	22	10	19	29
Indonesia	5.9	0.2	1.5	2.4	1.7	3	16	16	2
Mexico[a]	5.1	0.0	0.5	4.4	1.5	-7	-2	-13	-19
United States	4.3	3.1	2.4	4.4	1.2	-9	-1	-2	-12
Thailand	4.1	0.7	2.6	1.9	1.2	1	3	4	-4
Pakistan	3.8	0.3	0.9	1.1	1.1	9	19	8	-3
Morocco[a]	3.6	0.3	0.7	1.2	1.0	6	-6	14	11
Tunisia	3.6	0.8	1.0	1.1	1.0	7	-5	-3	18
Sri Lanka[b]	3.3	0.3	0.6	1.4	1.0	2	4	6	8
Above 15	298.1	—	—	79.2	86.3	—	—	—	—

Importers

European Union (27)	162.8	—	—	39.7	45.5	10	5	10	13
extra-EU (27) imports	84.2	—	—	19.2	23.5	11	9	13	13
United States	84.9	16.4	24.0	32.1	23.7	3	6	4	2
Japan	24.0	3.6	7.8	9.4	6.7	3	4	6	1
Hong Kong, China	19.1	1.6	6.2	7.6	5.4	3	8	2	2
retained imports	...	...	...	...	...	...	...	...	...
Russian Federation [b,c]	14.5	—	—	1.3	4.1	27	23	2	79
Canada [c]	7.6	1.7	2.1	1.8	2.1	11	14	14	12
Switzerland	5.2	3.4	3.1	1.5	1.4	7	2	5	11
United Arab Emirates [b]	5.0	0.6	0.5	0.4	1.4	29	7	72	64
Korea, Republic of	4.3	0.0	0.1	0.6	1.2	19	6	29	15
Australia [c]	3.7	0.8	0.6	0.9	1.0	10	17	5	13
Mexico [a,c]	2.5	0.3	0.5	1.7	0.7	-5	-2	0	-2
Singapore	2.4	0.3	0.8	0.9	0.7	4	-5	17	-3
retained imports	0.9	0.2	0.3	0.3	0.2	7	7	12	16
Norway	2.3	1.7	1.1	0.6	0.6	9	11	7	16
China [a]	2.0	0.1	0.0	0.6	0.6	7	6	7	15
Saudi Arabia	1.9	1.6	0.7	0.4	0.5	13	25	13	18
Above 15 [d]	323.1	—	—	91.8	90.3	—	—	—	—

[a] Includes significant shipments through processing zones
[b] Includes Secretariat estimates
[c] Imports are valued f.o.b. (free on board)
[d] Excludes retained imports of Hong Kong, China

Appendix III ─

The Garment Industry

IN ORDER TO PROVIDE the reader with more details about this industry, its history, and development, I shall discuss three important issues. It is of course possible to say much more on each of these points, but together they give further insight into the industry, as well as its relations to markets.

Production and Consumption Have Become Separated over Time

At the dawn of history, clothes were produced locally, but over time, when people met due to war, barter, and trade, this diffused ideas, materials, and techniques. The garment industry was also one of the first to be industrialized in the eighteenth century (Farnie and Jeremy 2004), and it has been global ever since.

The separation of production and consumption is a condition of the making of this market. In 1790, 80 percent of all clothes worn in the United States were made in the home, whereas by 1890, 90 percent were made outside the home (Swedberg 2003: 149). Another development came when fabric was cut in one place, but put together into garments by workers in their own houses (Weil et al. 1995: 181), commissioned by an entrepreneur. The next analytical step was when manufacturers concentrated production, including labor, first in workshops and later in factories. Weber ([1923] 1981: 162–77) says that the emergence of the textile industry in Britain was the first time labor was gathered in one place with equipment owned by one individual, for what we call a workshop (see also Weber [1904–1905] 1968: 66–68). In a workshop, several people worked together, though the tasks were specialized. Eventually, a mass market came about (Howe 2003: 156). These steps represent a gradual separation of production from consumption. The spread of mass markets, which made it easier to calculate production, was due to the more or less standardized taste patterns in Europe, reflecting the standard of living. This increased the demand for identical or almost identical clothes, which made it easier to organize production according to rational capitalist methods. Later, the separation took on global proportions,

with production in developing countries and consumption in developed
countries (and of course in developing countries, too). Though the routes
have been slightly different for individual European nations, it is clear
that the change is essentially cost-driven. The industry is labor-intensive
and so far, in contrast to the textile industry that experienced rational-
ization in the 1960s (Lindner 2002), it has not been rationalized, in the
sense of replacing labor with machines. The separation has been acceler-
ated, however, because of the deregulation of international trade—for example, by the World Trade Agreement on Textiles and Clothing of 1995
(Taplin and Winterton 2004), and of course the more recent abolition of
trade tariffs on imports into Europe in this sector since January 2005.
Other minor changes have occurred, all of which have led to more liber-
alization of international trade. States have played a major role by supporting and facilitating production in many developing countries (Taplin
and Winterton 2004: 256).

Today, few European retailers have their factories close to their market
(see the thematic issue of *Journal of Fashion Marketing and Management*, 8 (3), 2004 for articles discussing the industry in different European countries). I asked several representatives of BGRs whether they
had considered having their own factories. The answer of one BGR representative is clear: "I think it's going in the opposite direction." She argued
that the "retail business will be getting tougher and tougher." She also
made the point that price will be more important. Some BGRs still have
their own "assembly lines"—in other words, the capacity to put things
together. This enables firms to make minor changes late in the production
process, and thus adapt quickly to changing fashions in consumer markets. Other firms (like those in the UK) have invested money in factories
abroad. Having these "factories," especially under a quota system, also
provides flexibility, so the firm can put the label "Made in Italy" on the
garment, even though only a small portion of the production work actually takes place at the final production step.

Some production still exists in the West, both of expensive (cf. Gereffi 1999; cf. Arpan, De La Torre, and Toyne 1981) and less expensive
clothing. This production often relies on advanced technology (Weil et al.
1995: 177), and it is design-driven (Taplin and Winterton 2004: 259–60).
The kind of production that predominates is either related to national
needs (for example, military uniforms), special products (new materials
or newly invented products), or high fashion. In addition, immigrants
from certain countries have started up garment production in both Europe (Morokvasic 1993) and the United States (Bonacich and Applebaum
2000). This is a form of production that competes on the basis of speed
and relatively low cost.

Garment Production Is Hard Labor

Based on my own field trips, the accounts of other eyewitnesses, and literature on fashion, it is clear that working conditions are hard for many in this industry. Historically, this has always been the case, and Marx's descriptions of working conditions in garment production are still fairly accurate even today (Cawthorne 1995: 47). The production of many garments is still labor-intensive (cf. Bonacich and Applebaum 2000). Moreover, the principles of so-called "scientific management" are very much alive (cf. Braverman 1974).

Of course, the working conditions facing most workers in developing countries are hard, regardless of the industry. As a result, there has been a vibrant discussion of so-called "sweatshops" (Bonacich and Applebaum 2000; Cawthorne 1995: 54). There are also indications that the garment industry in particular has a large "reserve army" of labor to be employed, partly in factories (cf. Cawthorne 1995: 49) and partly in more home-based production (Knorringa 1995), reminiscent of the early phases of work organization (Weber [1923] 1981). Several studies of working conditions are available, as well as their affects on the labor force and their families (for example, Dobbs 1927).

Working conditions in the garment industry have been discussed intensively (cf. Hale and Wills 2005). The worst cases do not exist in the production chains of larger BGRs, however. Regardless of how sincere they are in wishing to improve the living conditions of these workers, BGRs have a number of reasons to make sure their suppliers maintain at least minimum working standards. They do not wish to be "named and shamed," for example, as this is likely to mean fewer consumers in their stores. Moreover, better working conditions are likely to attract workers who are more skilled.

The following excerpt from a magazine interview indicates how important it can be for manufacturers to implement the demands made on them by global buyers. "Mr. X's [name of the factory owner] spacious, well-ventilated and well-lit factories are designed to appeal to multinationals concerned about protecting their image from criticisms that they are exploiting workers in poor countries." Nonetheless, the effects of these demands and their implementation by manufacturers may have real and beneficial consequences for the workers.

There is thus no doubt that working conditions in the garment industry in emerging economies are harder than working conditions in Western countries, wages are low, and social benefits are of course much worse. The workers in this industry do not make much money—some reports indicate as little as 20 U.S. dollars a month. However, though the money they earn is not much compared to workers in any kind of factory in a Western country, it is still more than that earned by many others in the same country. Thus, from the standpoint of the large group of impoverished persons in India, a job in the garment industry may be preferable to trying to make a living as a farmer. One should see these working conditions in light of the transition from an agrarian society to an industrial society as described by Marx and others. The garment industry has also been targeted in the public debate because its production process is sometimes hazardous to the environment, as well as to the workers. The production of fabrics, not least the dying, is often a major cause of concern.

Markets Can Be Engines of Development

The problems and the sheer toil that characterize work in the garment industry are plain to see. Still, one cannot deny that some upgrading has taken place (Tokatli, and Eldener 2004; Tokatli, Wrigley, and Kizilgün 2008) and that workers have benefited, in contrast to people in other developing countries who have not been affected by the globalization of the garment industry (cf. Amsden 2001).

It is interesting in this context to examine the literature on the leading role played by the textile and apparel industries in industrialization throughout history in most countries—for instance in Sweden and Japan (for example, Heckscher 1948: 22; Kemp [1983] 1986: 35). Furthermore, modern industrialization began in Great Britain, spearheaded by the textile and apparel industries (Farnie and Jeremy 2004). In the early phases, low-paid workers are almost a necessity if a country is to develop into an industrial society. Naturally, other conditions must exist, such as basic transportation and a reasonably stable political and legal situation. Thus, history teaches us clear lessons concerning industrial development, and it is therefore easy to see that essentially the same process can be observed today in many developing countries.

The relocation of the textile and apparel industries from Northern Europe and the USA to southern Europe, and then to Asia and Latin America is correlated with industrialization. Once a country has gone through the phase of industrialization—which seems to be a regular part of development—a "deindustrialization" phase follows, in which services, design, and high technology become more important. It is therefore not inaccurate to talk of a (much simplified) technological–economic cycle: farming, industrialization, high technology, and services (all of which also exist simultaneously). This process is occurring in India, for example, and the conditions in an industry must be understood in relation to these larger societal changes. The process can be understood only in a global light. In Southeast Asia, for example, some segments of textile and apparel production are being relocated to less developed countries, where it is possible to produce at even lower costs. One way of grasping this multifaceted situation, in which apparel production is declining in the Western world, is to see it as a "natural" stage of development, as described by Bell (1973). This, however, is a simplification that leaves open as many questions as it answers. It does not explain, for example, why some garments are still designed, produced, and sold in the developed world.

The prediction among social scientists seems to be that the apparel industry in developed countries will employ even fewer people in the future. This is part of the larger picture, in which low-skill jobs are diminishing in the developed world across industries because of their less competitive wages (Hirst and Thompson 1999: 109). However, one can observe an increased usage of high technology in the industry, such as CAD (computer-aided design) and CAM (computer-aided manufacturing) (Weil et al. 1995). Having said this, it is still clear that technology is not the driving force in this industry. Rather, the logic of the market, with trade based on property rights embedded in trust and long-term relations, is a better candidate for explaining the relative success of manufacturers in some developing countries (cf. Collins 1990). To explain why some countries—for example, those in Africa—have done worse than Asian countries would require examination of the cultural and political dimensions. To pursue this analysis is beyond the scope of this study, however. It is clear that neither technology nor labor costs can explain the superior development of Asian countries in comparison with African countries.

Appendix IV _

Economic Sociology

THERE IS NO DOUBT THAT the new economic sociology has helped revitalize sociology as a whole, paving the way for sociological analyses of the economy (for example, Swedberg 1990, 1997, 2004a; Granovetter and Swedberg 1992; Smelser and Swedberg 2005; Beckert and Zafirovski 2005). This general tendency is a marvelous development. Here, however, I would like to raise five critical points—or shortcomings—within this field. My study tries to deal with them.

The reasonable reaction among leading U.S. sociologists to Parsons's value-based analysis—as a result of which social structure became a key element in the new economic sociology—had the unfortunate consequence that values were to a large extent excluded from sociological analyses.[1] Economic sociology by definition excludes the question of value (cf. Fevre 2003; Fligstein 2001), and this value deficit is the first problem with economic sociology. As Swedberg (2003: 220) notes, the value paradigm has been criticized in sociology, among others by Swidler and DiMaggio. But values were of central importance in classical economic sociology—such as in Weber ([1904] 1949; Swedberg 2003: 26–227), though he never defined values.

New economic sociologists share the idea of the economy as a social construction (Swedberg 1997: 165). However, examination of how this idea is used makes it clear that much of, say, U.S. network research is bound up with a naturalistic idea of associated units, and is underpinned by a naïve "ontological" realism. The nodes of the network are defined objectively—that is, from the researcher's perspective—as a consequence of which the social construction of actors is downplayed or even omitted. Network sociology is in practice often objectivistic, and at its worst the network is depicted as "traces in the snow": One can observe that people have walked there, but one does not know for what reasons. It is not the idea of networks that I find problematic—quite the contrary, since it plays a central role in the present study—but rather the reasoning of many network theorists, and their epistemological and "ontological" assumptions with regard to networks, in contrast to their phenomenologies (see Krippner 2001: 791–98, for a critical discussion of U.S. network theory). The naturalist assumption is the second problem with the new economic sociology.

U.S.-driven economic sociology has partly been formed contrary to the dominant theory of the economy: neoclassical economics. In many cases, economic sociology provides an "add on" to the insights, findings, or theories of economists. Mark Granovetter's important manifesto of economic sociology, "Economic Action and Social Structure: The Problem of Embeddedness" (1985), addresses the issue of actors' degrees of embeddedness in the contemporary economy. As a result, some have seen the text as supporting the idea that sociology merely supplements the existing economic explanation. For example, my reading of the contributions in the theme issue (2005) on economic sociology of the *Journal of Economic Perspectives* is that economic sociology is neither seen nor proposed as a true alternative to economic analysis, in the eyes of economists. In order to develop alternatives, I argue that we must move beyond what some see as "the highly protected market of American sociology" (Bourdieu 2005: 2, 232n2; cf. Krippner 2001). Krippner, as I read her, is critical of the sociologically naïve approach taken by some first-generation economic sociologists. For example, she refers critically to Fred Block who tends to see markets as "pure," but embedded in wider social networks (Krippner 2001: 784–85). I believe she is correct to assert that we must not be caught in the spell of economics if we want to further economic sociology.

It is, in my view, unlikely that economic sociology will provide a more systematic alternative to neoclassical economics if it continues tacitly to "adore" economics, often taking essentially non-sociological foundations as the starting point of analysis and argumentation.[2] This means that questions of identity, status, and money must be approached from a general sociological platform, and this calls for a rethink. The fact that the theoretical and empirical points made by economic sociology have predominantly been tailored to economics is the third problem.

We should view neoclassical economics in relation to the modernization processes that took place in Europe where the theories were developed. It is clear that there is a Western bias in many economic theories.[3] The same can also be said about economic sociology, old as well as new (cf. Swedberg 1997). A consequence of this is the relative lack of studies that seriously address the processes of globalization, though of course some attempts have been made to address this issue (for example, Fligstein 2001; Knorr-Cetina and Bruegger 2002; Biggart and Guillen 1999; Stark 1996).

There is a substantial body of sociological literature dealing with globalization and the global economy (for example, Kellner 2002; Sklair 2002; Kim and Shin 2002; Van der Land et al. 2000; Hirst and Thompson 1999; Bauman 1998), but these studies are not closely connected with contemporary economic sociology. Moreover, studies also exist on the globalization of culture, food consumption, tourism (Uddhammar 2006), financial markets (for example, Knorr-Cetina and Bruegger 2002), producer markets (for example, Bair and Gereffi 2001; Gereffi 1999), and other topics.

The so-called global commodity (or value) chain approach (GCC) (for example, Hopkins and Wallerstein 1994; Gereffi 1994, 1999; Gereffi, Humphrey, and Sturgeon 2005) addresses the economic link between producers in developing countries and consumers in developed countries. This literature, though it has gradually acknowledged the role of non-material dimensions and markets (Gereffi, Humphrey, and Sturgeon 2005), rests on a materialistic perception of the world, due to its Marxist heritage. This is why, in my opinion, it does not pay enough attention to the commodity as a social construction. I draw on three important insights from the GCC literature. The first is the global dimension of interconnected markets. The second is that consumer activities reverberate upstream in the chains that lead to the garment producers. Finally, the cultural, economic, and social contexts in which production and consumption take place are important. This issue is discussed also by Fligstein (2001: 94–97, 191–222). Both advocates of the GCC approach and Fligstein speak about global markets and control, but Fligstein puts more emphasis on the state and less on firms.

Moreover, Fligstein (2001: 191) seems to conclude that there is scant evidence of a global economy. This should come as no surprise, as his conditions for the existence of global markets are hard to meet. A market is global, according to Fligstein, only "if there are a small number of participants who know one another and operate across countries with a common conception of control" (Fligstein 1996: 663). This means Fligstein simply takes White's idea of the market as a definition of all markets. White himself would probably not agree with Fligstein, and I argue in this book that there are different kinds of markets. I also show that the standard market for production of garments is global, which is at odds with Fligstein's definition.

Phenomena such as "glocal" production (adaptation of products to local conditions by producers who sell globally) indicate that some markets are neither local nor global. Advertising campaigns are often examples of *glocalization* (cf. Slater and Tonkiss 2001: 190). It is obvious that today we live in a more global world than our predecessors. This does not mean that the arguments presented here give a complete picture, or even an accurate one. A great many authors argue that there is no clear picture of a global world, or even tendencies in that direction (for example, Hirst and Thompson 1999). It is also argued by some that even the sphere usually seen as the most "global," the economy, is not really global at all. Alan Rugman (2000), for example, argues that though there are multinational enterprises, their activities are essentially organized regionally or locally. The limited attention paid to the global dimension is the fourth problem with the current economic sociology literature.

Most economic sociological studies, old as well as new, tend to focus on the production of commodities, but few seem to realize that consumption, at least today, is at least as important. This book tries to bring consumption to the fore, and takes the consumer market for garments as its point of departure. The fifth problem with the new economic sociology literature, then, is that it does not pay enough attention to consumption (cf. Zukin and Smith Maguire 2004: 173).

Fashion Theory and Research

I DEVOTE THIS FINAL APPENDIX to the large literature on fashion, discussing its strengths and weaknesses. This is not a complete review of the field of fashion studies, but it does consider some of the more important works and discusses some of the problems in this field.

For good introductions, overviews, and accounts of the field of fashion, see Entwistle (2000), Wilson (2003), Kawamura (2005), Crane and Bovone (2006), and Welters and Lillethun (2007), as well as Entwistle and Wilson (2001) for an overview and a discussion of the origins of research in this field. See also Steel (1997) for a modern history of fashion, and the *Encyclopedia of Clothing and Fashion* (Steel 2004) and *Fashion: Critical and Primary Sources* (McNeil 2008a) as general sources. Though fashion appears to be identical to garment fashion, I prefer to see clothes as one example of the more general social process (cf. Lieberson 2000; Gerhards 2005). Students of fashion have seen it as elitist or irrational, but also as close to human needs, and they have often assigned particular functions to it. It is generally accepted that fashion matters to people because it is a way of enacting, expressing, playing with, and drawing on social roles and identities, thereby creating and sustaining, among other things, gender, group affiliations, and distance. The notion of identity, though often undertheorized, has been important in this literature (for example, Davis 1992).

Fashion became a force in society only with the emergence of capitalism around 1700 (Braudel 1981). König (1973: 139), however, argues that the history of fashion goes back earlier and says that the first spread of "fashion-oriented behavior" can be observed "within the upper ranks of the feudal system" at the end of the Middle Ages. Craik argues that we should see it as a general phenomenon, and not linked to the historical development of European societies (1993: 4). Researchers from many disciplines have discussed fashion but some look down on this field and on the relevant research. Nonetheless, the following quote is still essentially a correct summary: "The 'mystery' of fashion changes has fascinated not only economists and sociologists, social historians and cultural anthropologists, but also philosophers and moralists, poets, playwrights, and novelists" (Gregory 1947: 71). The "irrationality" of fashion is not only a theme of older economists; contemporary "thinkers" too cannot avoid imagining conditions under which consumers would be better off "by banning the use of fashion" (Pesendorfer 1995: 771). One should, however, remember that the history of fashion is essentially a history of women's fashion, which means that there is an important gender dimension in this field of research.

Fashion has also been of interest to historians, and more recently to feminists (Wilson 2003: 47–66), besides sociologists and economists. A central question in many studies has been the diffusion of fashion. Though focusing on the UK, Entwistle and Wilson (2001) argue that the field of fashion grew out of art history, and that it concentrated on haute couture.

In the main text, I explain how I see the field of fashion. Though my central idea—to relate production and consumption—is not new (cf. Aspers and Skov 2006: 807–8), few researchers have tried to analyze this relationship empirically. This study deviates from large parts of the existing fashion literature because it takes an economic sociological outlook on the field of fashion. The lack of a discussion of contemporary fashion is an obvious weakness of my study, from one perspective. However, any scholarly treatment of contemporary fashion becomes a history of fashion long before it gets into print. It has not been possible to include an account of the internal references and the internal narrative of fashion—made up of actors' references to past fashions when new fashions develop. The virtue of leaving out this "aesthetic" dimension is that it allows me to focus on the social structure of the industry in which these internal narratives are constructed.

In a sense, journalists who write on fashion and the fashion industry can be bracketed in sociological analyses. This literature (Agins 2000) is often very rich in detail and offers a good insight into the business from people who have access to arenas that are usually inaccessible to researchers. What this kind of work is unable to give us is accounts that are not just stories, but built on theory, thereby enabling them also to provide explanations. A first step in this direction is to draw a distinction between the phenomena of fashion and clothes (cf. Kawamura 2005), and to talk of fashion systems (Godart 2009). It is possible also to analyze fashions in art or cars, as well as in the sciences.

The second approach I want to mention is the humanistic–historical, which has provided many interesting studies and above all has shown the role of fashion in different historical and cultural settings (for example, Wilson 2003; Evans 2000; Rouse 1989; McNeil 2008b). This literature often overlaps with studies in dress history. It is very important that we have a knowledge of history, as we always draw on it in our interpretations (Gadamer [1960] 1990). This means that historical accounts of fashion play an important role (for example, Breward 1995).

The semiotic literature is the third body of work I shall mention. Ideally, visual studies can be used as a bridge between art history and social science (Schroeder 2003), to study, for example, fashion advertisements (Schroeder 2004). Used in this way, we can learn about the internal narrative of fashion advertisements, which can then be combined with the experiences of customers. This semiotic approach is often fused with cultural studies. I agree with those who criticize this approach (Entwistle and Wilson 2001: 2–3), but I would like to specify its weaknesses carefully. Briefly, it is misleading to think of fashion as a language or a code (cf. Barthes [1967] 1990; Corrigan 1997: 172–74; Davis 1992; Barnard 1996), and one sometimes speaks of uncovering the "hidden meaning" (van Leeuwe and Jevitt 2001: 91). The linguistic analogy becomes even more problematic given that the entities that carry meaning in fashion are replaced at a much faster rate than linguistic entities.

Malcolm Barnard's (1996) work relies on the semiotic approach, and I take it as a point of departure for a critical discussion. Barnard sees fashion and clothing as "communication," but it is a form of communication that is driven by "power and ideology" (1996: 4). Like many others, he stresses how clothes are part and parcel of class and gender distinctions, and few would deny this. The most fundamental difference between the perspective I propose and the semiotic approach is my argument that we have to start with the meaning of the actors studied, rather than with the "objective meaning" constructed by the researcher.

One idea of semiotics is that the signifier—a word or an item, such as a garment—is given meaning by the signified. A signifier stands for something, and only those who know the "code"—that is, "a set of shared rules"—can understand this meaning (cf. Barnard 1996: 78–79). The object, Barnard says, denotates and connotates. Denotation means that the characteristics of the garment are pinned down, such as its fabric. Connotation refers to the meaning of the garment in terms of, for example, its regular users. Only the connotative meaning is "an intersubjective and hermeneutic affair," according to Barnard (1996: 83). Barnard (1996: 84) uses this distinction to create different types of meanings. It is complicated if we have different kinds of meanings, especially since they are "understood at the same time" (Barnard 1996: 84). These meanings, according to Barnard (1996: 91), seem to correspond to the same categories as Barthes suggested: "class, sex, age and so on." The semiotic approach uses a mechanical theory of society, but this cuts off the most central dimension of meaning with reference to actors, namely the interpretations of the actors who form fashion. Actors, if one uses this kind of semiotic approach, become essentially meaningless.

It is above all non-ethnographic work that has perpetuated the idea of semiotics in the field of fashion. Semiotically influenced researchers hardly ever do ethnography. Instead, they ascribe meaning to reality, so to speak, over the heads of the people whose meanings construct reality to a much larger extent than the researchers' interpretations allow. The meaning-oriented perspective I advocate implies that actors, at the reflexive level, can combine clothes in ways that are interpreted by them and their fellow humans in a great number of ways, depending on their origin, history, and context, which we have to understand by accounting for actual meanings. This means that it is not the researcher's task to act as a judge to determine the meaning of clothes (or texts and pictures), especially without calling any witnesses. The project that I share with many others is to see how fashion is co-determined in social interaction at the same time as it co-determines its wearers—it is a social affair throughout. To speak of fashion systems that could be analyzed as language is sociologically naïve—merely a metaphor, not an explanation. The semiotic approach is largely unable to transform its findings into explanatory theory. What we get instead is "accounts" of the field "covered," but no indications of their generality. As the semiotic approach relies on sociology—age, sex, and class issues—to explain why people have certain meanings, I see few reasons why one should enter the field of semiotics in the first place.

Fashion, moreover, must always account for the bodies of the users of fashion (cf. Entwistle 2000; Entwistle and Wilson 2001: 4; Entwistle 2001). The body is often the material peg of the narratives that create peoples' discrete as well as unique identities. One should by no means see the body as given; it is an effect of social interaction, too. Body styles and shapes are not only literally formed by garments, but fashion also constructs values related to how bodies should look. The appearance of real people is normally the combined effect of the body—including hairstyle, tattoos, makeup, perfume, skin color (whether it is tanned or not), fitness and what the body gives off, such as smell—and the clothes and accessories used. Clothes are of course also an integral part of the understanding of sexuality. This means that one can analyze body fashions as an integral part of clothing fashions (Craik 1993: 4–5).

The body carries garments. The physical histories of different trades, such as carpenter or clerk, are also "inscribed on" the body, and these bodily postures, so to speak, are correspondingly part of what constitutes these trades. What people wore in the past, and to some extent still wear, to signal membership of collective identities—such as ice hockey players, fire fighters, or nurses—is usually not seen as the object of fashion studies, though one can study fashion within each group (cf. Craik 1993). Dress codes are part of what constructs order, and also a way of signaling status groups (Weber [1921–22] 1978). Religious groups, the military, royalty, and others have used clothes to separate themselves from other groups, and they have done this partly through consumption.

Finally, I would like to broach an area of research that is of great importance—and that I have already touched upon—which could be used to improve both the methods of fashion studies and theoretical development, namely visual sociology (for example, Pink 2001; Banks 2001). Sociology, in contrast to art history and anthropology, has only recently realized the importance of the visual. Fashion is visual and this is evident from looking at magazines, but also by observing dressed bodies, on the catwalk and in the streets, at parties, and on other occasions. These are just a few examples of our observation of others as wearers of garments. Studies of fashion must recognize this and use suitable theories and methods in empirical studies. Visual methods—for example, photo-elicitation (Gold 1991)—will most likely increase the quality of the evidence.

All these aspects are important, but I do not see any of them as the central starting point of the sociology of fashion. I argue that the central task of the sociology of fashion, in contrast to the history of fashion, dress history, and other disciplinary approaches, is to develop a theory that can be used to analyze the highly complex logic of fashion. Such a theory must be general enough to account for the constant changes of fashion, and also be able to handle more than fashions in clothes, though clothes are likely to continue to be the central empirical field of study. It must also be applicable to historical settings. In this book, I have not used it to study concrete instances of fashion, and the diffusion of fashion. However, there is great potential in the modern sociological approaches to diffusion (for example, Liljeros 2004; Camitz and Liljeros 2006).

Notes

Introduction

1. Quota systems are international trade agreements on the export and import of different kinds of garments. A quota restriction means that a country is allowed to export only a certain quantity of garments to another country or an economic union. In some production countries, there is an official exchange market for quotas, organized by the state, and sometimes unofficial markets exist. The international quota system was abolished on January 1, 2005, but was in force when I carried out most of my study.

2. Hobbes ([1651] 1968), who saw order as essentially a problem of "law and order," identified the state as the solution, but the question goes deeper. The "contract" that Hobbes sets up as an idea presupposes trust. There is no "rational" solution to the issue of trust; faith is essential (Möllering 2006), as Durkheim ([1893] 1984), following Rousseau (Wrong 1994: 9), stressed. It may be taken for granted that the state is the final guarantor of law and order in society, maintained ultimately by *Gewaltherrschaft* [control based on force]. It keeps track of and taxes all economic actors, but it does not govern how each market is constructed in detail. Markets can also be self-regulatory, and though "politics" in broad terms has not disappeared, it is taking new forms (Sörbom 2002). Today, political activism is also present in markets (Micheletti et al. 2004).

3. His later writings also include a discussion of cooperation (Beckert 2006). This means that order in Parsons's sociology essentially comes down to socialization (cf. Luhmann [1984] 1995: 104) of society's members to the existing consensus.

4. The problem with Fligstein's approach is a result of his interpretation of White's market model. Fligstein's (1996, 2001: 22, 30–31, 94) market definition assumes that all markets are like White's (1981) producer market model. However, White's theory does not deal with the neoclassical market model, which assumes standardized goods and actors who can switch between the roles of buyers and sellers.

5. All definitions in this book are in italics. My definition of order embraces the ontic level—the objects of study (cf. Heidegger [1927] 2001) discussed by sociologists—but I only touch upon the question of ontology. In sociology, the "question of order ... concerns the ultimate source of social patterns; it does not concern the ontological question of whether these patterns or the individuals who may or may not support them are real" (Alexander et al. 1987: 13). Philosophers, in contrast, have mainly debated the ontological—"ways of being"—level of order, though there have been some minor inroads into "sociology" (Hacking 2002). It is hence problematic that "ontology" in sociology—and we should therefore refer only to the "ontic"—is often tied, and sometimes also reduced, to

the epistemological question (Reed 2008)—that is, the question of how one can know what there is and the justification of such claims.

6. The notion of order or *Ordnung* can be traced to ancient Greece, in which armies were said to be "ordered." More generally, it refers to the relationship between the parts and the whole (Meinhardt 1984, 6: 1250). Xenophon stresses the importance of order in the dialogue *Oeconomicus*, in which Socrates takes part (Xenophon: 37–40). This means there is a clear connection with ontology as well as social order, but also to the order, in terms of categories, of nature. Later on, for example in the work of Aquinas, order was strongly linked to theology; the world order was more or less a product of God and connected to something good.

During the Enlightenment, order referred to both natural and social order, with the latter essentially mirroring the former. There is also a discussion of order in mathematics and logic (Erzog 1984). The use in this work of the notion of order carries no normative ideas.

7. Obviously, also people's identities are "social components" that have to be ordered, while at the same time one can talk of social construction only on the assumption that many people have similar references. Man, in other words, holds a special role, as part of the world, but as the "part" that can reflect upon itself (cf. Heidegger [1927] 2001). Consequently, the identities of human beings are also ordered, but they are, at the same time, the condition for talking about order. It is therefore incorrect to speak of order "as such," as Parsons and most sociologists do, unless one acknowledges and discusses the special role of man as constituting order.

8. Although meaning is a basic notion, it does not appear in the works of many prominent researchers. Many sociologists, especially in the U.S.—such as Parsons, Homans, and Coleman—have not taken up the issue of meaning. Among European sociologists, the importance of meaning in sociological analysis is more common, as evident in the works of Habermas, Giddens, Bourdieu, Luhmann, and others.

9. This means that order and the regional ontology (cf. Husserl [1952] 1980: 22; [1913a] 1962: 57) of the social sciences are connected (cf. Luhmann 1997: 896). These regional ontologies, that are of an ontic character, to follow Heidegger ([1927] 2001), are ultimately connected to the lifeworld (Husserl [1954] 1970). Thus, for practical reasons, to study all the social constructions that are preconditions for these markets would be impossible.

Chapter 1. Garment Sellers in Consumer Markets

1. The "material side" of the peg, is "material" only because it is social. This follows from the phenomenological-ontological approach of the book drawing on Martin Heidegger. It implies this, and means it is non-productive to divide the world into a ready-made material part and a social or cultural part, of which the latter attach meaning to the former.

2. Relational sociology can be traced back to the symbolic interactionists, who argued that social interaction is central to understanding social life. The relational approach (cf. Swidler 1986: 276–77; Emirbayer 1997) involves rejecting both

traditional structural analyses (see, for example, Burt 1992), or individualistic approaches, such as rational choice theory (for example, Coleman 1990). These approaches, like many others, simply take many of the questions—such as those of being, order, and identity, which I consider of central sociological importance—for granted. From a relational sociological perspective, one has to analyze how being, order, and other social phenomena are co-constructed.

The approach proposed here rejects the naïve sociology that treats actors and actions as the only units of social analyses. Pragmatic thinkers such as George Herbert Mead, and more sociological followers of the Chicago school, as well as phenomenologists, such as Martin Heidegger, realized that thinking is socially structured and that the relations between people and contexts are of great importance. But neither pragmatism nor phenomenology have built up general and systematic theoretical blocks.

3. See Aspers (2006a) for an introduction to White's market theory.

4. Values are thus tools for evaluation, both of things and people (see also Spates 1983; Hitlin and Piliavin 2004). Luhmann proposes the following definition: "any point of view specifying which consequences of action are to be preferred to others" (Luhmann 1982: 97). There are of course other definitions; for example, following Clyde Kluckhorn, "conceptions of the desirable" (Parsons and White [1961] 1970: 194).

Values have traditionally been seen as growing out of culture and specifying ultimate ends (cf. Swidler 1986: 273–76). They are important in all sociological analysis to explain order (cf. Devereux 1961: 23; Joas 1997: 32–34; Boltanski and Thèvenot [1991] 2006: 10), and sociologists usually assume that individuals have goals and orient their actions to values (cf. Heidegger [1940] 1986: 24–26).

Many sociologists connect values with structure. Radcliffe-Brown, who speaks of interest (1952: 199), and Weber ([1921–22] 1978), who speaks of meaning and interest, connect structure with values, as does Parsons (Lidz 1991: 31). Values should be separated from norms, which regulate what one ought to do or not do in certain situations, and attitudes, which are directed towards concrete states of affairs (Spates 1983: 30 n1, 32). Moreover, a value comes in degrees; it is not a matter of either/or.

5. A shopping center or a shopping district also tries to create an identity. This can be done by allowing certain brands and retailers to have stores in an area and denying others, to create the right mixture and profile. This strategy is used in shopping malls in Turkey, as well as in areas of London and elsewhere. This process may be more or less regulated. Carnaby Street in London, which is in fact more than just one street, hosts smaller shops with brands with a medium to high-fashion profile, such as Replay, Lee, Diesel, and Miss Sixty. This "street" has its own homepage [http://www.carnaby.co.uk/] (accessed October 5, 2006). The retail units that are available are, for example, always mentioned in relation to the neighboring stores. Oxford Street is the area of the large BGRs, such as Topshop, Zara, H&M, Benetton, and French Connection UK.

6. http://www.vogue.co.uk/Shows/Reports/Default.aspx?stID=34050 (accessed March 29, 2006).

7. http://www.vogue.co.uk/Shows/Reports/Default.aspx?stID=32597 (accessed March 29, 2006).

8. http://www.euratex.org/content/mission.html (accessed March 16, 2006).

9. http://www.fta-eu.org/ftatheftaen.cdb (accessed March 16, 2006).

10. http://www.fta-eu.org/ftamembersen.cdb (accessed March 16, 2006).

11. http://www.eureporter.co.uk/showarticle.php?newsid=1969 (accessed March 16, 2006).

12. http://www.eureporter.co.uk/showarticle.php?newsid=1957 (accessed March 16, 2006).

Chapter 2. Affordable Fashion

1. If a "consumer" starts to trade—that is, both sell and buy commodities—he or she becomes a trader, which sets him or her apart from consumers in the eyes of both producers and consumers.

2. Giddens talks about self-identity, which he defines as "the self as reflexively understood by the person in terms of her or his biography" (1991: 53). Reflexive identity represents the "existential baseline" for humans, and it is also in relation to reflexive identity that it is possible to talk of constitution. Actors' behavior can be understood in relation to what they want to achieve. Other actors, however, will orient to their egos according to how they perceive them, which resembles Mead's discussion of others' attitudes towards "me" (cf. Beckert 2003: 777). The approach suggested here opens up the possibility of analyzing how being (the reflexive identity of humans) is affected by what they do, as seen by others. In other words, it connects the existential-psychological level with the social, as well as levels of analysis represented by structurally determined identities (cf. Granovetter 1992: 5–6).

This kind of freedom is of course not the sociologically naïve freedom that one finds in the works of Sartre or Nozick. A reflexive identity is conditioned in terms of differentiation from other identities, but it has the peculiar characteristic that it is constituted by the ego. This means that the ego must come to grips with what and who it is—its being. I stress the interpretative role of being, without addressing the ontological level that is its precondition, discussed in different ways by Husserl and Heidegger.

In light of Husserl and, most of all, Heidegger, it is in the strictest sense only reflexive identity that is able to constitute meaning. It is this form of identity that bears the strongest resemblance to Heidegger's *Dasein* ("there-being" or just "existence") which, so to speak, is the baseline of the constitution of "everything." This idea is here given a more sociological twist. *Dasein* cannot be explained or proved, since it is the very precondition for "explanations" and "proofs" (Heidegger [1927] 2001: 205).

It is in this process of identity formation that *Dasein* recognizes itself among others, as well as a human being among things (cf. Werkmeister 1941: 86). This notion should also be related to Mead's "self" and Giddens's (1991) discussion of "self-identity." We have no room here to expand on this existential-phenomenological aspect. I also see this as a way of connecting the question of being with sociological questions that I regard as an essential component in understanding being.

Reflexive identity also touches on psychology (cf. Husserl [1954] 1970). This psychological level, of course, can be understood only in relation to the sociological level. Some "psychological problems" can be traced to people who fail to become what they wish or what society wants them to be. Such problems may have individual histories, but they are rooted in social conditions. Consequently, mentally ill actors may have a much-skewed perception of who they are, and this is in terms of their "reflexive" identity. Fashion is one way of trying to become what one wants to be. The conclusion, however, is that actors can think and reflect about their being without being completely *controlled* by social conditions.

3. Also, Lash and Urry stress the importance of consumption for "the constitution of individual and collective identity" (1987: 288–92). One aspect of this idea is expressed by Clammer: "shopping is not merely the acquisition of things: it is the buying of identity" (1992: 195). The relation between commodities and identity has also been discussed within the so-called "cultural economy" literature (cf. Slater and Tonkiss 2001: 176–81; Du Gay 1993: 579–80; Corrigan 1997; Miller, Jackson, Thrift, Holbrook and Rowlands 1998). It follows, on a more general level, that "without consumer goods, certain acts of self-definition and collective definition in this culture would be impossible" (McCracken 1988: x). Also, Bourdieu ([1979] 1984) stresses the role of consumption in differentiation and social order.

4. Economists have "invented" a number of different kinds of goods: Giffen goods, Veblen goods, positional goods, non-positional goods, inferior goods, rivalrous goods, public goods, normal goods, and so on.

The use of status, and also standards, cannot be understood in terms of the economic notion of positional goods, whose "value depends relatively strongly on how they compare with things owned by others" (Frank 1985: 101). The reason is that the focus of the distinction between positional and non-positional goods is on the goods as evaluated by actors in terms of whether they have a utility function. The assumption is that there is a way of evaluating the commodity as such. In status markets, actors have identities and their actions must be understood based on who they are.

5. It is important to realize that this argument does not fall back on the "quality" of the products. In reality there may of course be differences also in quality (for example, how many washes a blouse can go through without losing its shape). It is likely that the blouse will be discarded because it is out of fashion long before its "quality" reveals itself.

6. The value of diamonds cannot be explained by their functionality, and it cannot be understood in the tautological way as economists have explained it— namely in terms of marginal utility theory. It is the reason for the willingness to pay large sums for diamonds, "on the margin," which holds the key to the explanation. The explanation is thus sociological, and refers to their symbolic value (conditioned by scarcity, but not determined by scarcity).

7. Wilson (2003) devotes an entire chapter to "The Fashion Industry," but restricts the discussion almost exclusively to the history of working conditions. There are exceptions (White and Griffiths 2000) that at least combine discussion of the design and other dimensions of the fashion industry with clothes.

8. Uncertainty is turned into risk only when it is possible to assign probabilities to outcomes. To achieve probabilities, three conditions for means–ends relations must be met: "(1) similarity across cases; (2) similarity over time; and (3) sufficiently large numbers of past observations" (Guseva and Rona-Tas 2001: 626). Though the difference between the two is in some sense semantic, calculability, needless to say, is a precondition of prediction. However, it may be able to predict without making a calculation, which here is viewed as a task performed to establish means–ends relations.

9. Some, such as Simmel ([1907] 1978: 446) and Max Weber, relate culture to both meaning structure and values (Swedberg 2003: 226; Parsons and White [1961] 1970: 194).

10. See also DiMaggio and Cohen (2005) on the diffusion of goods. One may, in their language, characterize fashion garments as a commodity associated with prestige and negative externalities—that is, their value decreases the greater their number of buyers. Moreover, in some cases a network can be thought of in terms of "borders" for the diffusion of a fashion. Moreover, things go out of fashion at different times; people seem to have different thresholds (Granovetter 1978) in this respect.

11. See Simmel's ([1907] 1978: 452–56) discussion of subjective (personal) and objective culture, and Berger and Luckmann ([1966] 1991), who followed Schütz and speak of objective and subjective reality.

Chapter 3. Entrenching Identities

1. The UK-based company French Connection has even succeeded in using its own logo, spelled "FCUK," as a visual component of its garments.

2. Firms often have pictures that accepted and registered users, such as fashion journalists, can download and use free of charge. These pictures may be the same as those used in public advertising campaigns. In this way, BGRs can both control the visual output and get free "advertisement" space.

3. Compare Luhmann's description, "[I]t is precisely in the relationship of economy and advertising that we therefore find good arguments for an increasing differentiation of systems with a decrease in structural coupling" ([1996] 2000: 49).

4. It is thus not only the interest in being flexible that explains why many functions are outsourced (cf. Hirsch [1977] 1992). The insecurity that BGRs face when it comes to evaluating as well as judging advertisements can at least rhetorically be discussed by members of the marketing department at a BGR, who can say that they have hired a highly prestigious advertising agency to develop their campaign. This indirect way of securing and justifying decisions is also an indication of the values produced in the evaluation process in which advertising agencies determine what is good and what is not, and in which they are ranked.

5. Ben Crewe (2003) describes how the launch of a magazine is the result of gut feeling and instinct (2003: 67) rather than market research. The point is that there is no way one can ask people beforehand what they would like to see (Crewe 2003: 76). It is, moreover, very difficult to know in advance how a magazine will be received and who its readers will be (Crewe 2003: 76–77). In some

corners of the industry there is also a marked skepticism concerning market research, partly due to the belief that market research is a threat to the competence
of journalists and others whose task is to know what is in vogue before it is in
vogue (Crewe 2003: 78).

6. This visual dimension cannot be reduced to pure signaling of information
(as White's [2002: 16] adoption of Spence's work implies). It is not information unless the actors are capable of perceiving it, and it is therefore a form of
knowledge.

7. Many organizations focus on the environment. The German Otto group, for
example—named after its owner, Dr. Michael Otto—is a large firm that stresses
the importance of the environment. This is tied to the major debate on corporate
responsibility (cf. Hiß 2006).

8. The notion of standard is not identical with standardized commodities. In
my use of standard, I allow a "bliss point," which follows the *Oxford English
Dictionary* usage, in which a standard is the authoritative scale by which other
items are measured. This deviates somewhat from the economic and technological discussion of standards and standardized products. Standards in this latter
sense (see Wilson 2000: 57) facilitate communication and trade, and make it
possible to calculate and predict the environment of the firm (Brunsson and
Jacobsson 2000; Schmidt and Werle 1998: 81; Boltanski and Thèvenot [1991]
2006: 8; Barzel 2004), as, not least, members of the French convention-economist
school have stressed (cf. Favereau, Biencourt, and Eymard-Duvernay 2002; Biggart and Beamish 2003). Though standards refer to more than products, the following is an informative definition of a standardized product. Such a product is
"made with a known, widely diffused production technology in which quality is
so widely attainable that competition comes to be inevitably centered on price"
(Storper 1997: 109).

9. From http://www.ifat.org/whatisft.html (accessed October 10, 2003). Many
organizations like this can be found, focusing on different product categories.
Fruit is one example: see http://www.fairtrade.net (accessed October 10, 2003).
Specific standards exist for each type of fruit, such as bananas.

10. In 2000/2001, almost half of all retailers, from different industries, lacked
a code of conduct (Young and Welford 2003: 67–78).

11. NGOs are often united in a critical view of globalization. One Dutch organization, the Centre for Research on Multinational Corporations (SOMO), established in 1973, is a research and advisory bureau that "investigates the negative
consequences of Multinational Enterprises' (MNEs') policies and the consequences of the internationalization of business, particularly for developing countries"
(http://www.somo.nl/index_eng.php, accessed October 25, 2005).

Chapter 4. Branded Garment Retailers in the Production Market

1. As a result, I bracket (in the phenomenological sense) the role of agents or
others who can operate as intermediaries in a market like this. Moreover, when I
talk of buyers in this chapter, I refer also to firms. It is of course real people who
operate as actual buyers on the behalf of firms.

2. I became aware of this in a number of ways. When I was waiting to interview a buyer I sat in a reception area together with another person who also seemed to be waiting for someone. Both of us were led into a small meeting booth that served as an interface between the interior of the BGR and its visitors. I asked why they had these booths and was told they wanted to keep their "secrets."

In one contact I had with a large BGR, I was asked to hand in a detailed description of my project so they could decide whether I would be allowed to study their firm. I got the following reply in an e-mail:

> Dear Patrik!
> I have read your research proposal and your wish for interviews and a visit. Acceptance on our part, regardless of whatever confidentiality we might impose, would result in a study of the heart of [name of the BGR]'s business ideas, know-how, business relations, methods and organization, and I therefore have to say no to your request.
> [Signature]

They denied my request early in the research process, but this served only to indicate that I was on the right track.

3. The magazine *Fashion Forecast*, and different *Colleziones*, as well as many other magazines, feature pictures from catwalks. The Internet is the largest source of information, and sites such as [http://www.style.com] (accessed November 7, 2006) make it easy to find out what is being presented on the catwalk, regardless of where one is based.

In India, many manufacturers subscribe to the industry journal *Apparel Fortnightly*, which has articles on upcoming trends. I subscribed to this journal for a year. Many websites, of course, provide information on trends in color and fabrics, for example: http://www.apparelindia.com (accessed April 4, 2006). This site explains the fashion trends in terms of colors, style, and fabrics. It also distinguishes between babies (0–3), kids (3–8), preteens (8–12), and ladies. The following is an excerpt from this site, commenting on style:

> This summer [2006] almost all the styles will be based on comfort and basic cuts. Comfort means a simple straight cut in comfortable fabrics with stretching effect and tangibility. For a teenage girl, comfort means a tight fitted shirt in a stretchable fabric with any kind of tangibility and maybe baggy pants or an ankle length skirt with detachable pockets. A revival of the eighties is underway, and a lust for decoration and logo-mania.

4. Many actors are involved in the collective determination of a fashion line. Gronow's (1997: 110) finding, based on a study of Finnish fashion designers, supports Blumer's ideas on the collective selection of fashion. While there are other versions of this process, Gronow traces how the actors who are directly involved in the process make such decisions.

5. Though there is a general culture of competition, this can be mitigated by friendship. I asked a representative of a buying office if he had any kind of contact with other buying offices of a friendly nature? "Some kind of cooperation, for example?" He responded in a way that implied competition, but with excep-

tions: "It is an entirely different matter if [name of a firm] has a colleague of mine [working for it], whom I have worked with at [the name of another firm is mentioned]".

Q: So it is more like a network?

A: Yes ... If I have a colleague working [at another company], I pick up the phone and say "I need a good vendor—suggest me a name—I need help, I need a merchandiser or I need a good guy. Have you seen anyone in a factory, maybe I can take one from a factory?" I can certainly take one from my factories, or I can take someone from his factories . . . so it is basically a network.

6. See, for example, www.style.com (accessed October 6, 2006).

7. This is not to say that there is an underlying realist ontology. It is not implied that the social constructions made up of practice, pictures, and text are reflections of an underlying ontology that essentially could be revealed by a neutral language. That meanings overlap and make it possible to posit perspectives is merely a reflection of the fact that people live in the same world and that no interpretation can be made outside of the communal base of the lifeworld. This is one insight of continental thinkers inspired by Husserl, such as Heidegger and Gadamer, but it is also found among analytic philosophers drawing on pragmatism, such as Donald Davidson (Wachthauser 1994).

Chapter 5. Manufacturing Garments in the Global Market

1. The way they use the Internet is also instructive. See Internet sites that have links to manufacturers, such as:

http://www.iigf.trade-india.com (accessed August 24, 2006)

http://www.apparelindia.com (accessed August 24, 2006)

2. Culture can also mean that, for example, in India, people in the industry mix English with local languages—for example, Hindi—also in conversations in which only Indians take part.

Chapter 6. Branded Garment Retailers in the Investment Market

1. Obviously, an ethnography that also includes the activities of traders would probably show many more details, but this kind of research is beyond the scope of this study. See the site of the London Stock Exchange, which is full of general information for investors (of different kinds and sizes), as well as many other categories. This chapter draws only on experience of trading stocks using intermediaries: http://www.londonstockexchange.com/en-gb (accessed July 12, 2006).

2. The discussion of performativity (Callon 1998, 1999, 2005) is also contingent upon the neoclassical market model developed by Walras. Donald MacKenzie has shown that the price mechanism and the clearing function of "markets"

are "performed" in this sense (MacKenzie 2004, 2006; MacKenzie and Millo 2003; MacKenzie, Muniesa, and Siu 2007).

3. Clifford Geertz makes a point about the traders in the Modjokuto Pasar ("bazaar") market in Indonesia. He says, "there is little if any differentiation between the buying role and selling role as long as one remains within the pasar; the trader is either or both indifferently." Geertz also states that the market in which they operate shows cohesion also because "the characteristics of a 'good' buyer and a 'good' seller are thus identical" (Geertz 1963: 33).

4. For a more detailed description of how one advanced stock exchange operates, see http://www.stockholmsborsen.se/handelsinfo/index.asp?lank=1&lang=eng (accessed December 14, 2005).

5. Principles, strategies, tools, rules of thumbs, and ideas abound concerning how to evaluate stocks (cf. Smith 1981; MacKenzie 2006). The literature devoted to these issues is huge, and the idea of industries still reflects the fact that subject matter matters, despite how rules of thumb may differ between industries (cf. Hessling and Pahl 2006).

6. The reason is that the patterns that technical analysts react to, if they are to be useful, must be repeated. If not, there would be no historical data to form the bedrock for establishing these "rules of thumb" concerning when to buy and sell stocks. In sum, this form of knowledge is based on classic behaviorism.

7. It is obviously possible to question the centrality of profit, which I have not done here. Some firms may be founded for purposes entirely other than making a profit, but if they are seen as profitable by investors, they are included in the market. This is just another way of saying that the decision that makes a firm a member is not made by the firm alone. A firm that seeks investors, but that fails, cannot get off the ground. This firm will not become a member of the market. Moreover, firms that do not comply with the rules of the game may be expelled from the stock exchange, if they violate its rules or go bankrupt. There is currently much turmoil in stock exchanges, and acquisitions have taken place, indicating that several markets may become one.

8. The materials are from 2005–2006, and the study of their websites was mostly carried out in spring 2006. Quotations are in this case not connected to specific websites. BGRs present themselves in the written materials that they issue as information to the stock exchange. Representatives also make statements on their market strategies in interviews and through other channels of communication. This information is directed to investors and "the market," but not to the final consumers. This supports my general claim that they are two different audiences. The Internet site of a BGR is usually organized so that the consumers' interests and the interests of the investors ("investor relations") are catered to in different places.

Chapter 7. Markets as Partial Orders

1. Simmel draws on both Kant and Nietzsche. The notion of form comes from the Kantian idea of a-priori categories, though it is possible to concoct a more social constructivist interpretation of Simmel, his ideas are expressed in a language

that refers to a-priori categories. Simmel's idea is that certain values, interests, and needs are mediated through such forms, an idea that comes from Nietzsche (among others). Nonetheless, Simmel's subjectivism, his analyses at the level of interaction, and the attempt to combine social structure with values should be acknowledged as a step in the direction of combining several key components.

2. The varieties of capitalism approach has the advantage that it identifies commonalities of markets at the national level, though this does not mean that this level is important in itself. I think that the ambition "to bring firms back into the center of comparative capitalism" (Hall and Soskice 2001: 4) is less fruitful if one simultaneously sees variation as located at the national level.

Appendix IV. Economic Sociology

1. New economic sociology has its deepest roots in the Department of Sociology at Harvard University. The reaction against Parsonian sociology was particularly strong here, especially among Harrison White and his students (personal conversation with Mark Granovetter, September 11, 2004).

2. The sociology of the market literature is full of studies of individual markets, but they have not analyzed the social conditions of markets to the same degree. The literature on social conditions, in contrast, seldom addresses the issue of markets (Beckert 2002).

3. Some have argued that social science theories are not universal (Gudeman 2001: 4). As a corollary, the development of theories must be understood in relation to the societies in which they emerge.

References

Abelson, Raziel, and Kai Nielsen. 1967. "Ethics, History of," pp. 81–117 in vol. 3 of *The Encyclopedia of Philosophy*, edited by P. Edwards. New York: Macmillan Publishing.

Abernathy, Frederick, John Dunlop, Janice Hammond, and David Weil. 1999. *A Stitch in Time: Lean Retailing and the Transformation of Manufacturing—Lessons from the Apparel and Textile Industries*. New York: Oxford University Press.

Abolafia, Mitchel. 1996. *Making Markets, Opportunism and Restraint on Wall Street*. Cambridge, Mass.: Harvard University Press.

Agins, Teri. 2000. *The End of Fashion, How Marketing Changed the Clothing Business Forever*. New York: Harper Collins.

Agrawal, Jagdish, and Wagner A. Kamakura. 1995. "The Economic Worth of Celebrity Endorsers: An Event Study Analysis," *Journal of Marketing* 59: 56–62.

Ahrne, Göran, and Nils Brunsson. 2005. "Organizations and Meta-Organizations," *Scandinavian Journal of Management* 21: 429–49.

———. 2008. *Meta-Organizations*. Cheltenham: Edward Elgar.

Alexander, Jeffrey. 1987. *Twenty Lectures*. New York: Columbia University Press.

Alexander, Jeffrey, Bernhard Giesen, Richard Münch, and Neil Smelser, eds. 1987. *The Micro-Macro Link*. Berkeley: University of California Press.

Amsden, Alice. 2001. *The Rise of "The "Rest," Challenges to the West From Late-Industrializing Economies*. Oxford: Oxford University Press.

Arendt, Hannah. [1958] 1988. *The Human Condition*. Chicago: Chicago University Press.

Arpan, Jeffrey, Jose De La Torre, and Brian Toyne. 1981. "International Developments and the U.S. Apparel Industry, "*Journal of International Business Studies* 12, 3: 49–64.

Aspers, Patrik. 1999. "The Sociology of Alfred Marshall, an Overview," *American Journal of Economics and Sociology* 58, 4: 651–68.

———. 2001. "Crossing the Boundaries of Economics and Sociology: The Case of Vilfredo Pareto," *American Journal of Economics and Sociology* 60, 2: 519–45.

———. 2004. *Empirical Phenomenology, an Approach for Qualitative Research*. The Methodology Institute, London School of Economics.

———. 2006a. *Markets in Fashion, a Phenomenological Approach*. London: Routledge.

———. 2006b. "Contextual Knowledge," *Current Sociology* 54, 5: 745–63.

———. 2006c. "Ethics in Global Garment Market Chains," pp. 287–307 in *The Moralization of Markets*, edited by N. Stehr, C. Henning, and B. Weiler. London: Transaction Press.

———. 2007. "Theory, Reality and Performativity in Markets," *American Journal of Economics and Sociology* 66, 2: 379–98.

———. 2008. "Order in Garment Markets," *ACTA Sociologica* 51, 3: 187–202.

Aspers, Patrik. 2009. "Knowledge and Valuation in Markets," *Theory and Society* 39, 2: 111–31.

———. Forthcoming "Using Design for Upgrading in the Fashion Industry," *The Journal of Economic Geography*.

Aspers, Patrik, and Lise Skov. 2006. "Afterword to the theme 'Encounters in the Fashion Industry,'" *Current Sociology* 54, 5: 802–13.

Auty, Susan, and Richard Elliot. 1998. "Fashion involvement, self-monitoring and the meaning of brands," *Journal of Product and Brand Management* 7, 2: 109–23.

Bair, Jennifer, and Gary Gereffi. 2001. "Local Clusters in Global Chains: The Causes and Consequences of Export Dynamism in Torreon's Blue Jeans Industry," *World Development* 29, 11: 1885–903.

———. 2002. "NAFTA and the Apparel Commodity Chain: Corporate Strategies, Interfirm Networks, and Industrial Upgrading," pp. 23–50 in Free Trade and Uneven Development. The North American Apparel Industry after NAFTA, edited by D. Spener, G. Gereffi, and J. Bair. Philadelphia: Temple University Press.

Balkin, N. 1956. "Prices in the Clothing Industry," *Journal of Industrial Economics* 5, 1: 1–15.

Banks, Marcus. 2001. *Visual Methods in Social Research*. London: Sage Publications.

Barnard, Malcolm. 1996. *Fashion as Communication*. London: Routledge.

Barnes, Liz, and Gaynor Lea-Greenwood. 2006. "Fast Fashioning the Supply Chain: Shaping the Research Agenda," *Journal of Fashion Marketing and Management* 10, 3: 259–71.

Barry, Andrew, and Don Slater, eds. 2005. *The Technological Economy*. London: Routledge.

Barthes, Roland. [1967] 1990. *The Fashion System*. Berkeley: University of California Press.

Barzel, Yoram. 2004. "Standards and the Form of Agreement," *Economic Enquiry* 42, 1: 1–13.

Baudrillard, Jean. [1976] 1993. *Symbolic Exchange and Death*. London: Sage.

Bauman, Zygmunt. 1998. *Globalization: The Human Consequences*. Cambridge: Polity Press.

Beaudoin, Pierre, Marie Lachance, and Jean Robitaille. 2003. "Fashion Innovativeness, Fashion Diffusion, and Brand Sensitivity among Adolescents," *Journal of Fashion Marketing and Management* 7, 1: 23–30.

Beck, Ulrich. 1999. *World Risk Society*. Cambridge: Polity Press.

Becker, Howard. 1974. "Art as Collective Action," *American Sociological Review* 39, 6: 767–76.

———. 1978. "Arts and Crafts," *American Journal of Sociology* 83, 4: 862–89.

———. 1982. *Art Worlds*. Berkeley: University of California Press.

Becker, Karin. 2000. "Visualizing Events on the Front Page," pp. 146–73 in *Picturing Politics, Visual and Textual Formations of Modernity in Swedish Press*, edited by K. Becker, et al. Stockholm: Stockholm University.

Beckert, Jens. 1996. "What Is Sociological about Economic Sociology? Uncertainty and the Embeddedness of Economic Action," *Theory and Society* 25: 803–40.

———. 2002. *Beyond the Market. The Social Foundations of Economic Efficiency*. Princeton: Princeton University Press.

———. 2003. "Economic Sociology and Embeddedness: How Shall We Conceptualize Economic Action," *Journal of Economic Issues* 37, 3: 769–87.

———. 2006. "Interpretation versus Embeddedness: The Premature Dismissal of Talcott Parsons in the New Economic Sociology," *American Journal of Economics and Sociology* 65, 1: 161–88.

———. 2009. "The Social Order of Markets," *Theory and Society* 38, 3: 245–69.

Beckert, Jens, and Jörg Rössel. 2004. "Reputation als Mechanismus der Reduktion von Ungewissheit am Kunstmarkt," *Kölner Zeitschrift für Soziologie und Sozialpsychologie* 56, 1: 32–50.

Beckert, Jens, and Milan Zafirovski, eds. 2006. *International Encyclopedia of Economic Sociology*. London: Routledge Ltd.

Bell, Daniel. 1973. *The Coming of Post-Industrial Society: A Venture in Social Forecasting*. New York: Basic Books Inc.

Benjamin, Beth, and Joel Podolny. 1999. "Status, Quality, and Social Order in the California Wine Industry," *Administrative Science Quarterly* 44, 3: 563–89.

Berger, Peter, and Thomas Luckmann. [1966] 1991. *The Social Construction of Reality, A Treatise in the Sociology of Knowledge*. London: Penguin Books.

Biddle, B. J. 1986. "Recent Developments in Role Theory," *Annual Review of Sociology* 12: 67–92.

Biggart, Nicole, and Thomas Beamish. 2003. "The Economic Sociology of Convention: Habit, Custom, Practice, and Routine in Market Order," *Annual Review of Sociology* 29: 443–64.

Biggart, Nicole, and Mauro Guillen. 1999. "Developing Difference: Social Organization and the Rise of the Auto Industries of South Korea, Taiwan, Spain, and Argentina," *American Sociological Review* 64, 5: 722–47.

Birtwistle, Grete, and Linda Shearer. 2001. "Consumer Preference of Five UK Fashion Retailers," *Journal of Fashion Marketing and Management* 5, 1: 9–18.

Blumer, Herbert. 1968. "Fashion," pp. 341–45 in vol. 5 of the *International Encyclopedia of the Social Sciences*, edited by D. Sills. London: The Macmillan Company.

———. 1969. "Fashion: From Class Differentiation to Collective Selection," *The Sociological Quarterly* 10, 3: 275–91.

Boltanski, Luc, and Laurent Thèvenot. [1991] 2006. *On Justification, Economies of Worth*. Princeton: Princeton University Press.

Bonacich, Edna, and Richard Applebaum. 2000. *Behind the Label, Inequality in the Los Angeles Apparel Industry*. Berkeley: University of California Press.

Bourdieu, Pierre. [1979] 1984. *Distinction: A Social Critique of the Judgment of Taste*. Cambridge, Mass.: Harvard University Press.

———. 1987. "What Makes a Social Class? On the Theoretical and Practical Existence of Groups," *Berkeley Journal of Sociology* 22: 1–17.

———. [1980] 1990. *The Logic of Practice*. Cambridge: Polity Press.

———. 1990. *In Other Words, Essays Towards a Reflexive Sociology*. Cambridge: Polity Press.

———. 1993. *The Fields of Cultural Production, Essays on Art and Literature*. Oxford: Polity Press.

Bourdieu, Pierre. [1992] 1996. *The Rules of Art, Genesis and Structure of the Literary Field*. Stanford, Calif.: Stanford University Press.

———. 2005. *The Social Structures of the Economy*. Cambridge: Polity Press.

Bovone, Laura. 2006. "Urban Style Cultures and Urban Cultural Production in Milan: Postmodern Identity and the Transformation of Fashion," *Poetics* 34: 370–82.

Braham, Peter. 1997. "Fashion: Unpacking a Cultural Production," pp. 119–75 in *Production of Culture/Cultures of Production*, edited by P. du Gay. London: Sage.

Brannon, Evelyn. 2005. *Fashion Forecasting*. New York: Fairchild Books & Visuals.

Braudel, Fernand. 1981. *Civilization and Capitalism 15ᵗʰ–18ᵗʰ Century. Volume I: The Structures of Everyday Life, the Limits of the Possible*. London: Collins.

———. [1975] 1992. *Civilization and Capitalism 15ᵗʰ–18ᵗʰ Century. Volume II: The Wheels of Commerce*. London: Fontana Press.

Braverman, Harry. 1974. *Labor and Monopoly Capital: The Degradation of Work in the Twentieth Century*. New York: Monthly Review Press.

Breward, Christopher. 1995. *The Culture of Fashion, a New History of Fashionable Dress*. Manchester: Manchester University Press.

Brubaker, Rogers, and Frederick Cooper. 2000. "Beyond 'Identity,'" *Theory and Society* 29: 1–47.

Brunsson, Nils, and Bengt Jacobsson. 2000. "The Contemporary Expansion of Standardization," pp. 1–17 in *A World of Standards*, edited by N. Brunsson, and B. Jacobsson. Oxford: Oxford University Press.

Burt, Ronald. 1988. "The Stability of American Markets," *The American Journal of Sociology* 94, 356–95.

———. 1992. *Structural Holes. The Social Structure of Competition*. Cambridge. Mass.: Harvard University Press.

Callon, Michel, ed. 1998. *The Laws of the Market*. Oxford: Blackwell Publishers

Callon, Michel. 1999. "Actor-Network Theory—The Market Test," pp. 181–95 in *Actor Network Theory and After*, edited by J. Law, and J. Hassard. Oxford: Blackwell Publishers.

———. 2005. "Why Virtualism Paves the Way to Political Impotence: A Reply to Daniel Miller's Critique of the Laws of the Markets," *Economic Sociology, European Electronic Newsletter* 6, 2: 1–15.

Callon, Michel, Cécile Méadel, and Vololona Rabeharisoa. 2002. "The Economy of Qualities," *Economy and Society* 31, 2: 194–217.

Camitz, Martin, and Fredrik Liljeros. 2006. "The Effect of Travel Restrictions on the Spread of a Moderately Contagious Disease," *BMC Medicine* 4: 32.

Cannon, Aubrey 1998. "The Cultural and Historical Contexts of Fashion," pp. 23–38 in *Consuming Fashion, Adorning the Transnational Body*, edited by A. Brydon, and S. Niessen. Oxford: Berg.

Carrier, James, and Daniel Miller. 1998. *Virtualism: A New Political Economy*. Oxford: Oxford University Press.

Castells, Manuel. 1996. *The Information Age: Economy, Society and Culture, The Rise of the Network Society*. Oxford: Blackwell.

Cawthorne, Pamela. 1995. "Of Networks and Markets: The Rise of a South Indian Town, the Example of Tiruppur's Cotton Knitwear Industry," *World Development* 23, 1: 43–56.

Cerulo, Karen. 1997. "Identity Construction, New Issues, New Directions," *Annual Review of Sociology* 23: 385–409.

Chamberlin, Edward. [1933] 1948. *The Theory of Monopolistic Competition, A Re-orientation of the Theory of Value*. Cambridge, Mass.: Harvard University Press.

———. 1953. "The Product as an Economic Variable," *Quarterly Journal of Economics* 67, 1: 1–29.

Clammer, John. 1992. "Aesthetics of the Self, Shopping and Social Being in Contemporary Urban Japan," pp. 195–215 in *Lifestyle Shopping, the Subject of Consumption*, edited by R. Shields. London: Routledge.

Clark, Gordon, Nigel Thrift, and Adam Tickell. 2005. "Performing Finance, the Industry, the Media, and Its Image," pp. 165–82 in *The Technological Economy*, edited by A. Barry, and D. Slater. London: Routledge.

Coase, Ronald. [1937] 1988. "The Nature of the Firm," pp. 33–56 in *The Firm, The Market, and The Law*, edited by R. Coase. Chicago: Chicago University Press.

Coleman, James. 1990. *Foundations of Social Theory*. Cambridge, Mass.: Harvard University Press.

Collins, Jane. 2000. "Tracing Social Relationships in Commodity Chains: The Case of Grapes in Brazil," pp. 97–109 in *Commodities and Globalization, Anthropological Perspectives*, edited by A. Haugerud, M. P. Stone, and P. D. Little. London: Rowan and Littlefield Publishers, Inc.

Collins, Randall. 1990. "Market Dynamics as the Engine of Historical Change," *Sociological Theory* 8, 2: 111–35.

Cook, Daniel. 2000. "The Other 'Child Study': Figuring Children as Consumers in Market Research, 1910s–1990s," *The Sociological Quarterly* 41, 3: 487–507.

Corrigan, Peter. 1997. *The Sociology of Shopping*. London: Sage.

Craik, Jennifer. 1993. *The Face of Fashion, Cultural Studies of Fashion*. London: Routledge.

Crane, Diana. 1999. "Diffusion Models and Fashion: A Reassessment," *Annals of the American Academy of Political and Social Science* 566: 13–24.

———. 2000. *Fashion and Its Social Agenda, Class, Gender, and Identity in Clothing*. Chicago: The University of Chicago Press.

Crane, Diana, and Laura Bovone. 2006. "Approaches to Material Culture: The Sociology of Fashion and Clothing," *Poetics* 34: 319–33.

Creamer, Winfred. 2000. "The Impact of Colonial Contact on the Production and Distribution of Glaze-Paint Decorated Ceramics," pp. 151–62 in *Commodities and Globalization, Anthropological Perspectives*, edited by A. Haugerud, M. P. Stone, and P. D. Little. London: Rowan and Littlefield Publishers, Inc.

Crewe, Ben. 2003. *Representing Men, Cultural Production and Producers in the Men's Magazine Market*. Oxford: Berg.

Dalton, George, and Paul Bohannan. [1962] 1971. "Market in Africa: Introduction," pp. 143–66 in *Economic Anthropology and Development, Essays on Tribal and Peasant Economies*, edited by G. Dalton. London: Basic Books.

Darr, Asaf. 2006. *Selling Technology, the Changing Shape of Sales in an Information Economy*. Ithaca: Cornell University Press.

Davis, Fred. 1992. *Fashion, Culture and Identity*. Chicago: The University of Chicago Press.

Davis, Gerald, and Christopher Marquis. 2005. "The Globalization of Stock Markets and Convergence of Corporate Governance," pp. 352–90 in *The Economic Sociology of Capitalism*, edited by V. Nee, and R. Swedberg. Princeton: Princeton University Press.

De Bondt, Werner. 2005. "The Values and Beliefs of European Investors," pp. 163–86 in *The Sociology of Financial Markets*, edited by K. Knorr-Cetina, and A. Preda. Oxford: Oxford University Press.

Deeg, Richard, and Gregory Jackson. 2007. "Towards a More Dynamic Theory of Capitalist Variety," *Socio-Economic Review* 5, 1: 149–79.

Devereux, Edward. 1961. "Parsons' Sociological Theory," pp. 1–61 in *The Social Theories of Talcott Parsons*, edited by Max Black. Engelwood Cliffs, NJ.: Prentice Hill.

Dickerson, Kitty, and Jeannette Jarnow. 2003. *Inside the Fashion Business* (7th ed). New Jersey: Prentice Hall.

DiMaggio, Paul, and Joseph Cohen. 2005. "Information Inequality and Network Externalities: A Comparative Study of the Diffusion of the Television and the Internet," pp. 227–67 in *The Economic Sociology of Capitalism*, edited by V. Nee, and R. Swedberg. Princeton: Princeton University Press.

Dobbs, S. P. 1927. "Sweating in the Clothing Industry," *Economica*, 19: 74–90.

Dodd, Nigel. 1994. *The Sociology of Money: Economics, Reason and Contemporary Society*. Cambridge: Polity Press.

———. 2005. "Reinventing Monies in Europe," *Economy and Society* 34, 4: 558–83.

Douglas, Audrey. 1969. "Cotton Textiles in England: The East India Company's Attempt to Exploit Developments in Fashion 1660–1721," *Journal of British Studies* 8, 2: 28–43.

du Gay, Paul. 1993. "'Numbers and Souls': Retailing and the De-Differentiation of Economy and Culture," *The British Journal of Sociology* 44, 4: 563–87.

du Gay, Paul, and Michael Pryke, eds. 2002. *Cultural Economy, Cultural Analysis and Commercial Life*. London: Sage.

Durkheim, Émile. [1893] 1984. *The Division of Labour in Society*. London: Macmillan.

Eisenstadt, Shmuel. 1968. "The Development of Sociological Thought," pp. 23–36 in vol. 15 of the *International Encyclopedia of the Social Sciences*, edited by D. Sills. London: The Macmillan Company.

Emirbayer, Mustafa. 1997. "Manifesto for a Relational Sociology," *American Journal of Sociology* 103, 2: 281–317.

Emirbayer, Mustafa, and Ann Mische. 1998. "What is Agency?" *American Journal of Sociology* 103, 4: 962–1023.

England, Paula, and Nancy Folbre. 2005. "Gender in Economic Sociology," pp. 627–49 in *The Handbook of Economic Sociology*, edited by N. Smelser, and R. Swedberg. Princeton: Princeton University Press.

Entwistle, Joanne. 2000. *The Fashioned Body. Fashion, Dress and Modern Social Theory*. Cambridge: Polity Press.

———. 2001. "The Dressed Body," pp. 33–58 in *Body Dressing*, edited by J. Entwistle, and E. Wilson. Oxford: Berg.

———. 2002. "The Aesthetic Economy: The Production of Value in the Field of Fashion Modelling," *Journal of Consumer Culture* 2, 3: 317–40.

———. 2006. "The Cultural Economy of Fashion Buying," *Current Sociology* 54: 704–24.

Entwistle, Joanne, and Elisabeth Wilson, eds. 2001. *Body Dressing*. Oxford: Berg.

Erzog, R. 1984. "Ordnung," pp. 1252–310 in vol. 6 of the *Historisches Wörterbuch der Philopsophie*, edited by J. Ritter, and K. Gründer. Basel: Schwabe & Co AG.

Etzioni, Amitai. 1988. *The Moral Dimension: Toward a New Economics*. New York: Free Press.

Evans, Caroline. 2000. "John Galliano: Modernity and Spectacle," pp. 143–65 in *The Fashion Business, Theory, Practice and Image*, edited by N. White, and I. Griffiths. Oxford: Berg.

———. 2005. "Multiple, Movement, Model, Mode: The Mannequin Parade 1900–1929," pp. 125–45 in *Fashion and Modernity*, edited by C. Breward and C. Evans. Oxford: Berg.

Falk, Pasi, and Colin Campbell, eds. 1997. *The Shopping Experience*. London: Sage.

Farnie, Douglas, and David Jeremy, eds. 2004. *The Fibre That Changed the World*. Oxford: Oxford University Press.

Favereau, Olivier, Olivier Biencourt, and Francois Eymard-Duvernay. 2002. "Where Do Markets Come From? From (Quality) Conventions!" pp. 213–52 in *Conventions and Structures in Economic Organization: Markets, Networks and Hierarchies*, edited by O. Favereau, and E. Lazega. Cheltenham: Edward Elgar.

Featherstone, Mike. 1991. *Consumer Culture and Postmodernism*. London: Sage.

Fevre, Ralph. 2003. *The New Sociology of Economic Behaviour*. London Sage.

Fine, Ben, and Ellen Leopold. 1993. *The World of Consumption*. London: Routledge.

Finkelstein, Joanne. 1996. *After a Fashion*. Melbourne: Melbourne University Press.

Fligstein, Neil. 1996. "Markets as Politics: A Political-Cultural Approach to Market Institutions," *American Sociological Review* 61: 656–73.

———. 2001. *The Architecture of Markets, an Economic Sociology for the Twenty-First Century Capitalist Societies*. Princeton: Princeton University Press.

Fligstein, Neil, and Iona Mara-Drita. 1996. "How to Make a Market: Reflections on the Attempt to Create a Single Market in the European Union," *The American Journal of Sociology* 102, 1–33.

Foley, Caroline. 1893. "Fashion," *The Economic Journal* 3, 11: 458–74.

Forney, Judith, Eun Joo Park, and Lynn Brandon. 2005. "Effects of Evaluative Criteria on Fashion Brand Extension," *Journal of Fashion Marketing and Management* 9, 2: 156–65.

Frank, Lawrence. 1944. "What is Social Order?" *The American Journal of Sociology* 49, 5: 470–77.

Frank, Robert. 1985. "The Demand for Unobservable and Other Nonpositional Goods," *The American Economic Review* 75, 1: 101–16.

Freeman, John. 2005. "Venture Capital and Modern Capitalism," pp. 144–67 in *The Economic Sociology of Capitalism*, edited by V. Nee, and R. Swedberg. Princeton: Princeton University Press.

Frenzen, Jonathan, Paul Hirsch, and Philip Zerrillo. 1994. "Consumption, Preferences and Changing Lifestyles," pp. 403–25 in *The Handbook of Economic Sociology*, edited by N. Smelser, and R. Swedberg. Princeton: Princeton University Press.

Frings, Gini. 2004. Fashion: From Concept to Consumer. New Jersey: Prentice Hall.

Gadamer, Hans Gerorg. [1960] 1990. *Wahrheit und Methode, Grundzüge einer philosopischen Hermeneutik*. Tübingen: J.C.B. Mohr.

Gadde, Lars-Erik, and Håkan Håkansson. 2001. *Supply Network Strategies*. Chichester, England: Wiley.

Geertz, Clifford. 1963. *Peddlers and Princes, Social Change and Economic Modernization in Two Indonesian Towns*. Chicago: Chicago University Press.

———. 1973. *The Interpretations of Culture*. New York: Basic Books.

———. [1978] 1992. "The Bazaar Economy: Information and Search in Peasant Marketing," pp. 225–32 in *The Sociology of Economic Life*, edited by M. Granovetter, and R. Swedberg. Boulder: Westview Press.

Gereffi, Gary. 1994. "The Organization of Buyer-Driven Global Commodity Chains: How U.S. Retailers Shape Overseas Production Networks," pp. 95–123 in *Commodity Chains and Global Capitalism*, edited by G. Gereffi, and M. Korzeniewics. Westport: Praeger.

———. 1999. "International Trade and Industrial Upgrading in the Apparel Commodity Chain," *Journal of International Economics* 48: 37–70.

Gereffi, Gary, David Spener, and Jennifer Bair, eds. 2002. *Free Trade and Uneven Development. The North American Apparel Industry after NAFTA*, Philadelphia: Temple University Press.

Gereffi, Gary, John Humphrey, and Timothy Sturgeon. 2005. "The Governance of Global Value Chains," *Review of International Political Economy* 12, 1: 78–104.

Gerhards, Jürgen. 2005. *The Name Game. Cultural Modernization and First Names*. New Brunswick/London: Transaction Publishers.

Giddens, Anthony. 1976. New Rules of Sociological Method: A Positive Critique of Interpretive Sociologies. Stanford, Calif.: Stanford University Press.

———. 1991. *Modernity and Self-Identity: Self and Society in the Late Modern Age*. Cambridge: Polity Press.

Giertz-Mårtenson, Ingrid. 2006. *Att se in in framtiden, En undersökning av trendanalyser inom modebranschen*, Magisteruppsats. Stockholm: Etnologiska Institutionen.

Ginzel, Linda, Roderick Kramer, and Robert Sutton. [1993] 2004. "Organizational Impression Management as a Reciprocal Influence Process: The Neglected Role of the Organizational Audience," pp. 223–61 in *Organizational Identity: A Reader*, edited by M. Harch, and M. Schultz. Oxford: Oxford University Press.

Giuliani, Elisa, Carlo Pietrobelli, and Roberta Rabellotti. 2005. "Upgrading in Global Value Chains: Lessons from Latin American Clusters," *World Development* 33, 4: 549–73.

Gladwell, Malcolm. 2000. *The Tipping Point: How Little Things Can Make a Big Difference*. New York: Little Brown and Company.

Godart, Frédéric Clément. 2009. *Status and Style in Creative Industries: The Case of the Fashion System*. Columbia University: Dissertation at the Dep. of sociology.

Goffman, Erving. [1963] 1968. *Stigma, Notes on the Management of Spoiled Identity*. Ringwood: Penguin Books.

———. [1959] 1971. *The Presentation of Self in Everyday Life*. London: Penguin Books.

———. 1979. *Gender Advertisements*. London: MacMillan.

Gold, Steven. 1991. "Ethnic Boundaries and Ethnic Entrepreneurship: A Photo Elicitation Study," *Visual Sociology* 6, 2: 9–22.

Goodman, Nelson. 1984. *Of Mind and Other Matters*. Cambridge, Mass.: Harvard University Press.

Granovetter, Mark. 1974. *Getting a Job, a Study of Contacts and Careers*. Cambridge, Mass.: Harvard University Press.

———. 1978. "Threshold Models of Collective Behavior," *American Journal of Sociology* 83, 6: 1420–443.

———. 1985. "Economic Action and Social Structure: The Problem of Embeddedness," *American Journal of Sociology* 91, 3: 481–510.

———. 1992. "Economic Institutions as Social Framework for Analysis," *Acta Sociologica* 35, 3–11.

Granovetter, Mark, and Richard Swedberg, eds. 1992. *The Sociology of Economic Life*. Boulder: Westview Press.

Green, Nancy. 1994. "Art and Industry: The Language of Modernization in the Production of Fashion," *French Historical Studies* 18, 3: 722–48.

Gregory, Paul. 1947. "An Economic Interpretation of Women's Fashion," *Southern Economic Journal* 14, 2: 148–62.

———. 1948. "Fashion and Monopolistic Competition," *The Journal of Political Economy* 56, 1: 69–75.

Griffin, Abbie, and John Hauser. 1993. "The Voice of the Customer," *Marketing Science* 12, 1: 1–27.

Gronow, Jukka. 1997. *The Sociology of Taste*. London: Routledge.

Gudeman, Stephen. 2001. *The Anthropology of Economy, Community, Market and Culture*. Oxford: Blackwell Publishing.

Guseva, Alya, and Akos Rona-Tas. 2001. "Uncertainty, Risk and Trust: Russian and American Credit Card Markets Compared," *American Sociological Review* 66, 5: 623–46.

Hacking, Ian. 1999. *The Social Construction of What?* Cambridge, Mass.: Harvard University Press.

Hackings, Ian. 2002. *Historical Ontology*, Cambridge, Mass.: Harvard University Press.

Hale, Angela, and Jane Willis, eds. 2005. *Threads of Labour, Garment Industry Supply Chains from the Workers' Perspective*. Oxford: Blackwell Publishing.

Halepete, Jaya, Jan Hathcote, and Cara Peters. 2005. "A Qualitative Study of Micromarketing Merchandising in the U.S. Apparel Retail Industry," *Journal of Fashion Marketing and Management* 9, 1: 71–82.

Hall, Peter, and David Soskice. 2001. *Varieties of Capitalism, the Institutional Foundations of Comparative Advantages*. Oxford: Oxford University Press.

Hall, Peter, and Daniel Gingerich. 2004. *Varieties of Capitalism and Institutional Complementarities in the Macroeconomy, an Empirical Analysis*. Discussion Paper 04/5, Köln: MPIfG.

Hasselström, Anna. 2003. *On and Off the Trading Floor, an Inquiry into the Everyday Fashioning of Financial Market Knowledge*. Stockholm: Department of Social Anthropology, Stockholm University.

Hatch, Mary, and Majken Schultz, eds. 2004. *Organizational Identity, a Reader*. Oxford: Oxford University Press.

Hauge, Atle. 2007. *Dedicated Followers of Fashion, an Economic Geographic Analysis of the Swedish Fashion Industry*. Uppsala: Uppsala University.

Hayek, Friedrich. 1945. "The Use of Knowledge in Society," *The American Economic Review* 35, 4: 519–30.

———. 1973. *Law, Legislation and Liberty, a New Statement of the Liberal Principles of Justice and Political Economy, Volume 1: Rules and Order*. Chicago: Chicago University Press.

Hecksher, Eli. 1948. *Industrialismen. Den ekonomiska utvecklingen sedan 1750.* Stockholm: Kooperativa Förbundets Bokförlag.

Hedström, Peter. 2005. *Dissecting the Social, On the Principles of Analytical Sociology*. Cambridge: Cambridge University Press.

Hedström, Peter, and Richard Swedberg. 1996. "Social Mechanisms," *Acta Sociologica* 39, 3: 281–308.

———, eds. 1998. *Social Mechanisms, an Analytical Approach to Social Theory*. Cambridge: Cambridge University Press.

Heidegger, Martin. [1919] 1987. *Zur Bestimmung der Philosophie*, Gesamtausgabe, II Abteilung: Vorlesungen, Band 56/57. Frankfurt am Main: Vittorio Klostermann.

———. [1940] 1986. *Nietzsche: Der europäische Nihilismus*, Gesamtausgabe, II Abteilung: Vorlesungen, Band 48. Frankfurt am Main: Vittorio Klostermann.

———. 1997. *Nietzsche, Zweiter Band*, Gesamtausgabe, I Abteilung: Veröffentliche Schriften, Band 6.2. Frankfurt am Main: Vittorio Klostermann.

———. [1927] 2001. *Sein und Zeit.* Tübingen: Max Niemeyer Verlag.

Hessling, Alexandra, and Hanno Pahl. 2006. "Scanning Talcott Parsons and Niklas Luhmann for Theoretical Keystones," *American Journal of Economics and Sociology* 65, 1: 189–218.

Hirsch, Paul. [1977] 1992. "Processing Fads and Fashions: An Organization-Set Analysis of Cultural Industry Systems," pp. 363–83 in *The Sociology of Economic Life*, edited by M. Granovetter, and R. Swedberg. Boulder: Westview Press.

Hirst, Paul, and Grahame Thompson. 1999. *Globalization in Question*. Cambridge: Polity Press.

Hiß, Stefanie. 2006. *Warum übernehmen Unternehmen gesellschaftliche Verantwortung? Ein soziologischer Erklärungsversuch*. Frankfurt: Campus Forschung.

Hitlin, Steven, and Jane Piliavin. 2004. "Values: Reviving a Dormant Concept," *Annual Review of Sociology* 30: 259–393.

Hobbes, Thomas. [1651] 1968. *Leviathan*. London: Penguin Books.

Hogg, Margaret, ed. 2005. *Consumer Behavior I: Research and Influences*. (Six volumes.) London: Sage.

Hopkins, Terence, and Immanuel Wallerstein. 1994. "Commodity Chains: Constructs and Research," pp. 17–19 in *Commodity Chains and Global Capitalism*, edited by G. Gereffi, and M. Korzeniewics. Westport: Praeger.

Howe, Stewart. 2003. "United Kingdom," pp. 155–87 in *Retailing in the European Union*, edited by S. Howe. London: Routledge.

Huat Chua, Beng. 1992. "Shopping for Women's Fashion in Singapore," pp. 114–35 in *Lifestyle Shopping, the Subject of Consumption*, edited by R. Shields. London: Routledge.

Husserl Edmund. [1913a] 1962. *Ideas, General Introduction to Pure Phenomenology, Book I*. New York: Collier Books.

———. [1954] 1970. *The Crisis of European Sciences and Transcendental Phenomenology*. Evanston: Northwestern University Press.

———. [1952] 1980. *Ideas, Pertaining to a Pure Phenomenology and to a Phenomenological Philosophy, Book III, Phenomenology and the Foundations of the Sciences*. The Hauge: Martinus Nijhoff.

———. [1913b] 1989. Ideas Pertaining to a Pure Phenomenology and to a Phenomenological Philosophy, Second Book, Studies in the Phenomenology of Constitution. Dordrecht: Kluwer.

———. [1922] 1992. Logische Untersuchungen, Zweiter Teil, Untersuchungen zur Phänomenologie und Theorie der Erkenntnis. Hamburg: Felix Meiner Verlag.

Ingham, Geoffrey. 2004. *The Nature of Money*. Malden Mass: Polity Press.

Isaac, Barry. 2005. "Karl Polanyi," pp. 14–25 in *Handbook of Economic Anthropology*, edited by James Carrier. Cheltenham: Edward Elgar.

Jacobs, Dany. 2006. "The Promise of Demand Chain Management in Fashion," *Journal of Fashion Marketing and Management* 10, 1: 84–96.

Jacobson, Timothy, and George Smith. 2001. *Cotton's Renaissance, a Study in Market Innovation*. Cambridge: Cambridge University Press.

Joas, Hans. 1997. *Die Entstehung der Werte*. Frankfurt am Main: Suhrkamp.

Johnson, Merrill. 1985. "Postwar Industrial Development in the Southeast and the Pioneer Role of Labor-Intensive Industry," *Economic Geography* 61, 1: 46–65.

Jungbauer-Gans, Monika, and Peter Griwy. 2005. "Machen Kleider Leute?" *Zeitschrift für Soziologie* 34, 4: 311–22.

Karpic, Lucien. Forthcoming. *The Economics of Singularities*. Princeton: Princeton University Press.

Kawamura, Yuniya. 2004. *The Japanese Revolution in Paris Fashion*. Oxford: Berg.

Kawamura, Yuniya. 2005. *Fashion-ology, an Introduction to Fashion Studies*. Oxford: Berg.

———. 2006. "Japanese Teens as Producers of Street Fashion," *Current Sociology* 54, 5: 784–801.

Kellner, Douglas. 2002. "Theorizing Globalization," *Sociological Theory* 20, 3: 285–305.

Kemp, Tom. [1983] 1986. *Industrialiseringsförlopp*. Stockholm: Liber Förlag.

Kettis, Magdalena. 2004. *The Challenge of Political Risk. Exploring the Political Risk management of Swedish Multinational Corporations*. Stockholm. Stockholm University.

Keynes, John. [1936] 1973. *The General Theory of Employment, Interest and Money*. London: Macmillan.

Kim, Sangmoon, and Eui-Hang Shin. 2002. "A Longitudinal Analysis of Globalization and Regionalization in International Trade: A Social Network Approach," *Social Forces* 81, 2: 445–68.

Kirzner, Israel. 1973. *Competition and Entrepreneurship*. Chicago: Chicago University Press.

Knight, Frank. 1921. *Risk, Uncertainty and Profit*. Boston: Houghton Mifflin Company.

Knorr Cetina, Karin. 1999. *Epistemic Knowledge, How the Sciences Make Knowledge*. Cambridge, Mass.: Harvard University Press.

Knorr Cetina, Karin, and Urs Bruegger. 2002. "Global Microstructures: The Virtual Societies of Financial Markets," *American Journal of Sociology* 107, 4: 905–950.

Knorringa, Peter. 1995. *Economics of Collaboration in Producer-Trader Relations, Transaction Regimes between Markets and Hierarchy in the Agra Footwear Cluster*, India, (Doctoral Dissertation). Den Haag: CIP-DATA, Koninklijke Bibliotheek.

Kocka, Jürgen. 1980. "The Rise of the Modern Industrial Enterprise in Germany," pp. 77–117 in *Managerial Hierarchies. Comparative Perspective on the Rise of the Modern Industrial Enterprise*, edited by A. Chandler, and H. Daems. Cambridge, Mass.: Harvard University Press.

König, Rene. 1973. *The Restless Image, A Sociology of Fashion*. London: George Allen & Unwin Ltd.

Korpi, Walter. 1985. "Power Resources vs. Action and Conflict: On Causal and Intentional Explanations in the Study of Power," *Sociological Theory* 3, 2: 31–45.

———. 2001. "Contentious Institutions. An Augmented Rational-Action Analysis of the Origins and Path Dependency of Welfare State Institutions in the Western Countries," *Rationality and Society* 13, 2: 235–83.

Kotler, Philippe. 2004. *Principles of Marketing*. New Jersey: Prentice Hall.

Kregel, Jan. 1998. "Financial Markets and Economic Development: Myth and Institutional Reality," pp. 243–57 in *Institutions and Economic Change, New Perspectives on Markets, Firms and Technology*, edited by K. Nielsen, and B. Johansson. Cheltenham: Edward Elgar.

Krippner, Greta. 2001. "The Elusive Market: Embeddedness and the Paradigm of Economic Sociology," *Theory and Society* 30, 6: 775–810.

Kumar, Krishan. 1995. *From Post-Industrial to Post-Modern Society: New Theories of the Contemporary World*. Oxford: Blackwell.

Lane, Christel, and Jocelyn Probert. 2006. "Domestic Capabilities and Global Production Networks in the Clothing Industry: A Comparison of German and UK Firms' Strategies," *Socio-Economic Review* 4: 35–67.

Lash, Scott. 1994. "Reflexivity and its Doubles: Structure, Aesthetics, Community," pp. 110–73 in *Reflexive Modernization, Politics, Tradition and Aesthetics in the Modern Social Order*, edited by U. Beck, A. Giddens, and S. Lash. Cambridge: Polity Press.

Lash, Scott, and John Urry. 1987. *The End of Organized Capitalism*. Cambridge: Polity Press.

Latour, Bruno. 1996. *Aramis or the Love of Technology*. Cambridge, Mass.: Harvard University Press.

Law, Ka Ming, Zhang, Zhi-Ming, and Chung-Sun Leung. 2004. "Fashion Change and Fashion Consumption: The Chaotic Perspective," *Journal of Fashion Marketing and Management* 8, 4: 362–74.

Leeuwen van, Theo and Carey Jewitt, eds. 2001. *Handbook of Visual Analysis*. London: Sage.

Leifer, Eric, and Harrison White. 1987. "A Structural Approach to Markets," pp. 85–108 in *The Structural Analysis of Business*, edited by M. Mizruchi, and M. Schwartz. Cambridge: Cambridge University Press.

Lengnick-Hall, Cynthia. 1996. "Customer Contributions to Quality: A Different View of the Customer-Oriented Firm," *The Academy of Management Review* 21, 3: 791–824.

Lidz, Victor. 1991. "The American Value System," pp. 22–36 in *Talcott Parsons, Theorist of Modernity*, edited by R. Robertson, and B. Turner. London: Sage.

Lieberson, Stanley. 2000. *A Matter of Taste: How Names, Fashions, and Culture Change*. New Haven: Yale University Press.

Liljeros, Fredrik. 2004. "Social Simulations," *Sociologisk Forskning* 2: 19–22.

Lindblom, Charles. 2001. *The Market System: What It Is, How It Works, and What to Make of It*. New Haven: Yale University Press.

Lindner, Stephan. 2002. "Technology and Textiles Globalization," *History and Technology*. 18, 1: 1–22.

Luhmann, Niklas. 1981. *Gesellschaftsstruktur und Semantik, Studien zur Wissenssoziologie der modernen Gesellschaft* (Band 2). Frankfurt am Main: Suhrkamp.

———. 1982. *The Differentiation of Society*. New York: Columbia University Press.

———. [1984] 1995. *Social Systems*. Stanford, Calif.: Stanford University Press.

———. 1997. *Die Gesellschaft der Gesellschaft*. Frankfurt am Main: Suhrkamp.

———. [1996] 2000. *The Reality of the Mass Media*. Stanford, Calif.: Stanford University Press.

Lury, Celia. 2005. "The Objectivity of the Brand, Marketing, Law and Sociology," pp. 183–200 in *The Technological Economy*, edited by D. Slater, and A. Barry. London: Routledge.

Macaulay, Stewart. 1963. "Non-Contractual Relations in Business: A Preliminary Study," *American Sociological Review* 28, 1: 55–67.

MacKenzie, Donald. 2004. "The Big, Bad Wolf and the Rational Market: Portfolio Insurance, the 1987 Crash and the Performativity of Economics," *Economy and Society* 33, 3: 303–34.

MacKenzie, Donald. 2006. *An Engine, Not a Camera, How Financial Models Shape Markets*. Cambridge: Cambridge University Press.

MacKenzie, Donald, and Yuval Millo. 2003. "Constructing a Market, Performing Theory: The Historical Sociology of a Financial Derivatives Exchange," *American Journal of Sociology* 109, 1: 107–45.

MacKenzie, Donald, Fabian Muniesa, and Lucia Siu, eds. 2007. *Do Economics Make Markets? On the Performativity of Economics*. Princeton: Princeton University Press.

Marshall, Alfred. [1920a] 1961. *Principles of Economics*, edited with annotations by C. W. Guillebaud, two volumes. London: Macmillan and Co.

———. 1920b. *Industry and Trade. A Study of Industrial Technique and Business Organization; and of Their Influences on the Conditions of Various Classes and Nations*. London: Macmillan and Co.

Marshall, David. 1997. *Celebrity and Power Fame in Contemporary Culture*. Minneapolis: University of Minnesota Press.

Martin, Thomas. 1968. "Social Institutions: A Reformulation of the Concept," *The Pacific Sociological Review* 11, 2: 100–109.

Marzo-Navarro, Mercedes, Marta Pedraja-Iglesias, and Ma Pilar Rivera-Torres. 2004. "The Benefits of Relationship Marketing for the Consumer and for the Fashion Retailers," *Journal of Fashion Marketing and Management* 4, 4: 425–36.

McCracken, Grant. 1988. *Culture and Consumption: New Approaches to the Symbolic Character of Consumer Goods and Activities*. Bloomington and Indianapolis: Indiana University Press.

———. 1989. "Who is the Celebrity Endorser? Cultural Foundations of the Endorsement Process," *Journal of Consumer Research* 16: 310–21.

McNeil, Peter. 2008a. *Fashion: Critical and Primary Sources*. Oxford: Berg.

———. 2008b. "'We're Not in the Fashion Business:' Fashion in the Museum and the Academy," *Fashion Theory* 12: 1: 65–82.

McRobbie, Angela. 1998. *British Fashion Design: Rag Trade or Image Industry?* London: Routledge.

———. 2003. "From Clubs to Companies, Notes on the Decline of Political Culture in Speeded up Creative Worlds," *Cultural Studies* 16, 4: 616–31.

Meinhardt, H. 1984. "Ordnung," pp. 1250–52 in vol. 6 of the *Historisches Wörterbuch der Philosophie*, edited by J. Ritter, and K. Gründer. Basel: Schwabe & Co AG.

Merton, Robert. 1968. *Social Theory and Social Structure*. New York: The Free Press.

Meyer, Deborah, and Heather Anderson. 2000. "Preadolescents and Apparel Purchasing: Conformity to Parents and Peers in the Consumer Socialization Process," *Journal of Social Behavior and Personality* 15, 2: 243–57.

Micheletti, Michele, Andreas Føllesdal, and Dietlin Stolle. 2004. *Politics, Products and Markets, Exploring Political Consumerism Past and Present*. New Brunswick: Transaction Publishers.

Miller, Daniel, Peter Jackson, Nigel Thrift, and Beverly Holbrook. 1998. *Shopping, Place and Identity*. London: Routledge.

Miller, Gary. 1992. *Managerial Dilemmas*. New York: Press Syndicate.

Mises, Ludwig von. [1963] 1966. *Human Action: A Treatise on Economics.* Chicago: Henry Regnery Company.

Möllering, Guido. 2006. *Trust: Reason, Routine, Reflexivity.* Oxford: Elsevier, 2006.

Moeran, Brian. 1996. *A Japanese Advertising Agency, An Anthropology of Media and Markets.* Honolulu: University of Hawaii Press.

———. 2004. "Marketing Ethnography: Disciplines and Practices," pp. 23–45 in *Market Matters, Exploring Cultural Processes in the Global Marketplace,* edited by C. Garsten, and M. Lindh Montoya. Houndsville: Palgrave MacMillan.

———. 2005. "Tricks of the Trade: The Performance and Interpretation of Authenticity," *Journal of Management Studies* 42, 5: 901–22.

———. 2006. "More than Just a Fashion Magazine," *Current Sociology* 54, 5: 725–44.

Moor, Elizabeth. 2003. "Branded Spaces: The Scope of 'New Marketing'," *Journal of Consumer Culture* 3, 1: 39–60.

Mora, Emanuela. 2006. "Collective Production of Creativity in the Italian Fashion System," *Poetics* 34: 334–53.

Morokvasic, Mirjana. 1993. "Immigrants in Garment Production in Paris and in Berlin," pp. 75–95 in *Immigration and Entrepreneurship. Culture, Capital and Ethnic Networks,* edited by I. Leight, and P. Bhachu. New Brunswick: Transaction Publishers.

Moss, Laurence, and Andrew Savchenko. 2006. "Introduction," *American Journal of Economics and Sociology* 65, 1:xiii–xxviii.

Muggleton, David. 2000. *Inside Subculture, The Postmodern Meaning of Style.* Oxford: Berg.

Mützel, Sophie. 2007. "Marktkonstitution durch narrativen Wettbewerb," *Berliner Journal für Soziologie* 17: 451–64.

Negus, Keith. 2002. "Identities and Industries: The Cultural Formation of Aesthetic Economies," pp. 115–31 in *Cultural Economy, Cultural Analysis and Commercial Life,* edited by P. du Gay, and M. Pryke. London: Sage.

Nelson, Richard, and Sidney Winter. 2002. "Evolutionary Theorizing in Economics," *The Journal of Economic Perspectives* 16, 23–46.

Nietzsche, Friedrich. [1882] 1960. *Joyful Wisdom,* translated by Thomas Common. New York: Frederick Ungar Publishing Company.

Nixon, Sean. 1996. *Hard Looks, Masculinities, Spectatorship and Contemporary Consumption.* New York: St. Martin's Press.

Norberg, Peter. 2001. *Finansmarknadens amoralitet och det kalvinistiska kyrkorummet: en studie i ekonomisk mentalitet och etik.* Stockholm: Ekonomiska forskningsinstitutet vid Handelshögskolan.

Nozick, Robert. 1974. *Anarchy, State, and Utopia.* New York: Basic Books, Inc., Publishers.

Ogburn, William. 1937. "Culture and Sociology," *Social Forces* 16, 2: 161–69.

Offe, Claus. 2000. " Civil Society; Social Order," *Archives Européennes de Sociologie* XLI, 1: 71–94.

Pareto, Vilfredo. [1915–16] 1935. *Mind and Society, A Treatise on General Sociology.* New York: Dover Publications.

Parsons, Talcott. 1929. "'Capitalism' In Recent German Literature: Sombart and Weber (Concluded)." *The Journal of Political Economy* 37, 1: 31–51.

———. [1937] 1968. *The Structure of Social Action*, vol. I–II. New York: The Free Press.

———. [1951] 1970. *The Social System*. London: Routledge.

———. 1991. "A Tentative Outline of American Values," pp. 37–65 in Talcott Parsons, *Theorist of Modernity*, edited by R. Robertson, and B. Turner. London: Sage.

Parsons, Talcott, and Winston White. [1961] 1970. "The Link Between Character and Society," pp. 183–235 in T. Parsons, *Social Structure and Personality*. New York: The Free Press.

Pesendorfer, Wolfgang. 1995. "Design Innovation and Fashion Cycles," *The American Economic Review* 85, 4: 771–92.

Peters, Enrique Dussels , Celemente Ruiz Durán, and Michael Piore. 2002. "Learning and the Limits of Foreign Partners as Teachers," pp. 224–45 in *Free Trade and Uneven Development. The North American Apparel Industry after NAFTA*, edited by D. Spener, G. Gereffi, and J. Bair. Philadelphia: Temple University Press.

Pettinger, Lynne. 2004. "Brand Culture and Branded Workers: Service Work and Aesthetic Labour in Fashion Retail," *Consumption, Markets and Culture* 7, 2: 165–84.

Phillips, Damon, and Ezra Zuckerman. 2001. "Middle-Status Conformity: Theoretical Restatement and Empirical Demonstration in Two Markets," *The American Journal of Sociology* 107: 379–429.

Pink, Sarah. 2001. *Doing Visual Ethnography*. London: Sage.

Plattner, Stuart. 2000. "Profit Markets and Art Markets," pp. 113–34 in *Commodities and Globalization, Anthropological Perspectives*, edited by A. Haugerud, M. P. Stone, and P. D. Little. London: Rowan and Littlefield Publishers, Inc.

Podolny, Joel. 1993. "A Status-based Model of Market Competition," *American Journal of Sociology* 98, 4: 829–72.

———. 2005. *Status Signals, A Sociological Study of Market Competition*. Princeton, NJ.: Princeton University Press.

Powell, Michael. 1997. *The Audit Society, Rituals of Verification*. Oxford: Oxford University Press.

———. 2005. "Enterprise Risk Management and Organization of Uncertainty in Financial Institutions," pp. 269–89 in *The Sociology of Financial Markets*, edited by K. Knorr-Cetina, and A. Preda. Oxford: Oxford University Press.

Powell, Walter, and Kaisa Snellman. 2004. "The Knowledge Economy," *Annual Review of Sociology* 30: 199–220.

Power, Dominic, and Atle Hauge. 2008. "No Man's Brand— Brands, Institutions, Fashion and the Economy," *Growth and Change* 39, 1: 123–43.

Pradelle, Michele. [1996] 2006. *Market Day in Provence*. Chicago: The University of Chicago Press.

Preda, Alex. 2005. "Legitimacy and Status Groups in Financial Markets," *The British Journal of Sociology* 56, 3: 451–71.

Quante, Michael. 2007. "The Social Nature of Personal Identity," *Journal of Consciousness Studies* 14: 56–76.

Radcliffe-Brown, Alfred. 1952. *Structure and Function in Primitive Society, Essays and Addresses*. London: Cohen and West.

Reed, Isaac. 2008. "Justifying Sociological Knowledge: From Realism to Interpretation," *Sociological Theory* 26: 101–29.

Rich, Stuart, and Bernard Portis. 1964. "The 'Imageries' of Department Stores," *Journal of Marketing* 28: 10–15.

Ricoeur, Paul. 1992. *Oneself as Another*. Chicago: Chicago University Press.

Rogers, Everett. 2003. *Diffusion of Innovation*, Fifth Edition. New York, NY: Free Press.

Ross, Jill, and Rod Harradine. 2004. "I'm Not Wearing That! Branding and Young Children," *Journal of Fashion Marketing and Management* 8, 1: 11–26.

Rouse, Elizabeth. 1989. *Understanding Fashion*. Oxford: Blackwell.

Ruggerone, Lucia. 2006. "The Simulated (Fictitious) Body: The Production of Women's Images in Fashion Photography," *Poetics* 34: 354–69.

Rugman, Alan. 2000. *The End of Globalization*. London: Random House.

Sassen, Saskia. 2001. *The Global City*. New York, London, Tokyo, Princeton: Princeton University Press.

———. 2005. "How are Global Markets Global? The Architecture of a Flow World," pp. 17–37 in *The Sociology of Financial Markets*, edited by K. Knorr-Cetina, and A. Preda. Oxford: Oxford University Press.

Schmidt, Susanne, and Raymund Werle. 1998. *Coordinating Technology, Studies in the International Standardization of Telecommunications*. Cambridge, Mass.: MIT Press.

Schmitz, Hubert, and Peter Knorringa. 2000. "Learning from Global Buyers," *The Journal of Development Studies* 37, 2: 177–204.

Schroeder, Jonathan. 2003. "Visual Methodologies Analysis," *Visual Anthropology* 16, 1: 81–88.

———. 2004. "Produktion och Konsumtion av Reklambilder," pp. 45–96 in *Bilder i Samhällsanalysen*, edited by P. Aspers, et al. Lund: Studentlitteratur.

Schütz, Alfred. 1962. *Collected Papers I, the Problem of Social Reality*. The Hague: Nijhoff.

Schumpeter, Joseph. [1950] 1975. *Capitalism, Socialism and Democracy*. New York: Harper and Row.

Simmel, Georg. [1922] 1955. "The Web of Group-Affiliation," pp. 125–195 in *Conflict and the Web of Group-Affiliations*. New York: The Free Press.

———. 1964. *The Sociology of Georg Simmel*, edited by K. Wolff. New York: The Free Press.

———. [1904] 1971. "Fashion," pp. 294–323 in *George Simmel on Individuality and Social Form*, edited by D. Levine. Chicago: Chicago University Press.

———. [1907] 1978. *The Philosophy of Money*. London: Routledge.

———. [1908] 1983. *Soziologie, Untersuchungen über die Formen der Vergesellschaftung*, Georg Simmel Gesammelte Werke, 2. Berlin: Duncker und Humbold.

Sklair, Leslie. 2002. *Globalization: Capitalism and its Alternatives*. Oxford: Oxford University Press.

Skov, Lise. 2006. "The Role of Trade Fairs in the Global Fashion Business," *Current Sociology* 54, 5: 764–83.

Slater, Don. 1997. *Consumer Culture and Modernity*. Cambridge: Polity Press.

———. 2002. "Capturing Markets from the Economists," pp. 59–77 in *Cultural Economy, Cultural Analysis and Commercial Life*, edited by P. du Gay, and M. Pryke. London: Sage.

———. 2005. "From Calculation to Alienation, Disentangling Economic Alienation," pp. 51–65 in *The Technological Economy*, edited by D. Slater, and A. Barry. London: Routledge.

Slater, Don, and Fran Tonkiss. 2001. *Market Society, Markets and Modern Social Theory*. Cambridge: Polity Press.

Smart, Barry. 2003. *Economy, Culture and Society*. Buckingham: Open University Press.

Smelser, Neil, and Richard Swedberg, eds. 2005. *The Handbook of Economic Sociology* (2nd ed). Princeton: Princeton University Press.

Smith, Charles. 1981. *The Mind of the Market, a Study of Stock Market Philosophies, Their Use, and Their Implication*. Totowa: Rowman and Littlefield.

———. 1989. *Auctions, the Social Construction of Values*. California: California University Press.

———. 2007. "Markets as Definitional Practices," *Canadian Journal of Sociology* 32, 1–39.

Sörbom, Adrienne. 2002. *Vart tog politiken vägen? Om individualisering, reflexivitet och görbarhet i det politiska engangemang*. Stockholm: Almqvist & Wiksell International.

Sørensen, Jesper. 2002. "The Strength of Corporate Culture and the Reliability of Firm Performance," *Administrative Science Quarterly* 47, 1: 70–91.

Somers, Margaret. 1994. "The Narrative Constitution of Identity: A Relational and Network Approach," *Theory and Society* 23: 605–49.

Spates, James. 1983. "The Sociology of Values," *Annual Review of Sociology* 9: 27–49.

Spence Smith, Thomas. 1992. *Strong Interaction*. Chicago: The University of Chicago Press.

Stark, David. 1996. "Recombinant Property in East European Capitalism," *American Journal of Sociology* 101, 4: 993–1027.

Steel, Valerie. 1997. *Fifty Years of Fashion: New Look to Now*. New Haven: Yale University Press.

———, ed. 2004. *Encyclopedia of Clothing and Fashion*. New York: Charles Scribner's Sons.

Storper, Michael. 1997. *The Regional World, Territorial Development in a Global Economy*. New York: The Guilford Press.

Swedberg, Richard. 1990. *Economics and Sociology, On Redefining Their Boundaries: Conversations with Economists and Sociologists*. Princeton: Princeton University Press.

———. 1994. "Markets as Social Structures," pp. 255–82 in *Handbook of Economic Sociology*, edited by N. Smelser, and R. Swedberg. Princeton: Princeton University Press.

———. 1997. "New Economic Sociology: What Has Been Accomplished, What Is Ahead?" *Acta Sociologica* 40: 161–82.

———. 1998. *Max Weber and the Idea of Economic Sociology*. Princeton: Princeton University Press.

————. 1999. *Orientation to Others and Social Mechanisms.* Stockholm: Stockholm University: Department of Sociology. Working Papers in Social Mechanisms (2).

————. 2003. *Principles of Economic Sociology.* Princeton: Princeton University Press.

————. 2004a. "On the Present State of Economic Sociology," *Economic Sociology, European Electronic Newsletter* 5, 2: 2–17.

————. 2004b. *Interest.* London: Open University Press.

————. 2005. *The Max Weber Dictionary, Key Words and Central Concepts.* Stanford, Calif.: Stanford University Press.

Swidler, Ann. 1986. "Culture in Action: Symbols and Strategies," *American Sociological Review* 51: 273–86.

Taplin, Ian. 1994. "Strategic Reorientations of U.S. Apparel Firms," pp. 205–22 in *Commodity Chains and Global Capitalism*, edited by G. Gereffi, and M. Korzeniewics. Westport: Praeger.

Taplin, Ian, and Jonathan Winterton. 2004. "Introduction, The European Clothing Industry, Meeting the Competitive Challenge," *Journal of Fashion and Marketing and Management* 8, 3: 256–61.

Thaver, Ismat, and Anne Wilcock. 2006. "Identification of Overseas Vendor Selection Criteria Used by Canadian Apparel Buyers, Is ISO 9000 Relevant?" *Journal of Fashion Marketing and Management* 10, 1: 56–70.

Thompson, Grahame, Jennifer Frances, Rosalind Levacic, and Jeremy Mitchel, eds. 1991. *Markets, Hierarchies and Networks.* London: Sage.

Thompson, Graig, and Diana Haytko. 1997. "Speaking of Fashion: Consumers' Uses of Fashion Discourses and the Appropriation of Countervailing Cultural Meanings," *Journal of Consumer Research* 24: 15–42.

Tokatli, Nebahat. 2007. "Global Sourcing: Insights from the Global Clothing Industry–The Case of Zara, a Fast Fashion Retailer," *Journal of Economic Geography* 8: 21–38.

Tokatli, Nebahat, and Yonca Boyaci Eldener. 2004. "Upgrading in the Global Clothing Industry: The Transformation of Boyner Holding," *Competition and Change* 8, 2: 173–93.

Tokatli, Nebahat, Neil Wrigley, and Ömür Kizilgün. 2008. "Shifting Global Supply Networks and Fast Fashion: Made in Turkey for Marks & Spencer," *Global Networks* 8, 261–371.

Uddhammar, Emil. 2006. "Development, Conservatism, and Tourism: Conflict or Symbiosis," *Review of International Political Economy* 13, 4: 656–78.

Uzzi, Brian. 1997. "Social Structure in Interfirm Networks: The Paradox of Embeddedness," *Administrative Science Quarterly* 42: 35–67.

van Daal, Jan, and Albert Jolink. 1993. *The Equilibrium Economics of Leon Walras.* London: Routledge.

van der Land, Don, Marco Staring, Richard van Steenbergen, Bart Wilterdink, and Nico Kalb, eds. 2000. *The Ends of Globalization, Bringing Society Back In.* Lanham: Rowman and Littlefield Publishers Inc.

Veblen, Thorstein. [1899] 1953. *The Theory of the Leisure Class, an Economic Study of Institutions.* New York: New American Library.

Velthuis, Olav. 2005. *Talking Prices, Symbolic Meanings of Prices on the Market for Contemporary Art.* Princeton: Princeton University Press.

Volckart, Oliver, and Antje Mangels. 1999. "Are the Roots of the Modern Lex Maercatoria Really Medieval?" *Southern Economic Journal* 65, 3: 6: 427–50.

Wachthauser, Brice. 1994. "Introduction: Is There Truth after Interpretation," pp. 1–24 in *Hermeneutics and Truth*, edited by B. Wachthauser. Evanston: Northwestern University Press.

Waldenfels, Bernhard. 1998. *Grenzen der Normalisierung*. Frankfurt am Main: Suhrkamp.

Warde, Alan. 1994. "Consumption, Identity-formation and Uncertainty," *Sociology* 25, 4: 878–98.

———. 2005. "Consumption and Theories of Practice," *Journal of Consumer Society* 5, 2: 131–53.

Weber, Max. 1946. *From Max Weber: Essays in Sociology*, edited by H. Gerth, and C. Wright Mills. London: Routledge.

———. [1904] 1949. "'Objectivity' in Social Science and Social Policy," pp. 49–112 in *The Methodology of the Social Sciences*. New York: The Free Press.

———. [1904–5] 1968. *The Protestant Ethic and the Spirit of Capitalism*. London: Unwin University Books.

———. [1921–22] 1978. *Economy and Society: An Outline of Interpretive Sociology*, two volumes, edited by Guenther Roth, and Claus Wittich. Berkeley: University of California Press.

———. [1923] 1981. *General Economic History*. New Brunswick, NJ: Transaction Publishers.

———. [1894] 1999. "Die Börse I, Zweck und äußere Organisation der Börsen," pp. 135–74 in *Max Weber Börsenwesen, Schriften und Reden 1893–1898*, Max Weber Gesamtausgabe, vol. 1/5 1. Tübingen: J.C.B. Mohr.

———. [1896] 1999. "Die Börse II, Der Börsenverkeher," pp. 617–57 in *Börsenwesen, Schriften und Reden 1893–1898*, Max Weber Gesamtausgabe, 1/5. Two volumes. Tübingen: J.C.B. Mohr.

Weil, David, Timothy Bresnahan, Peter Pashigian, Frederick Abernathy, John Dunlop, and Janice Hammond, 1995. "The Information-Integrated Channel: A Study of the U.S. Apparel Industry," Brookings *Papers on Economic Activity*, vol. 1995: 175–246.

Welters, Linda, and Abby Lillethun. 2007. *The Fashion Reader*. Oxford: Berg.

Werkmeister, W. H. 1941. "An Introduction to Heidegger's 'Existential Philosophy,'" *Philosophy and Phenomenological Research* 2, 1: 79–87.

White, Harrison. 1981. "Where do Markets Come From?" *American Journal of Sociology* 87, 3: 517–47.

———. 1992. *Identity and Control, a Structural Theory of Social Action*. Princeton: Princeton University Press.

———. 1993. "Markets in Production Networks," pp. 161–75 in *Explorations in Economic Sociology*, edited by R. Swedberg. New York: Russel Sage Foundation.

———. 2002. *Markets from Networks, Socioeconomic Models of Production*. Princeton: Princeton University Press.

White, Harrison C., and Robert Eccles. 1987. "Producers' Markets," pp. 984–86 in *The New Palgrave Dictionary of Economic Theory and Doctrine*, edited by John Eatwell. London: Macmillan.

White, Nicola, and Ian Griffiths. 2000. *The Fashion Business, Theory, Practice, Image*. Oxford: Berg.

Whitford, Josh. 2005. *The New Old Economy, Networks, Institutions, and the Organizational Transformation of American Manufacturing*. Oxford: Oxford University Press.

Williamson, Oliver. 1981. "The Economics of Organization: The Transaction Cost Approach," *American Journal of Sociology* 87, 3: 548–77.

Wilson, Elisabeth. 2003. *Adorned in Dreams, Fashion and Modernity*. London: Tauris and Co.

Wilson, Ted. 2000. *Battles for the Standard: Bimetallism and the Spread of the Gold Standard in the Nineteenth Century*. Aldershot: Ashgate.

Wittgenstein, Ludwig. 1980. *Culture and Value*. Chicago: Chicago University Press.

Woll, Cornelia. 2005. "Learning to Act on World Trade: Preference Formation of Large Firms in the Unites States and the European Union," Max-Planck Institute for the Studies of Societies Discussion Paper 05/01.

Wrong, Dennis. 1994. *The Problem of Order, What Unities and Divides Society*. New York: The Free Press.

Xenophon. 1970. *Xenophon's Socratic Discourse, an Interpretation of the Oeconomics*. South Bend, Ind.: St. Augustine's Press.

Zelizer, Viviana. 1981. "The Price and Value of Children: The Case of Children's Insurance," *The American Journal of Sociology* 86: 1036–56.

———. 1988. "Beyond the Polemics on the Market: Establishing a Theoretical and Empirical Agenda," *Sociological Forum* 3: 614–34.

———. 2005. "Circuits within Capitalism," pp. 289–322 in *The Economic Sociology of Capitalism*, edited by R. Swedberg, and V. Nee. Princeton: Princeton University Press.

Zetterberg, Hans. 1997. *Sociological Endeavor: Selected Writings*. Stockholm: City University Press.

Zorn, Dirk, Frank Dobbin, Julian Dierkes, and Man-Shan Kwok. 2005. "Managing Investors: How Financial Markets Reshaped the American Firm," pp. 269–89 in *The Sociology of Financial Markets*, edited by K. Knorr-Cetina, and A. Preda. Oxford: Oxford University Press.

Zuckerman, Ezra. 1999. "The Categorical Imperative: Securities Analysts and the Illegitimacy Discount," *The American Journal of Sociology* 104: 1398–438.

———. 2000. "Focusing the Corporate Product: Securities Analysts and De-Diversification," *Administrative Science Quarterly* 45: 591–619.

Zuckerman, Ezra, et al. 2003. "Robust Identities or Nonentities? Typecasting in the Feature-Film Labor Market," *American Journal of Sociology* 108, 5: 1018–74.

Zukin, Sharon, and Jennifer Smith Maguire. 2004. "Consumers and Consumption," *Annual Review of Sociology* 30: 173–97.

Index --